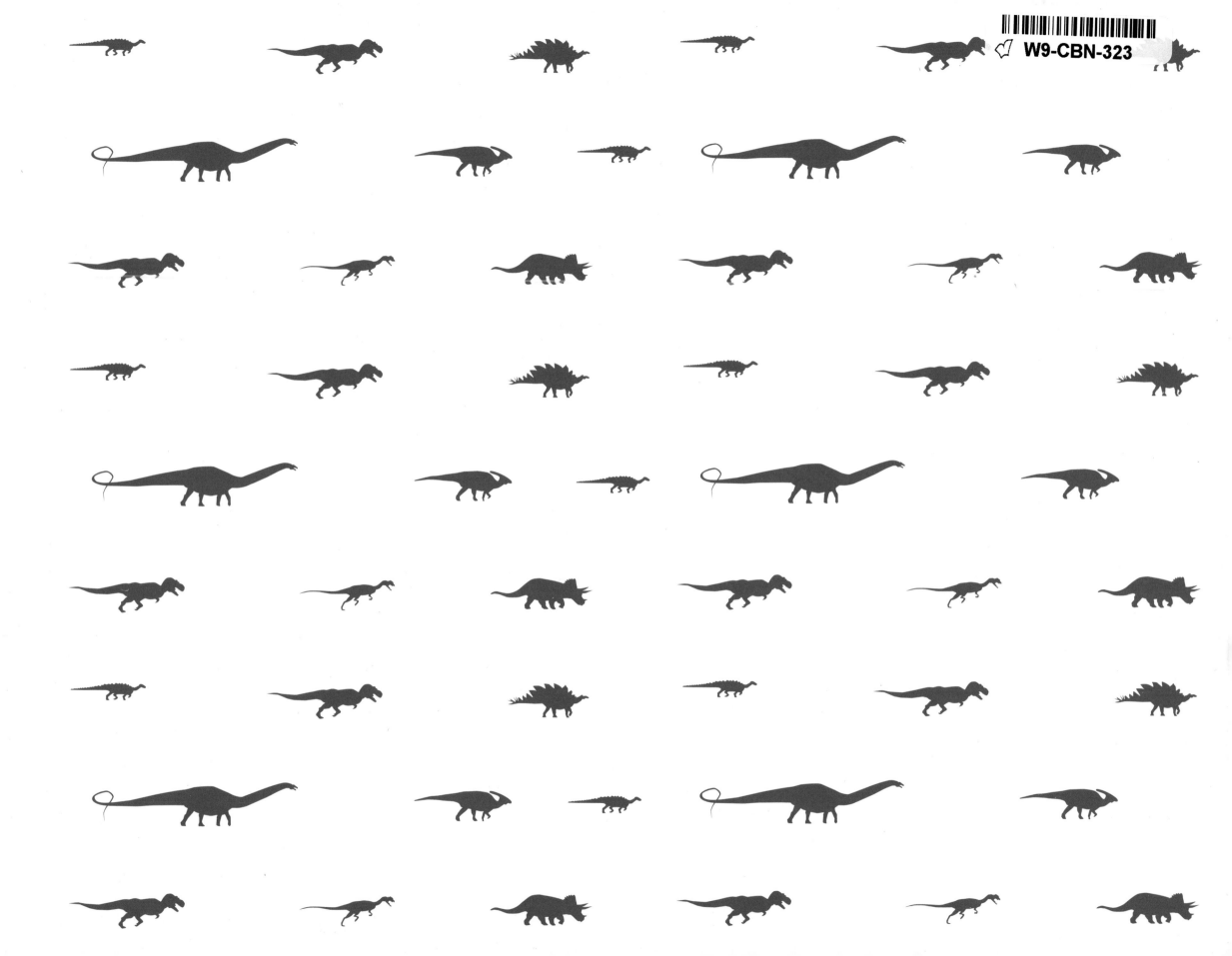

ENCYCLOPEDIA
OF DINOSAURS

Publications International Ltd.

Contributing Writers:

Brooks Britt, Ph.D., works at the Museum of Western Colorado in Grand Junction, Colorado.

Kenneth Carpenter, Ph.D., received his doctorate from the University of Colorado and works at the Denver Museum of Natural History.

Catherine A. Forster, Ph.D., is a professor and graduate director for the Department of Anatomical Sciences at State University of New York at Stony Brook.

David D. Gillette, Ph.D., is the Colbert Curator of Vertebrate Paleontology at the Museum of Northern Arizona at Flagstaff.

Mark A. Norell is curator and chair of the Department of Vertebrate Paleontology at the American Museum of Natural History in New York.

George Olshevsky is a freelance writer and editor who has published well over 50 books, including Mezaozoic Meanderings. In addition, he also has written articles for Dino-Frontline and Omni magazines.

J. Michael Parrish, Ph.D., is a professor and chair of the Department of Biological Sciences at Northern Illinois University. He also served as a consultant for this book.

David Weishampel, Ph.D. is a professor at Johns Hopkins University School of Medicine.

Consultant:

Peter Dodson, Ph.D., is a professor of Anatomy at the School of Veterinary Medicine at the University of Pennsylvania.

Photo Credits:

Front cover: **Joseph Tucciarone**

Back cover: **Luis V. Rey**

American Museum of Natural History: 15 (bottom left), 33 (bottom right); **Ann Ronan Picture Library:** 9, 10 (center), 11 (top & bottom right), 12 (bottom right), 14, 37, 123; **Donald Baird:** 15 (top), 18 (bottom left), 19 (top left), 43 (top center), 44 (bottom left), 75 (top right), 76 (right), 173; **John D. Bindon:** 254; **Black Hills Institute:** 175 (bottom right), 176 (top left), 243 (right), 244 (bottom); Peter Larson: 251 (left); **Brooks B. Britt:** 28 (bottom right), 41 (center), 44 (top right); **Tom Bynum:** 41 (right); **Ken Carpenter:** 15 (bottom right), 20 (right), 23, 28 (left), 39, 47, 61 (bottom), 96, 99 (left), 121, 129 (top), 141, 144 (top right), 146 (right), 147 (left), 157 (top), 170 (bottom right), 176 (bottom right), 178 (right), 179 (top), 183 (top), 188 (right), 199, 208 (top left), 214 (top), 216 (top), 229 (top left), 231 (top), 238, 241, 247 (left); **Corbis:** 250, 252 (top); UPI/Bettmann: 10 (left, right), 11 (bottom left); **Kent and Donna Dannen:** 43 (left), 92 (left); **Dinosaur National Monument:** 84 (right); **Dinosaur State Park:** 43 (bottom center); **Brian Franczak:** 1, 4, 7, 13, 26-27, 40 (right), 50, 54, 55, 56, 57, 58, 59 (right), 60, 62 (left), 63 (top), 64, 66 (right), 67, 69, 90, 91, 96 (bottom), 97, 102, 104, 105, 109, 113, 115, 124, 125, 127, 134, 137, 144 (top left), 149, 150, 151 (right), 154 (left), 156, 157 (bottom), 159, 164, 170 (top left), 171, 174, 175 (bottom left), 177, 178 (left), 179 (bottom), 182 (bottom), 183 (bottom), 185, 187, 196, 198 (bottom), 201, 202 (bottom), 203, 205, 208 (bottom left), 209, 215, 216 (bottom), 218 (bottom), 219, 220, 221, 224, 226, 229 (bottom left & top right), 230, 234, 235, 240; **Patrick Gulley/Chicago Academy of Sciences:** 29 (right), 36 (bottom), 73, 232; **Dennis Hallinan/FPG International:** 228 (bottom); **Doug Henderson:** 18 (top), 52, 53, 72, 78, 98, 108, 130, 133, 148, 190, 191, 192, 193 (right), 206, 227; **Blair Howard:** 32 (right), 115 (top), 243 (left); **James A. Jensen:** 40 (left), 117; **Eleanor M. Kish/Canadian Museum of Nature, Ottawa, Canada:** 22, 30, 38, 45, 46, 48, 65, 68, 94-95, 120, 138-139, 140, 152-153, 162, 166-167, 168 (left), 172, 180-181, 194-195, 210-211, 222-223, 236, 242, 245, 246; **Berislav Krzic:** 4; **Wade E. Miller/Brigham Young University:** 114, 116; **National Park Service:** 43 (right), 110 (left); **Natural History Museum of Los Angeles County:** 85 (top); **New Mexico Museum of Natural History:** 51 (bottom); **Gregory Paul:** 12 (top & bottom right), 16, 17, 19 (bottom), 20 (left), 25, 28 (top right), 31 (top), 34, 44 (top left & bottom right), 49, 51 (top), 54 (top), 55 (right), 59 (left), 61 (top), 63 (bottom), 66 (left), 70 (right), 74, 75 (left, center & bottom right), 76 (left), 77, 80-81, 85 (bottom), 86, 87, 88, 92 (right), 93, 99 (right), 100, 101, 103, 106-107, 110, 111, 112 (left), 118 (top & bottom), 119 (top & bottom), 126, 127 (left), 128, 131, 132, 143, 144 (bottom), 146, 155, 163, 165 (top), 168 (right), 169, 170 (bottom left), 175 (top left), 182 (top), 186, 188 (left), 189, 193 (left), 197, 198 (top left), 200, 204, 207 (top left & bottom left), 213, 217, 233, 237, 239, 247 (right); **Gary Raham:** 79 (right), 89; **Luis V. Rey:** 248, 251 (right), 252 (bottom), 253, 255; **Royal Ontario Museum:** 42, 151 (left), 165 (bottom), 198 (top right), 213 (left); **Lowell T. Seaich/Utah Field House:** 84 (left); **Paul Sereno:** 58 (right), 62 (right), 135, 136 (right), 207 (right), 208 (top right), 213 (top right), 218 (top); **John Sibbick:** 19 (top right), 21; **Tom Stack & Associates:** Jeff Foott: 41 (left); Brian Parker: 18 (bottom right); Kevin Schafer: 79 (left); **Tyrell Museum of Paleontology:** 8, 83, 160, 161, 202 (top); **Daniel Varner:** 24, 71; **Bob Walters:** 31 (bottom right), 33 (left, top right), 36 (top), 112 (right), 129 (bottom), 136 (left), 154 (right), 158, 176 (bottom left), 184, 214 (bottom), 225, 228 (top), 231 (bottom), 244 (top); **Peter Zallinger/Random House, Inc.:** 147 (right).

INTRODUCTION
PAGE 4

INTRODUCTION

Triceratops *are chased by a* Tyrannosaurus.

The distant thundering sounds signal the arrival of some of the largest animals ever to have roamed the earth. A herd of *Brachiosaurus* arrive to trample every plant they don't eat. The sounds also let an *Allosaurus* know that its next meal could be arriving. Though *Allosaurus* has no chance of catching and killing a healthy adult *Brachiosaurus,* it could try to separate a young or sick member from the herd.

It isn't hard to imagine this scene even though dinosaurs haven't walked the earth for millions of years. Dinosaurs have captured our imaginations. The *Encyclopedia of Dinosaurs* has been written to lead you into the exciting world of dinosaur research and back to the "Age of Dinosaurs." So start your adventure at the beginning of the book when humans first found dinosaur bones.

Early discoveries of dinosaur bones were baffling and probably inspired the legends of dragons. But by the 1800s, paleontology was beginning to be a science. Find out how explorers came to believe that dinosaurs existed and their early ideas about dinosaurs. The trail leading to our present knowledge of dinosaurs was paved by dedicated scientists and explorers.

Dinosaurs pose a special problem for scientists who classify them. With little information and few animals represented, trying to find clues about the dinosaur family tree has turned taxonomists into detectives. Learn what makes dinosaurs different from other reptiles and what makes them similar. A complete, updated, easy-to-follow classification chart is included.

Even though there are few fossils, paleontologists can learn much about dinosaur behavior. The study of these fossils is an important and interesting science. Find out what we know about the lifestyle, behavior, and appearance of dinosaurs. Many dinosaurs were complex creatures.

After learning about the background and history of dinosaurs, you will be introduced to over 140 dinosaurs, grouped by the time periods in which they lived. The first group of dinosaurs lived in the Late Triassic and Early Jurassic Periods, when the world was a much different place. Not only was there only one continent, called Pangaea, but there were no flowering plants and the animals were quite different from today. The Triassic was a time when the ancestors of the dinosaurs were evolving and changing. By the Late Triassic and Early Jurassic, the first dinosaurs had appeared.

The Middle and Late Jurassic saw the rise and dominance of dinosaurs. Sauropods, such as *Apatosaurus* and *Brachiosau-*

rus, became the dominant land animals. Fierce predators, such as *Allosaurus,* looked for their next victims. Slow, plodding *Stegosaurus* had its armor for protection.

The Early Cretaceous was a time of more changes. Flowering plants appeared and dinosaurs became more diverse. But the Late Cretaceous was the most exciting time of all.

By the Late Cretaceous, dinosaurs had become amazingly diverse. The largest predators roamed the land for food. There were dinosaurs that built nests and cared for their young, much like modern birds. There were also dinosaurs that built nests but left their young to fend for themselves, like some modern reptiles. One of the most remarkable features of some Late Cretaceous dinosaurs was a crest. Some dinosaurs could "bugle" to other dinosaurs by blowing air through their crests. One dinosaur even looked like it had a trombone attached to its head!

And then dinosaurs died out. The reasons are not yet understood, but scientists are exploring possibilities and studying the available information. Every day scientists get closer to solving the mystery of why dinosaurs died.

So begin your adventure in the world of dinosaurs. The *Encyclopedia of Dinosaurs* will be your travel guide and companion. And don't fear *Allosaurus* with its large teeth; after all, now it only lives in your imagination!

CHAPTER 1

THE HISTORY OF DINOSAUR DISCOVERIES

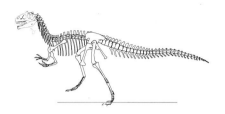

Dinosaur bones have been firing people's imaginations for hundreds of years. People in the Middle Ages found huge bones that were probably fossils of dinosaurs and large aquatic reptiles, such as plesiosaurs and mosasaurs. These may have inspired the legends of dragons and giants. The oldest record of possible fossil dinosaur bones is in a Chinese book written between 265 and 317 A.D. It mentions "dragon bones" found at Wucheng, in Sichuan Province. This area has produced many dinosaur bones.

Since those first discoveries, scientists have been trying to complete the picture of dinosaurs and their lives. All we have left of these amazing creatures are their fossil bones. Paleontologists continue their search to find all they can; each new fossil bone reveals a little more about dinosaurs. And each new dinosaur discovered tells us not only about that dinosaur but also about its place in evolution.

The study of dinosaur fossils has come a long way from the first scientific description when scientists thought a *Megalosaurus* thigh bone belonged to a very large man. Now, scientists can tell what type of diet an animal ate, when it lived, even sometimes how it raised its young. Paleontologists are indebted to the work of the early dinosaur hunters. Their dedication laid the groundwork for today's research.

Left: Megalosaurus *watches the scelidosaurs as two pterosaurs fly by.*

Early Dinosaur Discoveries

In 1677, Robert Plot, an Oxford professor, described the bottom portion of a huge dinosaur thigh bone of *Megalosaurus* in *The Natural History of Oxfordshire*, though he thought it was from a giant human. Almost 90 years later, this bone was illustrated in an academic paper on British natural history.

Dinosaur trackways, or fossilized footprints, are more common than dinosaur bones and there are many in the Connecticut Valley in New England. In the early 1800s, a farm boy named Pliny Moody described birdlike tracks of many shapes and sizes in a rock slab in South Hadley, Massachusetts. He called them traces of "Noah's raven." Later, the Reverend Edward Hitchcock wrote about these and other tracks. He thought they were the footprints of giant prehistoric birds.

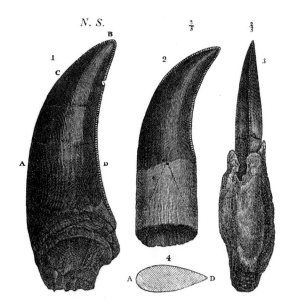

Teeth of Megalosaurus, *from a book by William Buckland.*

Dinosaur Discoveries in 19th Century England

Fossil dinosaur bones and teeth continued to turn up in England. The first dinosaur name was *Megalosaurus*, meaning "giant lizard." In 1824, William Buckland, a clergyman, published the first scientific dinosaur account. He described a tooth-filled lower jaw and other *Megalosaurus* specimens.

British scientists knew that dinosaurs were reptiles, though they considered them large, overgrown lizards. In a fossil-hunting expedition in the British countryside in 1822, Mary Ann Woodhouse Mantell found fossil teeth that showed dinosaurs were different from other reptiles. She gave them to her husband, a physician. A worker at the Hunterian Museum in London noticed their resemblance to an iguana's teeth, though they were much larger. French comparative anatomist Baron

Georges Cuvier agreed that they were from a giant plant-eating reptile. In 1825, Dr. Mantell described the teeth and other bones he had found as a new reptilian genus, *Iguanodon*. He later named his second dinosaur, *Hylaeosaurus*, in 1833.

Sir Richard Owen, England's greatest anatomist, studied Buckland's and Mantell's fossils. In 1841, he created the name Dinosauria, meaning "terrible lizard." This was a separate "tribe or sub-order" of reptiles. Owen also supervised the construction in 1854 of huge, life-size models of *Megalosaurus, Iguanodon, Hylaeosaurus,* and other fossil reptiles. These models were built by Waterhouse Hawkins. They still stand at Crystal Palace Park in Sydenham as a monument to the early days of dinosaur research in England.

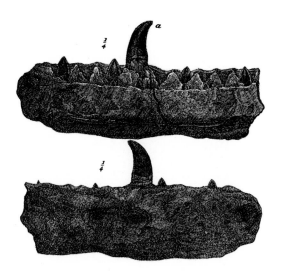

Jaws of Megalosaurus, *from the same book by Buckland.*

Cartoon of Gideon Mantell that appeared in 1836.

Left: *Mosasaurs, whose fossil bones may have inspired legends of dragons.* Top: *William Buckland, ready to explore a glacier.*

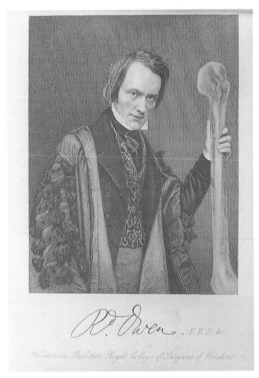

Sir Richard Owen

Once the idea of dinosaurs became established, more and more dinosaur fossils were recognized. In the following decades, European paleontologists Thomas Henry Huxley, Richard Lydekker, H.-E. Sauvage, Philippe Matheron, A. G. Melville, Ludwig Rutimeyer, and Hermann von Meyer described many new dinosaur species. Unfortunately, they often had little to work with—mostly pieces of bones and teeth. Scientists are still sorting out the tangle of species and genera.

Harry Govier Seeley, an amateur paleontologist and professor, made a major contribution to dinosaur classification in 1887. He concluded that there were two groups of dinosaurs: the saurischians, with a lizardlike pelvis; and the ornithischians, with a birdlike pelvis. With a few changes, scientists still use this same classification system today.

Waterhouse Hawkins prepares models of extinct animals for Crystal Palace Park.

The Great American Dinosaur Rush

In 1855, Ferdinand Vandiveer Hayden, a surveyor for the U.S. Geological Survey, took fossil teeth and other remains that he had found along the Judith River in Montana to Philadelphia. A year later, Joseph Leidy published his work on *Troodon, Palaeoscincus, Trachodon, Thespesius,* and *Deinodon.* He did not consider all of them to be dinosaurs.

Two years later, William Parker Foulke made an amazing discovery while vacationing in Haddonfield, New Jersey. John E. Hopkins had found some large vertebrae on his property two decades before. Souvenir hunters had carried off many of the bones, but Foulke and his workers found the rest of the skeleton. Leidy described the headless specimen as a new dinosaur, *Hadrosaurus foulkii.* It was the first dinosaur skeleton found in North America and one of the best found anywhere up to that time.

Edward Drinker Cope

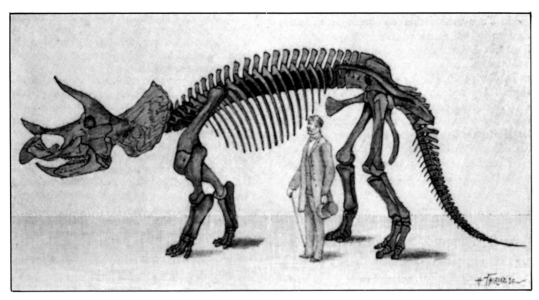

Reconstruction of a dinosaur by Othniel C. Marsh.

scribed more dinosaurs than Cope. Cope's interests in paleontology were wider than Marsh's, though, and he made the greater contribution. The techniques of prospecting, recording, excavating, and shipping large fossils are perhaps the two scientists' greatest legacy.

Henry Fairfield Osborn had just graduated from Princeton University when news of Marsh's expeditions inspired him to organize an expedition to Wyoming. He gained little but experience. Later he worked with Cope, where he picked up knowledge of vertebrate anatomy and paleontology. Osborn then worked at the American Museum of Natural History.

The size and appearance of dinosaurs impressed Osborn. He realized that they also fascinated the general public. Using his connections, he secured funding to find, prepare, and display dinosaur skeletons. By 1940, the American Museum had the greatest collection of dinosaurs on display.

As the 19th century was ending, Andrew Carnegie endowed a large natural history museum in Pittsburgh. After reading about the American Museum's discoveries, he instructed William J. Holland, the museum director, to find dinosaurs to exhibit. Museum employees Jacob Wortman and Arthur S. Coggeshall found a huge partial

In the late 1860s, two scientists took the spotlight. Their rivalry has become legend. Othniel Charles Marsh, nephew of multimillionaire George Peabody, was a Yale University graduate. He persuaded his uncle to finance the Peabody Museum at Yale, which supported his field work.

Edward Drinker Cope grew up a Quaker in Philadelphia. He was a child prodigy, who, by age 18, had published his first scientific paper. Cope was wealthy and he later inherited a small fortune that allowed him to pursue his studies.

Cope and Marsh's rivalry grew out of their ambition to be the greatest paleontologist. By 1866, Cope had described his first dinosaur, the meat-eating *Laelaps aquilunguis*. Marsh had not yet described a dinosaur. He pointed out errors in Cope's 1868 description of the aquatic reptile from Kansas, *Elasmosaurus*. Embarrassed, Cope tried to buy all the copies of his article, but Marsh kept several copies. Cope never forgot the insult.

Schoolmaster Arthur Lakes came across fossil bones in Morrison, Colorado, in

1877. He sent fossils to both Marsh and Cope. Marsh immediately secured rights and began digging. Fortunately for Cope, another schoolmaster found bigger bones near Cañon City, Colorado. Later that summer, two employees of the Union Pacific Railroad located some well-preserved bones at Como Bluff, Wyoming. Marsh sent his field man to supervise the excavation. These three locations fostered a revolution in our understanding of dinosaurs.

Marsh's and Cope's ambition to be the first to describe the largest and most spectacular fossils started the "dinosaur rush" that lasted for a decade. They hired teams of men to find new locations, to dig for dinosaurs, and to send bones to New Haven and Philadelphia for description. Each scrambled to be the first in print with new dinosaurs. As a result, many dinosaurs received two or more names. For example, Marsh described *Apatosaurus* in 1877 and *Brontosaurus* in 1879. Because they are the same animal, the older name has priority.

Cope died in 1897, and Marsh in 1899. After the smoke cleared, Marsh had de-

Above: *Othniel Charles Marsh.* Right: *Cartoon of Marsh from* Punch, *1890.*

PROFESSOR MARSH'S PRIMEVAL TROUPE.

HE SHOWS HIS PERFECT MASTERY OVER THE CERATOPSIDÆ.

(See Proceedings of the British Association at Leeds.)

dinosaur skeleton at Sheep Creek, Wyoming. They unearthed another of the same species nearby. Together with bones from related dinosaurs, workers made the two into a spectacular 84-foot-long mounted skeleton that Holland named *Diplodocus carnegii.*

Earl Douglass went to work for the Carnegie Museum. Prospecting in the Uinta Basin near Vernal, Utah, in 1908, he and Holland found a *Diplodocus* thigh bone. Douglass returned the following year and discovered the giant skeleton (over 70 feet long) that Holland named *Apatosaurus louisae,* in honor of Carnegie's wife. That skeleton proved to be the "tip of the iceberg" of dinosaur fossils. With Carnegie's support, Douglass started a large excavation that produced thousands of dinosaur bones. President Woodrow Wilson designated the quarry Dinosaur National Monument in 1915, and excavations continue even today.

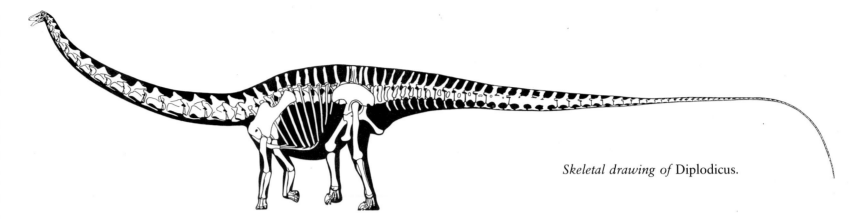

Skeletal drawing of Diplodicus.

Dinosaur Discoveries in Canada

About the time Douglass was collecting dinosaurs for the Carnegie Museum, western Canada opened to dinosaur prospec-

tors. In the early 1870s, George Mercer Dawson had found dinosaur bones in Saskatchewan while surveying the Canada-United States boundary. In 1884, Dawson's assistant, George B. Tyrrell, unearthed a large partial skull of a meat-eating dinosaur, which was later named *Albertosaurus sarcophagus,* in Alberta.

Geologist Thomas Chesmer Weston boated along the Red Deer River to scan the shore for dinosaur fossils. By the turn of the century, Canadian paleontologist Lawrence M. Lambe had collected many dinosaur specimens using the same technique. A few years later, in 1910, Barnum Brown specially outfitted a barge and continued Weston's and Lambe's work.

Charles Hazelius Sternberg's childhood interest in fossil plants led to a job as a fossil collector for Cope. The Canadian Geological Survey hired Sternberg in 1912 to find dinosaur skeletons and send them to Ottawa. He and his sons George, Charles, and Levi competed with Brown in Alberta for several years. Among the many fossils they found were two duckbilled dinosaur "mummies," preserved with extensive skin impressions. The wealth of specimens discovered by Brown and the Sternbergs showed the amazing diversity of crests, frills, and horns that had arisen among the Late Cretaceous dinosaurs.

Workers have found more dinosaur specimens in southern Alberta than anyplace else in the world. The Alberta government protected this resource by designating a 40-square-mile area along the Red Deer River as Dinosaur Provincial Park.

Top: Albertosaurus *with a juvenile.* Right: Albertosaurus libratus

Collecting fossils in Cherry Hinton chalk pit in Cambridgeshire, England.

Left: *Early drawing (1895) of an* Iguanodon. Right: *Excavating fossils in the great bone cave in Maestricht, Holland.*

Dinosaur Discoveries in Europe

In 1878, the feud between Cope and Marsh was getting into full swing. Meanwhile, coal miners at Bernissart, Belgium, discovered well-preserved dinosaur skeletons over a thousand feet beneath the ground. Soon the mining company Charbonnage de Bernissart diverted its resources to excavating the skeletons, a task that took several years.

Louis Dollo devoted his life to preparing, mounting, and studying these skeletons, making *Iguanodon* the best-known European dinosaur. Dollo's work inspired younger European paleontologists, who carried the study of dinosaurs forward.

One colorful character was Franz Baron Nopcsa von Felsö-Szilvás, a Transylvanian nobleman. He became intrigued with dinosaurs when his sister chanced upon some bones on her property in what is now Hungary. He published a scientific description of the new dinosaur in 1899, as a first-year student at the University of Vienna.

Much of Nopcsa's work was to describe the dinosaurs of central Europe, which we know from many pieces of fossils. He also speculated—sometimes outlandishly—about dinosaur origins, classification, and lifestyle. Other scientists quickly discredited his idea that the crested duckbilled dinosaurs were males and the flat-headed ones females. Scientists today accept a modern version of his hypothesis: that the sizes and shapes of the crests of duckbilled dinosaurs suggest the animal's maturity.

Europe's premier vertebrate paleontologist at that time was Friedrich Freiherr von Huene. Like Nopcsa, Huene was a nobleman—with the time and means to pursue a university education. At the University of Tübingen, he began his long career with a study of the Triassic dinosaurs of Germany. When workers found dinosaur bones at Trossingen, Huene investigated. The excavations uncovered an enormous bed of *Plateosaurus* bones. This animal lived during the Late Triassic.

Opening Asia to Paleontology

The Canadian dinosaur rush was ending. Meanwhile, Henry Fairfield Osborn decided the place to look for fossil mammals and the origins of the human race was in the Gobi Desert. The American Museum of Natural History sent expeditions led by Roy Chapman Andrews and Walter Granger to the Gobi. They first set out in 1922, but they did not find human remains. Instead, the prospectors found ancient mammal bones, and in one place, dinosaur bones. Heartened by these discoveries, the expedition returned in 1923. At Shabarakh Usu (now called Bayn Dzak), they identified the first dinosaur eggs ever found, many still arranged in nests. Workers also unearthed skeletons of *Protoceratops andrewsi,* the dinosaur that

laid the eggs. There were skeletons from hatchling to adult. They found many other new dinosaurs on that and later expeditions to the Gobi.

During the 1930s, political turmoil in China prevented further exploration of the Gobi Desert. After World War II, paleontologists from the Soviet Union, led by Ivan Antonovich Efremov, found many fossils in the Nemegt Basin. The huge meat-eater *Tarbosaurus bataar* and the giant plant-eater *Saurolophus angustirostris* were two new finds. These animals were closely related to North American dinosaurs *Tyrannosaurus rex* and *Saurolophus osborni.* This suggests that during the Late Cretaceous, a strip of land joined western North America and eastern Asia. There also could have been a group of islands between the two continents. Dinosaurs and other animals may have been able to roam between these areas.

Protoceratops *egg.*

In 1902, a Russian colonel named Manakin found the first dinosaurs from China along the Chinese bank of the Amur River (this river forms part of the boundary between Russia and China). In 1915, A. N. Kryshtofovitch and V. P. Renngarten led expeditions to the region. The first named dinosaur from China, *Mandschurosaurus amurensis,* was mounted in Leningrad.

Meanwhile, American paleontologist G. D. Louderback had unearthed dinosaur remains in the Sichuan Basin of southwestern China in 1913. That same year, mis-

sionary R. Mertens found a large partial skeleton in the Shandong Province. Otto Zdansky and Tan Xichou excavated the site in 1922. The well-preserved remains of a long-necked plant-eating dinosaur, *Euhelopus zdanskyi,* went to the University of Uppsala, Sweden, for examination.

China and Sweden sponsored the Sino-Swedish Northwest China Expeditions of 1927-31, led by Swedish geographer Sven Hedin and Chinese geologist F. Yuan. In 1953, Birger Bohlin wrote about some of the dinosaurs discovered during those expeditions, though many were only fragmentary remains.

China's foremost paleontologist from the 1930s until his death in 1979, Young Chung Chien studied vertebrate paleontology under Huene in Germany. On returning to China in 1928, he worked for the Geological Survey of China, starting excavations for fossil reptiles in several places. Young wrote up and supervised the mounting of *Lufengosaurus,* discovered in Yunnan Province at Lufeng. It was the first mounted dinosaur skeleton displayed in China. After the Chinese revolution, Young founded the Institute of Vertebrate Paleontology and Paleoanthropology. This institute supported the excavation and study of many dinosaurs and other fossils. It was almost entirely through the work of Young and his students that China became one of the centers of dinosaur research.

Reconstruction of Protoceratops *and nest.*

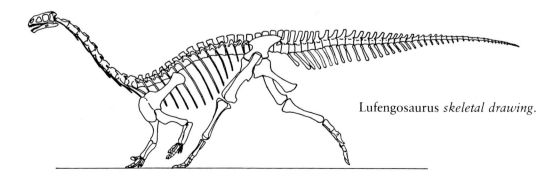

Lufengosaurus *skeletal drawing.*

Brachiosaurus, *with* Ceratosaurus *in the background.*

Dinosaurs of Africa

W. B. Sattler found the most interesting African dinosaurs in 1907 near Tendaguru Hill, Tanzania (in what was then German East Africa). Berlin paleontologists Werner Janensch and Edwin Hennig led an expedition to the site. From 1909 to 1912, several hundred untrained native workers toiled in the hot, humid climate to excavate the deep bone-pits. They crated and hand-carried thousands of bones, some weighing hundreds of pounds, cross-country to the port of Lindi for shipment to Berlin.

One spectacular result was the 40-foot-tall skeleton of *Brachiosaurus brancai,* which now stands in the East Berlin Natural History Museum. Assembled from the bones of several animals, it is the tallest mounted dinosaur skeleton in the world. Also found were skeletons of the spiny-plated dinosaur *Kentrosaurus* and remains of the huge plant-eaters *Barosaurus africanus* and *Dicraeosaurus.* The Tendaguru finds resembled the dinosaurs discovered in the western United States. This proved that the same kinds of dinosaurs (though not the same species) lived throughout the world during the Late Jurassic.

After World War I, the English continued the work at Tendaguru. By 1929, work at Tendaguru ceased. Recently, paleontologists have returned to the region to continue the search for dinosaurs.

In the autumn of 1912, word of a find of large dinosaur bones reached Ernst Freiherr Stromer von Reichenbach at the University of Munich. R. Markgraf had discovered the bones at the Baharia Oasis in Egypt. The bones belonged to a new meat-eating dinosaur, *Spinosaurus,* which had a six-foot-high sail on its back. Later surveys of the region uncovered more dinosaur bones. World War I ended German field work in Egypt.

In the early 1930s, Stromer wrote up three Egyptian dinosaurs: *Aegyptosaurus,* a giant plant-eater; *Bahariasaurus,* a giant meat-eater rivaling *Tyrannosaurus;* and *Carcharodontosaurus,* a smaller carnivore. Unfortunately, a bombing raid during World War II destroyed Stromer's specimens, including some that had not been described.

From the late 19th century until the 1950s, French paleontologists studied the dinosaurs of Morocco, Algeria, and Madagascar. In 1896, Charles Déperet had described a long-necked herbivore, *Lapparentosaurus,* and a large carnivore, *Majungasaurus,* from Madagascar. After World War II, Albert F. de Lapparent and Réné Lavocat described several new dinosaurs from Morocco and the Sahara. The most curious was *Rebbachisaurus,* a huge plant-eater with vertebrae nearly five feet tall. The animal may have resembled *Apatosaurus* with a tall ridge or sail along its back.

Dinosaurs from South America, India, and Australia

Huene's Trossingen studies brought him worldwide recognition and stimulated interest in dinosaurs everywhere, including South America. Commandante Buratovich at Neuquén was the first to discover dinosaurs in Argentina in 1882. The Museum of La Plata, which stored many of the fossils, invited Huene to work on the collection.

In 1936, an expedition sponsored by the Museum of Comparative Zoology of Harvard University went to the Santa Maria Formation of Rio Grande do Sul. Headed by Llewellyn Ivor Price and Theodore E. White, the prospectors brought back a large collection of fossils that included the

partial skeleton of *Staurikosaurus pricei.* It was described by Edwin Colbert in 1970. Scientists consider this the oldest known "true" dinosaur.

Price remained in Brazil, and his work inspired a generation of native South American paleontologists. Among these was Osvaldo A. Reig of the Institut Lillo of Tucuman in Argentina. Reig worked in the Ischigualasto Valley in the San Juan Province, where goat farmer Victorino Herrera found dinosaur remains slightly younger than *Staurikosaurus.* The Talampaya-Ischigualasto region is a remote, forbidding desert in central Argentina. In 1958, Alfred Sherwood Romer and Bryan Patterson uncovered reptile fossils from a period when dinosaurs were establishing themselves. In 1963, Reig described the primitive dinosaurs *Herrerasaurus* and *Ischisaurus,* which opened a hidden chapter of dinosaur evolution.

In 1958, Sohan Lall Jain, Tapan K. Roy-Chowdhury, and Pamela Lamplugh Robinson led an expedition in India. They located dinosaur bones near where the River Pranhita joins the River Godavari. Known as the Kota Formation, the rocks are layers of limestone, "fossilized" lake remains nearly 200 million years old. A rich bone bed excavated in 1961 yielded bones of several specimens of a new large, long-necked plant-eater, *Barapasaurus tagorei.* Also found was *Kotasaurus yamanpalliensis,* another plant-eater.

Although Australia has yielded other fascinating reptile fossils, the dinosaur record remains fragmentary. The first dinosaur remains discovered in Australia were a claw and some leg bones. In 1891, Seeley described a new sheep-size dinosaur, *Agrosaurus macgillivrayi,* a small relative of *Plateosaurus.*

Workers found more dinosaur fossil pieces later at Cape Paterson in Victoria and at Lightning Ridge in Queensland. In

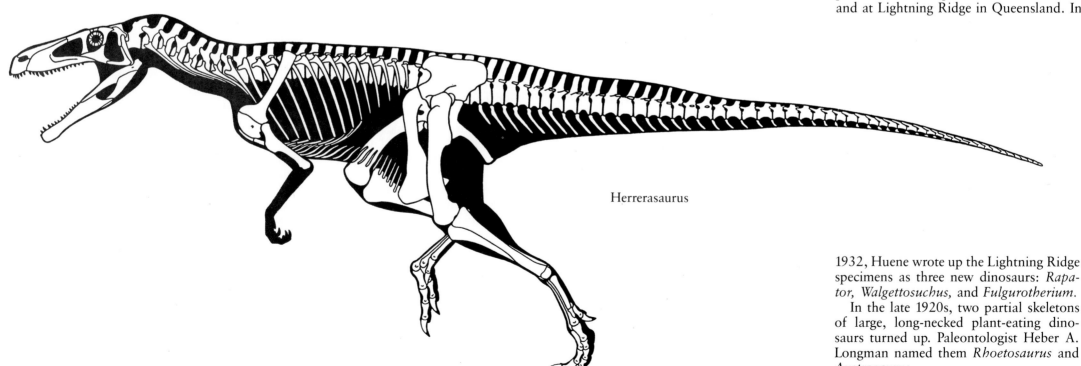

Herrerasaurus

1932, Huene wrote up the Lightning Ridge specimens as three new dinosaurs: *Rapator, Walgettosuchus,* and *Fulgurotherium.*

In the late 1920s, two partial skeletons of large, long-necked plant-eating dinosaurs turned up. Paleontologist Heber A. Longman named them *Rhoetosaurus* and *Austrosaurus.*

DINOSAUR RESEARCH EVOLVES (1960S TO 1980S)

Beginning in the 1960s, a rising number of scientists turned to the study of dinosaurs as a career—despite the low pay. Also, more museums and universities developed dinosaur research programs. Since the '60s, the number of known dinosaurs species has more than doubled, and our understanding of dinosaurs greatly increased.

The United States and Canada became home to the most vigorous dinosaur research in the world. The Tyrrell Museum of Paleontology in Alberta is located in the middle of a fertile dinosaur burial ground. Led by Philip J. Currie, Tyrrell researchers found bone beds that apparently were the remains of dinosaur herds. These provided information about growth changes, individual differences, disease, and herd structure.

John R. "Jack" Horner discovered hatchling duckbilled dinosaurs, dinosaur eggs, embryos, and nesting grounds in Montana's Two Medicine Formation. One kind of egg belonged to a duckbilled dinosaur that he and Robert Makela named

Dinosaur egg found in Two Medicine Formation in Montana.

Maiasaura *hatchlings.*

Maiasaura. Another egg was from a small ornithischian dinosaur that he and David B. Weishampel called *Orodromeus.* Horner also pioneered new techniques for examining dinosaur fossils, such as CAT-scanning the remains of dinosaur eggs to find embryos. Horner and his team found a *Maiasaura* bone bed that covered several square miles and contained the remains of at least 10,000 animals.

Farther south, in Utah and Colorado, the late James A. Jensen's work left an enormous amount of material—enough to fill a warehouse. These included remains of the immense plant-eaters *Supersaurus, Ultrasauros,* and *Dystylosaurus,* the more modest-size herbivore *Cathetosaurus,* the carnivore *Torvosaurus,* and several others. One of Jensen's most productive sites, the Late Jurassic Dry Mesa Quarry, yielded a six-foot-tall pelvis.

In Arizona, New Mexico, and Texas dinosaur-bearing rocks were discovered from Late Triassic to Late Cretaceous. Petrified Forest National Park and its surroundings are of Triassic age and have been studied by Robert A. Long, J. Michael Parrish, and several others. They studied fossils of North America's oldest known dinosaurs. Sankar Chatterjee examined fossils of dinosaurs and related animals from Triassic rocks in Texas. His prize fossil was what may be the oldest known bird.

Spencer G. Lucas and Adrian Hunt started several projects in New Mexico, including a survey of dinosaurs and their locations. The San Juan and Raton Basins contained rocks deposited when the Mesozoic Era ended. In 1947, an American Museum of Natural History field party led by Edwin Colbert discovered an extensive dinosaur burial site at Ghost Ranch, New

Mexico. Dozens of skeletons of *Coelophysis bauri* had become tangled in an ancient stream. In 1989, Colbert published his work on *Coelophysis,* making it the best-known Late Triassic predatory dinosaur.

In the mid-1980s, the first Alaskan North Slope dinosaur bones were discovered. They were from the duck-billed *Edmontosaurus,* which stood ten feet tall and were 40 feet long. Scientists speculated that these dinosaurs lived in social groups, or even herds.

In the early 1970s, Robert T. Bakker drew on the work of anatomist Gerhard Heilmann and paleontologist John Ostrom and argued that dinosaurs were not slow moving, but rather warm-blooded, active, and mobile. He also argued that dinosaurs are the direct ancestors of birds, a theory that received further support with new discoveries in the 1990s (see Chapter 9).

Petrified wood in Petrified National Forest.

Coelophysis *skeleton found at Ghost Ranch in New Mexico.*

dinosaur. These were the only dinosaurs known from Mexico from more than scraps.

James M. Clark, Rene Hernandez, and other paleontologists worked a site of roughly Middle Jurassic age in Tamaulipas, Mexico. Middle Jurassic dinosaur-bearing rocks are rare; the Mexican site was the first one found in North America. Another Mexican site yielded the remains of Late Cretaceous dinosaurs, especially duckbills.

South America saw an explosion of dinosaur research with the work of Reig and Romer. Jose F. Bonaparte and his colleagues worked in dinosaur-bearing formations in Argentina. One find was a bizarre relative of *Diplodocus.* This animal evidently had a pair of tall, parallel sails along its neck and back. South American Cretaceous dinosaurs were unusual, having evolved on their own after the continent broke free of Africa in the Late Jurassic Period.

Bonaparte also discovered dinosaurs from the Middle Jurassic in Argentina, including the giant herbivores *Patagosaurus* and *Volkheimeria* and the meat-eating *Piatnitzkysaurus.* This predator strongly

Lambeosaurus

resembles the Late Jurassic *Allosaurus* from North America and may be its closest known ancestor.

In China, the Cultural Revolution of the 1960s stopped most research, but in the mid-1970s there was an explosion of dis-

The eastern half of North America has produced few dinosaur fossils. In the 1980s, Paul E. Olsen studied the East Coast from Nova Scotia to New Jersey. He discovered the remains of several new Triassic dinosaurs. Olsen also found evidence of a large asteroid impact near the end of the Triassic, which may have killed other animals and allowed dinosaurs to rise to dominance.

In the past, Mexico was not well explored for dinosaurs. From 1968 to 1974, William J. Morris and his colleagues worked in the El Gallo Formation of Baja, California. They collected partial skeletons of the large duckbilled dinosaurs *Lambeosaurus laticaudus,* which was estimated to be as long as 54 feet. Also collected from the somewhat older La Bocana Roja Formation were the fragmentary remains of *Labocania anomala,* a heavily built, meat-eating

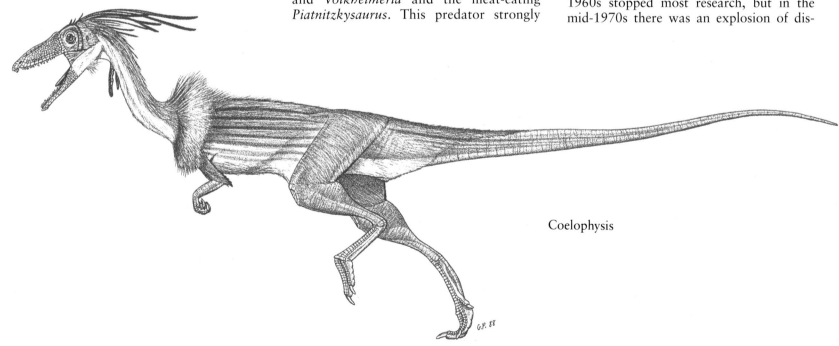

Coelophysis

coveries. Dinosaurs from the Lower Jurassic through the Late Cretaceous are now represented in China by excellent material. Paleontologists from the United States, Canada, and Europe visited China to examine the material and to exchange knowledge. The result was a new "Chinese dinosaur rush" (see Chapter 9).

The Polish-Mongolian Paleontological Expeditions of the late 1960s and early 1970s returned to the Gobi Desert. Zofia Kielan-Jaworowska led the expeditions, and they were rewarded with the discovery of new kids of dinosaurs and more complete remains of other known dinosaurs. Inspired by the success of the Polish scientists, the USSR Academy of Sciences took over field work in the Gobi in the mid-1970s. Almost every year since, the Joint Soviet-Mongolian Paleontological Expeditions unearthed more dinosaur remains. The discoveries inspired the exchange of ideas between Chinese and Western paleontologists.

Eric Buffetaut participated in several recent discoveries. In the late 1970s, while searching for crocodile remains in Thailand,

he and coworkers uncovered a huge dinosaur bed in the Upper Jurassic Sao Khua Formation. They found several partial skeletons of large plant-eaters, many scattered teeth of large predators, and the remains of a small meat-eater.

Because much of the Soviet Union is hard to reach, workers rarely discover dinosaurs there. Still, scientists from the Paleontological Institute of the USSR Academy of Sciences began to examine the dinosaur material in their collections. They also organized expeditions to regions south of the Ural Mountains, to the Caucasus, and to eastern Siberia.

Even England still yielded a new dinosaur find or two. Amateur fossil collector William J. Walker chanced upon a huge, foot-long dinosaur claw weathering out of a clay pit in Surrey. This new dinosaur, *Baryonyx walkeri*, revealed a new family of meat-eating dinosaurs.

Studies by Madrid paleontologist Jose Luis Sanz and his colleagues began to show how much Spain had to contribute to the study of dinosaurs. They found small and

Iguanodon *skeleton.*

Baryonyx walkeri

large predators, huge long-necked herbivores (including the new species *Aragosaurus ischiaticus),* small plant-eaters, large plant-eaters (*Iguanodon*), and armored dinosaurs (*Hylaeosaurus*). Topping off their work was the discovery at Las Hoyas of a new genus of Early Cretaceous fossil bird. This bird, which was between the "feathered dinosaur" *Archaeopteryx* and more modern birds, was a key to understanding bird evolution.

In the 1970s, French paleontologists discovered interesting Middle Cretaceous African dinosaurs near the Tenere Oasis in the southern Sahara Desert. Besides claws

and teeth identified as *Carcharodontosaurus,* they found the skeletons of two new dinosaurs related to *Iguanodon*.

Ralph Molnar of the Queensland Museum researched dinosaurs in Australia. In 1980, he described Australia's first armored dinosaur, *Minmi*. With Neville Pledge, he wrote up the small predator *Kakuru*, which was known only from pieces of fossils. These were the first dinosaurs to be described from Australia since Huene's work in 1932. In 1981, Alan Bartholomai and Molnar wrote up the herbivore *Muttaburrasaurus*, which is similar to *Iguanodon. Muttaburrasaurus* was the first almost complete Australian dinosaur ever skeleton found.

Also working in Australia were the husband-and-wife team of Thomas and Patricia Rich. They worked along the southern shore, where they found dinosaur-bearing Early Cretaceous rocks. The fossils were fragmentary and were in hard stone that was difficult to work, but they found enough material to show an unusual dinosaur fauna.

During much of the Cretaceous Period, Australia was close to the South Pole. For two or three months each year, the region was nearly always dark and the winter temperature must have been extremely cold. The dinosaurs that the Riches found were small and active, with oversize eyes that they believed adapted to life in semidarkness.

No paleontologist has doubted that dinosaurs lived in Antarctica during the Mesozoic Era, but it is difficult to find dinosaurs when ice caps two miles thick cover most of the continent. In the 1980s, however, an expedition led by Zulma de Gasparini and her coworkers at Argentina's Museum of La Plata brought back the remains of Antarctica's first known dinosaur. It was an armored form resembling North America's *Ankylosaurus*. The find was perplexing, since that type of dinosaur is rare.

Some of the most interesting work is not always the discovery of new and unusual dinosaurs. For some paleontologists, the most interesting work is the analysis of fossils gathered years, decades, or even a century ago. We do not know what piece of fossil may lead to new insights into dinosaur behavior or evolution. With the continuing work of dedicated scientists, our knowledge of these wonderful creatures increases almost daily.

Right: Iguanodon *with young.*

CHAPTER 2

DINOSAUR CLASSIFICATION AND EVOLUTION

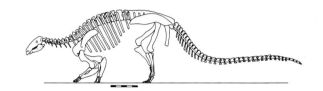

Dinosaurs ruled the world during the Mesozoic Era, which is divided into three Periods. During the Triassic Period, dinosaur ancestors were evolving. In the Late Triassic, the world saw the first true dinosaurs. In the Jurassic Period, the number of dinosaurs grew. By the Cretaceous Period, many different types of dinosaurs had evolved.

Paleontologists study the different kinds of dinosaurs to find their relationships to other dinosaurs and to find the ancestors of the dinosaurs. This can tell scientists much about evolution. It can also tell them some things about the world the dinosaurs lived in. Dinosaurs that could migrate were similar, but those dinosaurs that were isolated evolved differently. Dinosaurs and other organisms have historically been placed into hierarchical categories, using a system of classification called the Linnaean system. Today, research on dinosaur relationships uses an approach called cladistics, which uses the presence of shared morphological features to recreate the branching tree of dinosaur evolution.

Because scientists have incomplete information for dinosaurs, groupings may change when new information is found. So each new dinosaur fossil that is discovered could be a key that unlocks some of the information about dinosaur evolution and ancestry.

Left: *The dome-headed dinosaur* Pachycephalosaurus.

Tyrannosaurus, *the "tyrant lizard king."*

Kingdom
Phylum
Class
Order
Family
Genus
Species

The Linnaean System of Classification

In the 1750s, Swedish botanist Carl von Linné (who is known by the Latin form of his name, Linnaeus) developed a system to classify all living things. Each living thing has two scientific names, a genus and a species name. The scientist who first describes a new organism (any living thing) names it. Since Linnaeus began using this system, over a million species have been named.

A scientific name is given in the Linnaean System because living organisms are called different things in different languages. The house cat, for example, is *die Katze* in German; *le chat* in French; but English, French, and German biologists call it *Felis catus*.

In choosing a name, a scientist may highlight an interesting feature of the organism or may name it in honor of a person or the place it was found. So, the enormous meat-eating dinosaur *Tyrannosaurus rex* is the "tyrant lizard king" that reigned over other dinosaurs.

In the Linnaean System, similar *species* are grouped into a *genus*, similar *genera* into a *family*, similar *families* into an *order*, similar *orders* into a *class*, similar *classes* into a *phylum*, and similar *phyla* into a *kingdom*.

Dogs, coyotes, and wolves are in the genus *Canis*. *Vulpes*, the fox genus, and *Canis* are both in the dog family Canidae. Canidae and Ursidae, the bear family, are part of the order Carnivora (meat-eating animals). Carnivores and people are in the class Mammalia (all mammals). Mammals and fishes are in the phylum Chordata (animals with backbones, or chordates). Chordates and corals are members of the kingdom Animalia (animals). These categories are known as *taxa* (singular: *taxon*), and the study of these classifications is called *taxonomy*.

USING CLADISTICS TO ANALYZE EVOLUTIONARY RELATIONSHIPS

One of the most active areas of dinosaur research in the last two decades has been a thorough reconsideration of their relationships using a new approach called cladistics, which is also known as phylogenetic systematics. Unlike the Linnean system, which puts organisms into hierarchical categories, cladistics attempts to determine the many speciation events that resulted in the separation by branching of all organisms, living and extinct. In simpler terms, cladistics is a method of analyzing the evolutionary relationships between groups to construct their family tree.

Cladistics groups organisms on the basis of shared derived characters (synapomorphies) and uses a philosophical concept called parsimony, which holds that the simplest branching pattern (the one with the fewest steps) is most likely close to the true

one. Scientists using cladistics do not place organisms into nested categories like the Linnean system, because they assume that each branch occurs by the same simple process of speciation. However, the various Linnean categories are still widely used for placement of groups into categories, as is done in this book.

CLASSIFICATION AND EVOLUTION

After Charles Darwin published his theory of evolution, biologists began to understand why organisms fall into natural groupings. For example, species in the dog genus *Canis* look like one another because they all had a common ancestor. Foxes (genus *Vulpes*) and dogs (genus *Canis*) do not look as much alike because their common ancestor was farther back in time. The farther back a common ancestor lived, the longer its descendants have had to evolve and change.

It is almost impossible to prove that two species share a common ancestor. But by making an extensive list of characteristics, scientists can show how likely it is that two species are related. The more traits two species share, the more likely they are closely related and got those traits from a shared ancestor.

For example, both sparrows and bats have arms and hands that are wings, but sparrow wings and bat wings are much different. Sparrow wings and bat wings evolved separately, and not because of a common ancestor. This is called *convergent evolution*. On the other hand, the wings of sparrows, eagles, ostriches, and all other birds are alike. This shows that today's bird species are closely related and came from a common ancestor.

Two Quetzalcoetlus *and a small tyrannosaur.* Quetzalcoetlus *was a flying reptile that had a much different wing structure than* Archaeopteryx.

CLASSIFICATION CHART

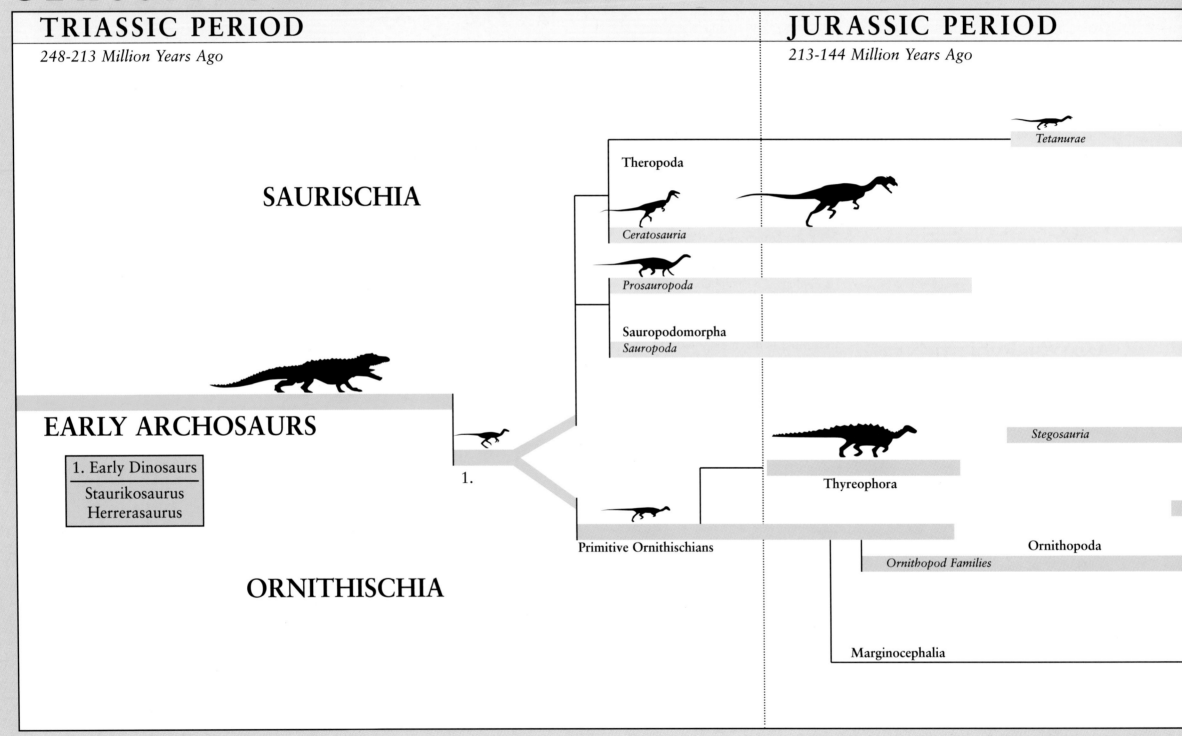

TRIASSIC PERIOD
248-213 Million Years Ago

JURASSIC PERIOD
213-144 Million Years Ago

SAURISCHIA

EARLY ARCHOSAURS

1. Early Dinosaurs
Staurikosaurus
Herrerasaurus

ORNITHISCHIA

Theropoda

Tetanurae

Ceratosauria

Prosauropoda

Sauropodomorpha
Sauropoda

1.

Primitive Ornithischians

Stegosauria

Thyreophora

Ornithopod Families

Ornithopoda

Marginocephalia

CRETACEOUS PERIOD

144-65 Million Years Ago

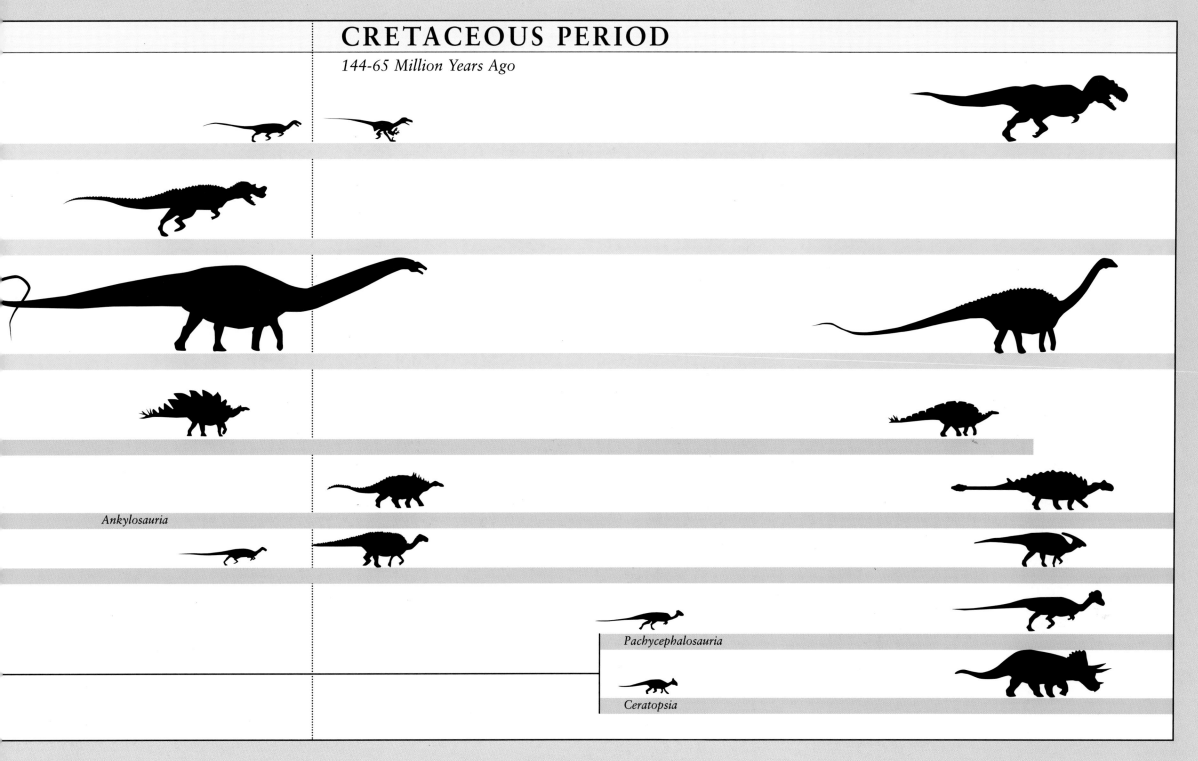

Ankylosauria

Pachycephalosauria

Ceratopsia

Dinosaurs as Archosaurs

Only a few dinosaurs are known from complete or nearly complete skeletons; almost half of the known species are based only on teeth or bone fragments. The shapes of bones are used for dinosaur classification. Only the hundred or so dinosaurs for which good remains are known can be studied for relationships.

Bones are rarely fossilized. Living things usually decay and vanish after death. It is difficult for paleontologists to describe an incomplete fossil skeleton and to decide what the animal looked and acted like from just a few fossilized remains. The discovery of a new dinosaur—or new fossils of a poorly known dinosaur—may change the family tree. We will never know all the different dinosaur groups that lived, so their family tree will always be incomplete.

Dinosaurs are classified as reptiles, but all reptiles do not form a single *clade* (a group that includes a common ancestral species and all the species that descended from it). There are two reptilian clades. One clade includes all living reptiles, dinosaurs, ichthyosaurs, plesiosaurs, and birds (the Sauropsida). The other clade is the mammals and the extinct mammallike reptiles (the Theropsida).

Crocodilians and birds are more closely related to each other than either is to lizards and snakes. They are part of a smaller sauropsid clade, the Archosauria. Lizards and snakes are in the clade Lepidosauria. Archosaurs had a large opening in the front of each eye. As the many groups of archo-

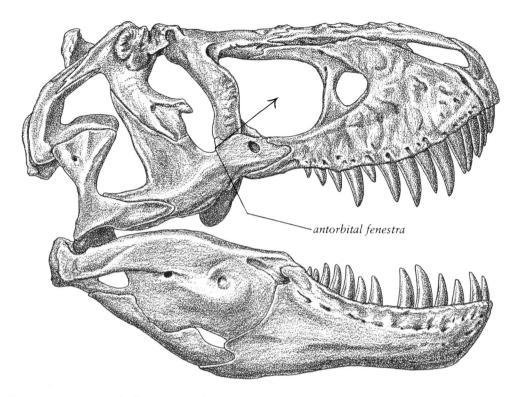

Tyrannosaurus rex skull drawing, showing the large antorbital fenestra.

saurs evolved, this *antorbital fenestra* ("window in front of the eye") sometimes closed (in crocodilians and the later plant-eating dinosaurs) or merged with the nostril (in pterosaurs). It was the largest opening in the skull of the large predatory dinosaurs, such as *Allosaurus* and *Tyrannosaurus*.

The earliest archosaurs are found in Permian rocks, formed before the Mesozoic Era began. In the beginning of the Mesozoic, when animal life was recovering from the worst mass extinction in the world's history, the archosaurs expanded and quickly spread. Most of those first archosaurs were extinct by the end of the Triassic Period, but the Pterosauria, Saurischia, and Ornithischia survived to the end of the Mesozoic, and the Crocodilia survived to the present. Birds have not been found in the Triassic, although some puzzling Triassic birdlike animals have recently been discovered in Asia, Europe, and Texas.

A Tyrannosaurus skeleton.

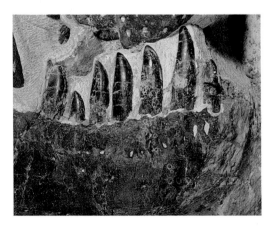

Tyrannosaurus rex fossil teeth.

Archosaurs Evolve

Two important evolutionary changes took place among the archosaurs. They changed from sprawling, lizardlike animals to animals that walked with their legs held directly under their bodies. The other change was from a cold-blooded, lizardlike metabolism (the way a body uses energy) to a warm-blooded, birdlike metabolism. These changes did not take place in all archosaurs, but they happened in the dinosaurs. Crocodilians are the only surviving example in which those changes did not occur; birds are the only surviving group in which they did occur.

Warm-bloodedness may have appeared early in the dinosaur-bird clade, so that almost all dinosaurs were warm-blooded. This trait may have been inherited from a common ancestor dinosaurs shared with birds. Or, these changes may have happened after dinosaurs and birds separated, so that only a few advanced predatory dinosaurs were warm-blooded.

The ancestors of dinosaurs developed a stronger ankle. This kind of ankle occurs in pterosaurs, dinosaurs, and birds. *Lagosuchus*, *Lagerpeton*, and *Pseudolagosuchus* were small, bipedal (they walked on two legs) archosaurs with advanced ankles and other features that suggest they were closely related to dinosaurs.

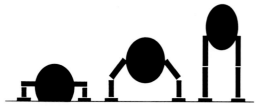

Above: *Archosaurs changed from lizardlike animals to animals with their legs held directly under their bodies, such as the dinosaurs. Right: Lagosuchus had an advanced ankle, like the ankles of dinosaurs.*

TRUE DINOSAURS AT LAST

Harry Govier Seeley split dinosaurs into two groups, the Order Saurischia ("lizard-hipped" dinosaurs) and the Order Ornithischia ("bird-hipped" dinosaurs). Both orders probably had a common ancestor that lived sometime during the Middle Triassic. Birds belong to the saurischian dinosaur clade.

As in all land animals, there were three bones in each side of the pelvis. The left and right *ilia* (singular: *ilium*) firmly gripped the spine in the sacrum. The left and right *pubes* (singular: *pubis*) extended down beneath the *ilia*. The left and right *ischia* (singular: *ischium*) extended down and back beneath the ilia and behind the pubes. In some dinosaurs, the pubes extended down and forward, as they do in lizards. This is why Seeley called them saurischian, or "lizard-hipped" dinosaurs. In other dinosaurs, the pubes extended down and back, running

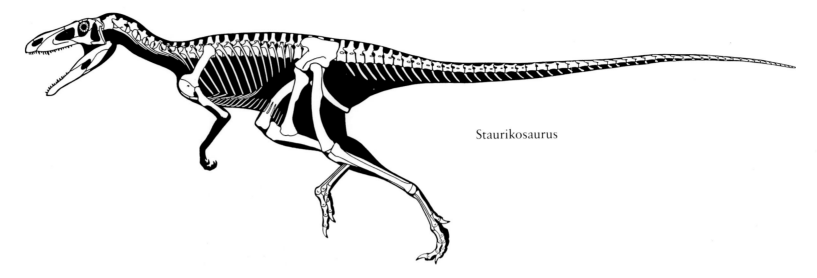

Staurikosaurus

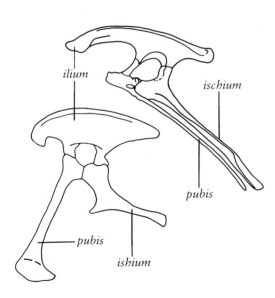

ilium

ischium

pubis

pubis

ishium

The top pelvis is typical for an ornithischian, or "bird-hipped," dinosaur. The bottom is typical for a saurischian, or "lizard-hipped," dinosaur.

beneath and parallel to the ischia, as they do in birds. Seeley called these dinosaurs ornithischian, or "bird-hipped" dinosaurs.

Ornithischian dinosaur pelves (the plural of pelvis) developed from evolutionary changes of the primitive saurischian pelvis. Ornithischians also had other traits that grouped them together: a bone, called the predentary, was at the front of the lower jaw. Also, an "eyelid" bone rimmed the upper part of the eye socket.

Some dinosaurs were neither saurischians nor ornithischians. The earliest, most primitive dinosaurs, such as *Staurikosaurus* and *Herrerasaurus*, fit into neither order. They were too specialized to be the direct ancestors of the dinosaurs.

DINOSAUR FAMILIES

Families: Staurikosauridae and Herrerasauridae. *Staurikosaurus*, a medium-size predator from the latest Middle Triassic of South America, is the oldest known true dinosaur and is the only member of the family Staurikosauridae. *Herrerasaurus* and *Ischisaurus*, also medium-size, two-legged

meat-eaters from South America, were more advanced and lived in the early part of the Late Triassic. They belong in the family Herrerasauridae. They lived in South America.

ORDER: SAURISCHIA
SUBORDER: SAUROPODOMORPHA
Infraorder: Prosauropoda

The sauropodomorphs quickly evolved into two major groups, the Prosauropoda and the Sauropoda. Although prosauropods appeared earlier, no known prosauropod could have been the ancestor of the sauropods. The prosauropods were wide-

spread and had at least seven families. They lived until the Early Jurassic. The largest prosauropods, some as long as 40 or more feet, were straight-limbed dinosaurs that resembled the later sauropods in some ways. All prosauropods were plant-eaters.

Family: Thecodontosauridae. The most primitive prosauropod, Thecodontosaurus, was also one of the smallest. It was about six to ten feet long. Like all prosauropods and most sauropods, it had a prominent claw on each front foot and a large claw on each back foot.

Family: Plateosauridae. This is the best-known family of prosauropods, with ani-

Plateosaurus

Left: Hesperornis, a Late Cretaceous bird, had wings simliar to Archaeopteryx.

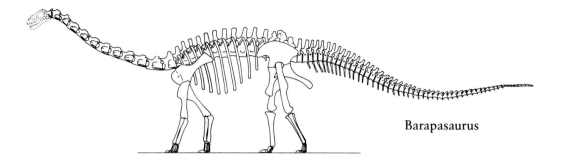

Barapasaurus

mals found in Europe, China, and North and South America. They were 25 to 30 feet long with narrow, long snouts, long necks, powerful front and back limbs, and heavy bodies.

Infraorder: Sauropoda

The second group of sauropodomorphs, the Sauropoda, probably came from an ancestor much like *Thecodontosaurus*. This probably happened sometime in the Late Triassic, when sauropods first appeared. All sauropods were giants and four-legged plant-eaters.

Like today's elephants, sauropods had little fear of predators because of their size. Being large also helped them reach food, such as leaves in treetops, that was too high for smaller plant-eaters. Sauropods had many features because of their large size. They lost the grasping function of their front feet, and their legs looked like long, straight columns. Their vertebrae (bones in the spine) had deep hollows to lighten the weight of their backbone. Also, to add strength they had more vertebrae where the pelvis and spine joined.

Sauropod skulls were either blunt (flat) or tapering (came to a point) and the nostrils were back from the tip of the snout. Sauropod heads, which were lightly built and fragile, often broke off after death.

Family: Vulcanodontidae. The earliest true sauropod is *Vulcanodon* from the Early Jurassic of Zimbabwe. The only skeleton is missing the head, neck, and much of the tail. It had a bulky body and its legs were long and straight. The front limbs were almost as long as the back, and each back foot had five toes.

Family: Barapasauridae. The next most primitive sauropod, *Barapasaurus*, is known from parts of several skeletons from the Early Jurassic of India. It was up to 60 feet long, with a slender body and a long neck, tail, and limbs.

Family: Euhelopodidae. Most of the sauropods known from the Middle and Late Jurassic of China are now placed in a separate family, the Euhelopodidae. Euhelopodids are one of the more primitive sauropod families, but they include such exotic animals as the extremely long-necked *Mamenchisaurus* and *Omeisaurus*.

Family: Cetiosauridae. This family is from the Middle Jurassic, perhaps from an ancestor from the Vulcanodontidae family. The cetiosaurids had expanded and spread into Europe, North and South America, Africa, and Australia by the Middle Jurassic.

Cetiosaurid skulls were blunt and box-like, with nostrils at the side of the snout. The neck was short, usually with 12 vertebrae. They ranged from small to large for sauropods; most were 35 to 60 feet long. The best-known genus is *Shunosaurus* from the Middle Jurassic of China. It had a small, bony club at the end of its tail. Cetiosaurids lasted until the Late Jurassic.

Family: Brachiosauridae. The front limbs of the brachiosaurids were as long or

Shunosaurus

longer than the back limbs. This gave the body a backward slope from the neck to the tail. The number of neck vertebrae in this family increased to 13 or more. The nostrils were farther back from the tip of the blunt snout and above the eyes in the skull of *Brachiosaurus*. Most brachiosaurids were larger than the cetiosaurids, 80 or more feet long even though they had shorter tails. They were among the heaviest land animals known. To reduce weight, their huge vertebrae were almost completely hollow. Known worldwide, brachiosaurids appear in the fossil record during the Middle Jurassic, were most numerous in the Late Jurassic, and almost vanished by the end of the Early Cretaceous.

Family: Camarasauridae. In this family the skull was boxlike. They still had 12 neck

vertebrae and the front limbs were slightly shorter than the back limbs. One of the last known camarasaurids was *Opisthocoelicaudia* from Mongolia, a heavy-bodied sauropod with a short tail that probably helped support it when it stood on its hind limbs to reach food.

Family: Diplodocidae. This family includes some of the most well known sauropods, including *Apatosaurus* and *Diplodocus*. Diplodocid skulls were long and tapered to a spoon-shaped snout and had nostrils on top of the skull. Their small, rod-shaped teeth were in the front of their snout. Diplodocids had long necks, with up to 15 vertebrae. Their backs were short compared to the length of their back limbs, and their tails ended in a whiplash that was probably used as a weapon. The long necks and tails made some diplodocids the longest animals that ever lived.

Family: Titanosauridae. Almost all southern-hemisphere sauropods from the Late Cretaceous, and many earlier ones, were titanosaurids. Their limbs were stocky. The vertebrae from the front and middle of the tail were unique and are the best feature that distinguishes the family. Not one complete or nearly complete titanosaurid skull has been found. One of the most interesting titanosaurids was *Saltasaurus*, which was

squat and covered with armor similar to the ankylosaurs.

Most titanosaurids were about 40 to 50 feet long, but a few became gigantic. The titanosaurids lived mainly in the southern hemisphere during the Cretaceous Period, surviving there as the northern-hemisphere sauropods became extinct.

SUBORDER: THEROPODA

The theropods were all the predatory dinosaurs except the herrerasaurians. From the smallest dinosaurs to the largest meat-eaters, the theropods had the most different kinds of saurischian dinosaurs of all suborders. These two-legged meat-eaters had clawed feet with no more than three functional toes.

The wings and feet of birds are similar to the arms and feet of theropod skeletons. Also like birds, all theropods to some extent had hollow bones. The best ancestral bird is the small, feathered, theropodlike *Archaeopteryx* from the Late Jurassic.

Brachiosaurus

Apatosaurus *skull.*

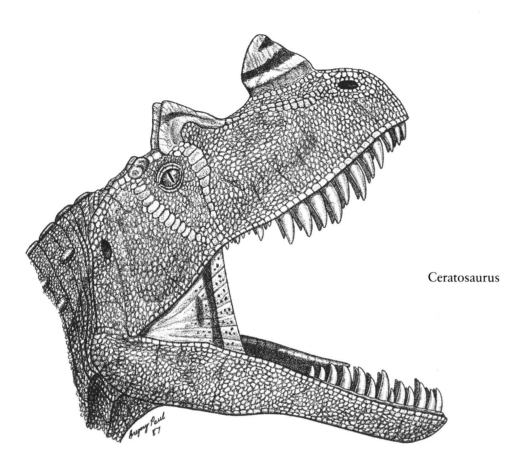

Ceratosaurus

were usually not present. Their hands had three or fewer fingers, and the "thumb" usually had the largest claw.

Family: Compsognathidae. The most primitive tetanuran was *Compsognathus* from the Late Jurassic of Europe. It was the smallest theropod, about three feet long and lightly built.

Family: Coeluridae. *Ornitholestes* and *Coelurus*, which lived during the Late Jurassic in western North America, were fast-running, lightly built theropods that were two to three feet tall at the hips and from six to ten feet long.

Family: Carcharodontosauridae. This group of giant theropods from Gondwana includes enormous predatory dinosaurs, *Giganotosaurus* from Argentina and *Carcharodontosaurus* from North Africa.

Family: Therizinosauridae: The therizinosaurids were apparently herbivorous or omnivorous theropods known from the

Late Cretaceous of Asia and North America. The unusual, birdlike pelves and almost prosauropod-like skulls of therizinosaurids have resulted in uncertainty about their evolutionary position, but they have recently been shown to be theropods closely related to the Ornithomimidae.

Family: Spinosauridae. Spinosaurids are a distinctive group of theropods with long, crocodile-like snouts and elongated vertebral spines that may have formed sail-like structures on their backs. Spinosaurids are restricted to the Cretaceous but are known from Africa, South America, and Europe.

Family: Oviraptorisauridae. Another curious theropod from the Cretaceous of Asia is *Oviraptor*, which has a tall, highly pneumatic skull with a turtle-like beak. *Oviraptor* got its name ("egg predator") because specimens were found in Mongolia with what were originally thought to be nests of ceratopsian eggs.

The theropods evolved into two major groups: the Ceratosauria, with flexible tails; and the Tetanurae, with stiff tails. All the earliest theropods were ceratosaurians. Their fossil record is from the Late Triassic through the Late Jurassic. The tetanurans appeared in the Middle Jurassic, diversified in the Late Jurassic, and were the main northern-hemisphere predators until the Late Cretaceous.

Infraorder: Ceratosauria

Family: Podokesauridae. The earliest ceratosaurians include Coelophysis from the Late Triassic of western North America. It was small and nimble and had a long, slender skull with many teeth.

Families: Halticosauridae and Ceratosauridae. *Dilophosaurus*, which lived during the Early Jurassic, had a double crest on

its head. *Ceratosaurus* was from the Late Jurassic and had a horn on its head. Both were from North America and are examples of later members of the ceratosaurians. After the Late Jurassic, ceratosaurians apparently vanished in the northern hemisphere but survived in South America.

Family: Abelisauridae. The abelisaurids are a group of medium to large African and South American theropods characterized by short, tall skulls. *Carnotaurus* from Argentina and *Majungatholus* from Madagascar are similar with the exception that *Carnotaurus* has two large horns on the skull.

Infraorder: Tetanurae

The tetanurans, the most advanced theropods, included several groups where the relationships are not well understood. Crests and other decorations on the head

Dilophosaurus, *front and side view.*

Family: Allosauridae. This family is typical of the larger Jurassic and Early Cretaceous theropods that were from 15 to 35 feet long or longer. The biggest allosaurid may have been more than 40 feet long. Allosaurids were slender but dangerous predators.

Family: Tyrannosauridae. Most dramatic of all the theropods were the tyrannosaurids, which probably came from allosauridlike ancestors at the beginning of the Late Cretaceous. Unlike other tetanurans, they had massive bodies, unusually shaped heads, and small two-fingered hands. Some tyrannosaurids were nearly 50 feet long and became the largest meat-eating land animals known. The smallest, such as *Nanotyrannus*, were about 18 feet long. The medium-size tyrannosaurids, such as *Albertosaurus* and *Daspletosaurus*, were about 30 feet long

Family: Ornithomimidae. Many kinds of small theropods also arose in the Cretaceous. Their skeletons were birdlike. Most had changes in their front legs and hands for a powerful striking action. The "quick-strike" motion of the front limbs may have been the beginning of the power stroke of birds' wings.

The "ostrich dinosaurs" or Ornithomimidae are known best from the Late Cretaceous of eastern Asia and western North America. They had small heads and they usually had no teeth. They had long necks and short, stiff backs. Their front limbs were long, and their powerful rear legs were built for speed. They are thought to have been the fastest dinosaurs.

Family: Dromaeosauridae. *Deinonychus* and other "sickle claw" theropods are among the best-studied dinosaurs. The discovery of *Deinonychus* supported the idea of a bird-dinosaur relationship and started the debate about dinosaurs being warm-blooded. Each foot had a large, sickle-shaped claw on the second toe. The end of the tail had vertebrae that locked together to make it stiff.

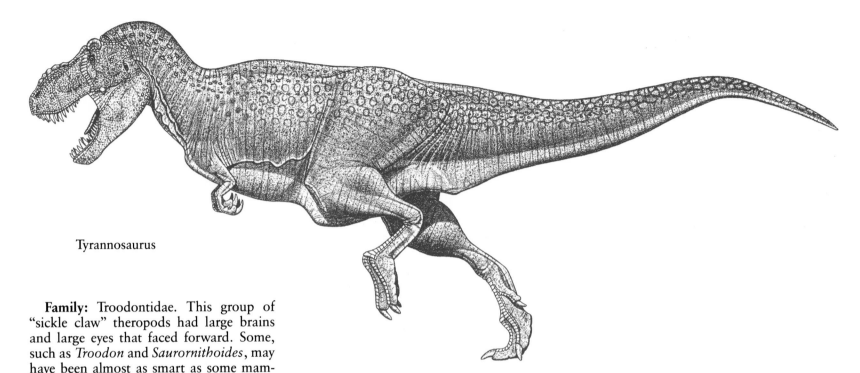

Tyrannosaurus

Family: Troodontidae. This group of "sickle claw" theropods had large brains and large eyes that faced forward. Some, such as *Troodon* and *Saurornithoides*, may have been almost as smart as some mammals.

ORDER: ORNITHISCHIA

The earliest ornithischian dinosaur was *Pisanosaurus*, a three-foot-long, two-legged (bipedal) plant-eater from the late Middle Triassic of Argentina. All ornithischians were plant-eaters.

Later ornithischians split into three advanced groups: heavy, armored plant-eaters that walked on all fours; specialized dome-headed dinosaurs and horned dinosaurs; and two-legged plant-eaters that included *Iguanodon* and duckbilled dinosaurs.

Family: Fabrosauridae. This family is found in Late Triassic through Late Jurassic rocks on several continents. Other primitive ornithischians are usually classified in this family. It was named after *Fabrosaurus*, from the Early Jurassic of South Africa. All fabrosaurids were small bipedal plant-eaters. The best-known fabrosaurid is *Lesothosaurus*, also from the Early Jurassic of southern Africa. The pelvis of *Le-*sothosaurus shows some features that put it at the bottom of ornithischians. *Scutellosaurus* from the Early Jurassic of western North America was protected by small bony plates resembling the larger plates of later armored ornithischians.

SUBORDER: THYREOPHORA
Infraorder: Stegosauria

Stegosaurs were the main armored dinosaurs of the Jurassic Period; ankylosaurs remained in the background. But ankylosaurs replaced stegosaurs in the Cretaceous Period. *Scelidosaurus* was very much like both groups. It was from the Early Jurassic of England and it walked on all four limbs (quadrupedal). It had stegosaurlike teeth, an ankylosaurlike pattern of armor plates and spines, and a pelvis like *Scutellosaurus*.

Family: Stegosauridae. These armored dinosaurs probably evolved in China during the Early Jurassic. By the Late Jurassic, they were in Europe (*Dacentrurus*), North America (*Stegosaurus*), and Africa (*Kentrosaurus*). The armor was a double row of large bony plates that ran along the back from behind the head to the tail. Sharp spines on the end of the tail were used as a weapon against predators.

Infraorder: Ankylosauria

During the Early Cretaceous, ankylosaurs replaced stegosaurs everywhere except in India. Ankylosaurs were different from stegosaurs because they had flexible body armor rather than a double row of tall plates. They were also closer to the ground, with only a slight arch, if any, to their backs. The heads of stegosaurs were long and narrow, but ankylosaurs had short, broad skulls. Instead of tail spines, ankylosaurs had shoulder spines or tail clubs for defense.

Family: Nodosauridae. The more primitive ankylosaurians, including all Jurassic and southern-hemisphere genera, belong in this family. Some nodosaurids had large,

Pachycephalosaurus

© '85 Walters

cone-shaped spines along the neck and shoulders for protection.

Family: Ankylosauridae. This family may have arisen during the Early Cretaceous from a nodosaurid ancestor. Ankylosaurid skulls had horns projecting from the back, giving them a triangular shape when viewed from above. All ankylosaurids had massive, bony tail clubs for defense.

SUBORDER: MARGINOCEPHALIA
Infraorder: Pachycephalosauria

Yaverlandia, from the Early Cretaceous of England, is the oldest known pachycephalosaur. But the only known specimen is a small, thick, skull-cap with two bony lumps that shows little about what the animal may have looked like or its relationships. The dome-headed dinosaurs were scarce, small to medium-size animals of the Cretaceous Period. Most lived in the northern hemisphere but one genus, *Majungatholus*, is known from the Late Cretaceous in Madagascar.

The back of the head of dome-headed dinosaurs was broadened into a shelf that often had bony lumps or short spikes. One

family, the Homalocephalidae, had bones on the top of the skull that were flat and thick (as in *Homalocephale* and *Goyocephale* from Mongolia). In the other family, the Pachycephalosauridae, the bones were raised into a very thick, high dome that was the main feature of the animal's appearance and even grew over the shelf (as in *Stegoceras*). Pachycephalosaur skeletons are rare, but their skull-domes, since they were solid bone, often were fossilized. They are quite common in some places.

Pachycephalosaurs had broad, chubby bodies. They were bipedal plant-eaters. As an animal grew, its dome got larger. The thick domes were used to compete for mates in head-butting contests between males or to fight predators by butting them in the side.

Infraorder: Ceratopsia

The Ceratopsia were the horned dinosaurs and their relatives. They were different from the pachycephalosaurs—and all other dinosaurs—because they had a special bone, the *rostral*, which formed part of a large, parrotlike beak.

Family: Psittacosauridae. The oldest and most primitive ceratopsians belong in this family of small, bipedal runners such as *Psittacosaurus* from the Early Cretaceous of China and Mongolia.

Family: Protoceratopsidae. In this family, the back of the skull was expanded into a wide frill over the back of the neck. *Microceratops* was a bipedal animal, like its possible psittacosaurid ancestors. The other protoceratopsids walked on all fours, making their larger heads easier to support.

Triceratops skeleton on the river's edge.

Family: Ceratopsidae. The Ceratopsidae had the shortest range of any dinosaur family. They arose during the Late Cretaceous in western North America. They quickly evolved into many unusual forms and lived until the end of the Mesozoic Era. From cow to elephant size, the quadrupedal (four-legged) ceratopsids had horns and frills on their heads. They had powerful jaws with hundreds of teeth for slicing tough plants. *Triceratops* had the most powerful jaw muscles of any land animal. The horns were used as weapons. The frills may have protected the neck and may have been brightly colored for mating season. The frills may also have helped keep its body temperature even.

SUBORDER: ORNITHOPODA

Except an increase in size and the evolution of the most remarkable chewing arrangement of all dinosaurs, different ornithopod families varied from one another in minor details. All were bipedal plant-eaters.

Family: Heterodontosauridae. These small, nimble bipedal plant-eaters have been found mainly in Early Jurassic rocks of southern Africa. Their teeth were sharp and tusklike in front, but the teeth at the sides of the jaw were built for chewing and slicing plants. They had large caninelike teeth (cone-shaped, pointed teeth) at the corners of the upper and lower jaws.

Family: Hypsilophodontidae. This was the most widespread and longest-lived ornithopod family. It flourished almost worldwide from the Middle Jurassic until the end of the Cretaceous.

Hypsilophodontids were small but had relatively large heads. Their feet were primitive with four functional toes. The first toe was smaller than the others; the fifth toe was only a splint. Hypsilophodontids had small front limbs with tiny hands. Bony tendons strengthened the back and stiffened the tail. Most were small dinosaurs about six to ten feet long, but some *Tenon-*

tosaurus species were as long as 22 feet. The Late Cretaceous *Thescelosaurus* grew to about 18 feet long.

Family: Dryosauridae. This short-lived family arose about the same time as the Hypsilophodontidae. The earliest dryosaurid was *Dryosaurus* from the Late Jurassic of western North America and eastern Africa. *Valdosaurus* from the Early Cretaceous of Europe and northern Africa and *Kangnasaurus* from Africa are the other two genera in this family. Dryosaurids, with small front limbs and heads, were larger and more powerful than hypsilophodontids. They lacked teeth at the front of the snout and instead had a well-developed beak that may have had a horny covering.

Family: Camptosauridae. The Late Jurassic genus *Camptosaurus* from western North America was a chubby, medium-size ornithopod about 15 feet long. It had specialized feet and skull.

Family: Iguanodontidae. *Iguanodon* is one of the best-known dinosaurs. This bulky, 35-foot-long ornithopod had a deep, narrow skull; a strong, well-developed pelvis; rows of bony tendons running along its back; a hand in which the thumb had become a sharp spike; and three broad toes plus an inner toe, which was reduced to a splint. The teeth were thick and were always being replaced. It ate tough plants. *Iguanodon* walked on two legs, but it could also use its hands to walk on all fours.

Iguanodontids have been found in Early and Late Cretaceous formations in North America, northern Africa, Europe, and Asia. The most advanced were *Probactrosaurus* from central Asia and *Ouranosaurus* from northern Africa. The teeth of *Probactrosaurus* had a more complicated pattern of replacement than those of *Iguanodon*. The vertebrae of *Ouranosaurus* had very long spines, creating a sail. With the rise of duckbilled dinosaurs, iguanodontids faded away.

Iguanodon skeleton on display at the Brussels Museum in 1883.

Family: Hadrosauridae. This group consists of two groups, the Hadrosaurinae and the Lambeosaurinae. They were both duckbilled dinosaurs that were closely related. They were large to very large plant-eaters of the Late Cretaceous in North and South America and Eurasia. The largest were *Shantungosaurus* from China and *Lambeosaurus laticaudus* from Mexico, both of which may have grown over 50 feet long and weighed over 20 tons. They may have been the largest known animals able to walk on two feet. Most duckbilled dinosaurs were about 30 feet long.

The teeth were in thirty to forty vertical rows like steps on a moving escalator. As each tooth wore away, it was replaced by the tooth directly below it. This process started when (or even before) the animal hatched and continued as long as it lived.

The skulls of hadrosaurines were generally longer and not as deep as those of lambeosaurines, and their ducklike beaks were flatter and broader.

Some hadrosaurines lacked cranial crests (*Edmontosaurus*); others had arched nasal bones (*Kritosaurus*); others had solid cranial crests (*Prosaurolophus* and *Maiasaura*). But all lambeosaurines in which the skulls are well known (*Hypacrosaurus*, *Corythosaurus*, *Lambeosaurus*, and *Parasaurolophus*) had hollow crests with looping nasal passages that may have been used to make sounds.

The duckbilled dinosaurs were perhaps the most advanced of all the dinosaurs. They had excellent hearing, eyesight, voice, and sense of smell. They lived in huge herds and may have migrated seasonally, returning to the same place each year to mate and lay their eggs.

CHAPTER 3

INTERPRETING DINOSAUR FOSSILS

Our knowledge of dinosaurs comes from what they left on earth as fossils. But very little dinosaur material has been fossilized by nature, and then nature itself often becomes the fossils' enemy. Wind and weather can damage fragile fossils, but erosion also uncovers them for collectors and paleontologists.

Scientists study dinosaur skeletons to learn about the animals' behavior and appearance. The skull is especially important. A dinosaur's teeth can tell us whether it was an advanced or primitive dinosaur, whether it ate plants or meat, or even whether it ate soft or tough plants. Its skull will tell if it had a large or small brain or if it had good or bad eyesight, hearing, and sense of smell. The shape of a dinosaur skull can also tell us what other dinosaurs it was related to and where it fits in the family tree.

Though the skull is important, paleontologists can tell much about a dinosaur skeleton without a head; many skeletons are found without skulls. And there are other clues that dinosaurs left behind, all giving information about their lifestyles and habits. Scientists have discovered dinosaur trackways (fossilized footprints), nests, and eggs. But even with this information, there is much that will never be known. The fossil record is incomplete and can be misleading. Paleontologists continue to search, hoping to uncover other clues that will give them more information about dinosaurs.

Left: *A mother* Maiasaura *tends her young.*

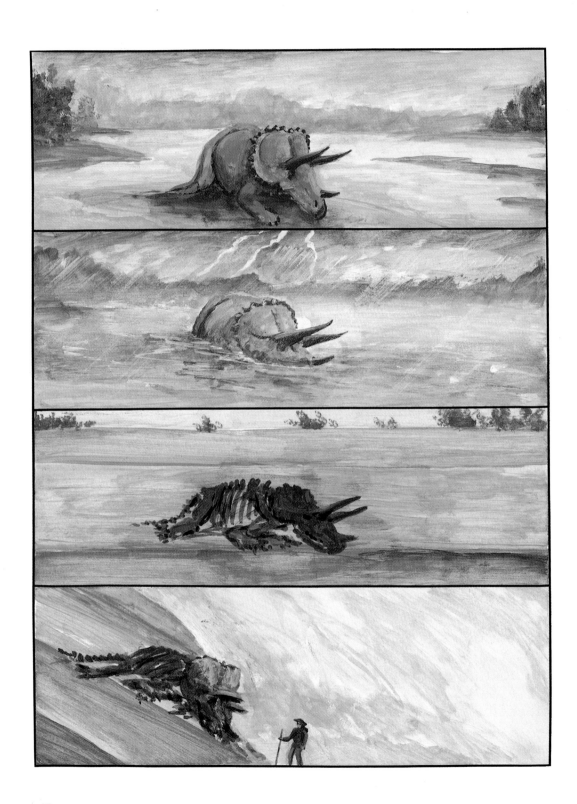

Fossilization

(1) *If an animal dies where conditions are right, such as near water or in a desert, the fossilization process begins.*

(2) *The dead animal is covered by sediment, which may be water, mud, or sand. The animal's soft parts (flesh, muscles, tendons) decay, leaving only its bones.*

(3) *More sediment layers build up over millions of years. During this time, minerals in the ground fill in the tiny holes in the bones. Sometimes the bones dissolve completely.*

(4) *Through natural erosion and sometimes movement of the earth (earthquakes), the fossils are exposed and can be excavated.*

How Dinosaurs Became Fossils

The term *fossilized* is important. It is not the dinosaur bones themselves that paleontologists find, but their stony replicas. Fossil bones are created by the slow replacement of bone molecules with the molecules of minerals in ground water. This process sometimes preserves even the delicate cell structure of the bones. Other times the bones dissolve completely and only their imprint is left on the rocks.

Teeth and bones are the most durable parts of a vertebrate's body. They may survive long after the animal's soft parts have rotted or been eaten. Except for fossilized footprints, skeletal remains are the most common fossils. Unfortunately, few animals ever become fossilized, compared to the millions that lived.

Animals seldom die where they can be fossilized. A recently deceased animal that remains above ground will be dissolved by the chemicals in soil and converted into plant food. This is why the bodies of even large animals are seldom found in the woods—and why fossils are most often found in deserts and other "bone-dry" places where there are not many plants.

Fossils being prepared for shipment at the Dry Mesa Quarry in Colorado.

Fossil bones being excavated at Dinosaur National Monument in Utah.

In order for a skeleton to become a fossil, a layer of sediment must quickly cover the body. This prevents the skeleton from being destroyed by other animals or nature. Over the following thousands and millions of years, this sediment hardens into a protective layer of rock, such as shale, siltstone, mudstone, or sandstone.

Dinosaur bones could have been covered by sediment in still water, such as at the bottoms of lakes, slow-moving rivers and river deltas, shallow seas, and seacoasts. The sediment could also have been brought by the air, such as sand from dust storms or volcanic ash falls. The places where conditions are right for skeletons to become fossils are only a small percentage of the world's land area at any time. Many species of dinosaurs lived where no fossils could form. Partly for this reason, there are many evolutionary "missing links" between groups of dinosaurs. So there is an incomplete picture of dinosaurs from the fossil record.

Problems with the Fossil Record

The fossil record can give us large amounts of knowledge. But there are many other ways that the fossil record is incomplete or misleading. Scientists must keep these problems in mind when they are reading the fossil record to come to conclusions about dinosaurs and their lifestyles.

Large, heavy bones are more likely to be preserved than small, lightly built bones. So, although small vertebrates usually outnumber large, fossils of small vertebrates are scarce. This might seem to suggest that big dinosaurs dominated the landscape and that there were fewer small animals. This was probably not the case.

For dinosaur fossils to be found, the rocks where the fossils are located must be accessible. Many dinosaur-bearing formations were eroded by wind and weather long before humans were around, so their

fossils have been lost forever. Other dinosaur-bearing formations are buried beneath hundreds of feet, even miles, of rock. These fossils are waiting to be excavated in the future. Only dinosaur-bearing formations that are now at the earth's surface are ready to be researched. So there is much information about the fossil record that has already been lost to erosion, but there is still much that today's paleontologists will never be able to find and evaluate.

We can also get a wrong idea about dinosaurs when scientists and paleontologists make mistakes. In the past, researchers were interested mainly in well-preserved skeletons that could be displayed in museums, so they sometimes ignored dinosaur bones unless they were new dinosaurs. Other times, they removed only the most interesting parts of the skeleton, such as the skull. They may have done this because they did not have the time or the money to excavate the whole skeleton, so they left the rest to erode.

Some museum specimens are useless because important information was recorded incorrectly or not at all. Dinosaurs have occasionally been mounted in museums with

Workers carefully dig out the fragile fossil bones of a dinosaur.

the bones in the wrong places. Museum workers have sometimes used too much plaster, restoring missing parts incorrectly. This may have mislead other researchers who relied on the published drawings and photographs of the restored skeletons. Modern methods of fossil collection and preparation have eliminated many of these problems with newly collected material. But museums have many fossils in their collections that need to be restudied.

So, everything we know about dinosaurs comes to us through an incomplete fossil record and the imperfect people who investigate it. But there is still much information that this fossil record gives us.

Limb bones of a Diplodocus *(left) and an* Apatosaurus *(right) at Dinosaur National Monument in Utah.*

Dinosaur Appearance and Behavior

Dinosaurs with almost complete fossil skeletons give us clues about what they were like. We get a good idea of the dinosaurs' size, weight, and appearance in life. The cell structure of fossilized dinosaur bones can tell us about the biology of a dinosaur. We then have information about how rapidly they grew, and perhaps about whether they were warm-blooded or cold-blooded. Fossilized bones sometimes leave evidence of bone diseases and the tooth marks of predators. Muscle tissue is almost never preserved (only two good "dinosaur mummies," with soft parts intact, have been discovered). But we can still tell how dinosaurs moved from the traces of ligaments and muscle scars on the bones.

Dinosaurs' teeth can tell us what kinds of foods they ate. Occasionally the actual stomach contents are preserved, so scientists can study what a dinosaur had for its last meal. The smooth "stomach stones" with which some dinosaurs ground up their food are sometimes preserved, and even fossilized dinosaur droppings, which are known as *coprolites,* have been found. All this gives us more information on dinosaur diets.

Fossilized skin impressions can be seen on very well preserved skeletons. The fine-grained sandy rocks of Dinosaur Provincial Park in Alberta, Canada, have preserved the skin impressions of duckbilled and horned dinosaurs. These provide an idea of what dinosaur skin looked like. No dinosaur has ever been found with feather traces, so there is no evidence that any dinosaur had feathers.

Scientists study locations and distribution of dinosaur bones for information about the dinosaurs' environments. The direction in which bones are pointed and the way they are arranged in dinosaur bone

Lambeosaurus *on display at the Royal Ontario Museum.*

beds are clues about the size and strength of rivers dinosaurs had to wade through. Scientists compare the number of different types of dinosaurs from one location to find out about dinosaur habits and lifestyles. For example, if there were few predators and many animals that would have been their prey, it would show that the predatory dinosaurs had a quick metabolism and were probably warm-blooded.

Fossil dinosaur jaw with teeth found at Dinosaur National Monument in Utah.

Dinosaur Tracks

Fossilized dinosaur footprints are more common than dinosaur skeletal remains. This is not surprising because each dinosaur could have left hundreds of thousands of prints over its lifetime. Unfortunately, footprints give few details about what the dinosaur looked like and what species it belonged to, though the skin texture of the soles of its feet is sometimes imprinted. The tracks can tell us an enormous amount about how the trackmakers walked, cruised, ran, sprinted, and even swam.

We know from their footprints, for example, that large theropod dinosaurs either roamed by themselves or in small groups. Smaller dinosaurs, both plant-eaters and

meat-eaters, often gathered in herds that left many directionless footprints. Large sauropods also probably lived in herds. After more study by paleontologists, trackways may show that dinosaurs migrated along thousand-mile-long "highways" in search of food.

By measuring stride lengths and footprint sizes, and comparing them with modern animals, it is possible to estimate how fast dinosaurs walked and ran. Typical walking speeds were about four or five miles per hour, though large sauropods may have walked two or three miles per hour. Since animals do not run at top speed for any length of time, tracks of fast-running dinosaurs are rare. Estimated theropod speeds may be more than 30 miles per hour, and ornithomimids may have been faster than ostriches.

A dinosaur footprint from Dinosaur State Park in Connecticut.

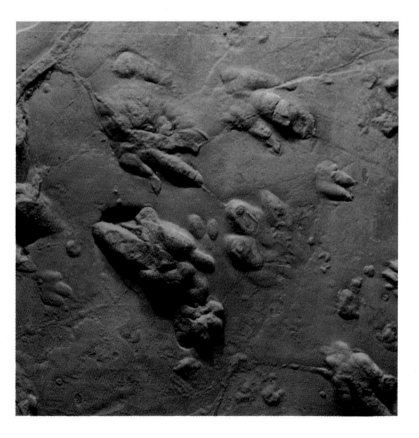

Upper Triassic dinosaur tracks found in Nova Scotia.

A fossil dinosaur egg.

Dinosaur Eggs

Fossilized dinosaur eggs were first unearthed in Mongolia during the 1920s. Dinosaur eggs usually are rare fossils, but they have been found in China, Mongolia, India, France, and South America. Besides shedding light on dinosaur nest structure, the eggs seemed to tell little.

But the recent discoveries of dinosaur nests, nurseries, eggs, embryos, hatchlings, nestlings, and juveniles in Montana have greatly increased our knowledge. Dinosaurs that began life as helpless hatchlings—the embryos show whether the animal could walk once it hatched—must have required parental care to survive. Other dinosaur hatchlings that could have walked once they hatched probably were left by themselves. To confirm this, the eggs of dinosaurs that required parental care are found smashed to bits, as if the hatchlings lived in their nests. The eggs of dinosaurs that were able to take care of themselves are usually found unbroken. By studying the sizes of the dinosaurs in the Montana nurseries, scientists may find out how many seasons it took for a particular species to grow big enough to leave the nursery and venture into the dangerous world. Unfortunately, nest structures and eggs have been found for only a small number of species.

Dinosaur Skeletal Structures

Dinosaurs are known for the special skeletal structures they evolved. These include the horns and frills of the ceratopsians; the sailbacks of certain iguanodontids and theropods; the domed skulls of the pachycephalosaurians; the cranial crests of the hadrosaurs and certain theropods; and the plates and spines of the stegosaurians and ankylosaurians. These special skeletal structures would have been bold and obvious, so these structures may have been for display. Many also had other uses, including regulation of body heat, making noise, and defense.

The thick-domed skull of a Pachycephalosaurus, *which it used in head-butting contests.*

Far left: Triceratops skeletal drawing, top view. Left: A Triceratops skull showing its frill and large brow horns.

Sight was an important sense to dinosaurs; their eyes were large. Dinosaurs were closely related to birds and crocodiles; both see colors and have a wide range of visual signals. So, these special skeletal structures of dinosaurs may have been brightly colored or boldly patterned. Closely related but different species may have been differently colored so they could be told apart during mating season.

Some of these structures, such as stegosaurian plates and ceratopsian frills, were made of thin bone that had many passages for blood vessels. Blood must have run through these passages, either to cool the animal off (if the dinosaur were warm-blooded) or to warm it up (if the dinosaur were cold-blooded). By regulating the blood flow to these structures, a dinosaur could regulate heat loss or heat gain and maintain a reasonably constant body temperature. The dinosaur may also have been able to change the structure's color by changing the blood flow. This would have given dinosaurs a way of expressing their emotional state to others of their kind.

Birds and crocodiles have excellent hearing, and their relatives the dinosaurs probably did, too. Some dinosaur skulls have the delicate bony structures of their middle and inner ears preserved. By examining these, scientists can confirm that most dinosaur groups could hear very well. Since that is true, they may have been able to vocalize. The head crests of the lambeosaurines were part of their nasal passages. An animal inhaled air into its crest, which then went down through the back of its head into the lungs. This was a very complicated pathway, but it may have been used for making sounds. The lambeosaurine could have inhaled air and vibrated its looping nasal passage, emitting a deep, low-frequency call. As far as we know, no two lambeosaurines had exactly the same crest shape, so no two would have made the same call. Their crests may have vocally distinguished individuals from one another.

The function of the horns of ceratopsids seems obvious: To fight an attacking tyrannosaurid. Also, rival ceratopsids probably locked horns in shoving matches over mates. Today's moose and elk use their antlers like this and fight predators by using their sharp-hoofed feet, not their antlers. Ceratopsids could also have used their sharp beaks to inflict painful, sometimes fatal wounds on predators.

It is difficult to understand that the world was a far different place 65 to 240 million years ago and that it was populated by huge and strange-looking creatures. All the large animals in today's zoos, from elephants to zebras to kangaroos (except crocodiles), evolved well after dinosaurs were gone. We are fortunate that some of the dinosaurs left their traces in rocks, which scientists have been able to study and compare with living animals. Scientists can then make educated assumptions about dinosaur lifestyles. In a world with a history that spans four and a half billion years, perhaps the most interesting thing about dinosaurs is that we have been able to learn anything about them at all.

Parasaurolophus walkeri, a hollow-crested hadrosaurid.

Right: *If covered by sand, these young* Diplodocus *specimens would have become fossils for paleontologists to study.*

CHAPTER 4

DINOSAUR BEGINNINGS

The Triassic and Early Jurassic Periods

Dinosaurs had not arrived as the Permian Period ended and the Triassic began. The earth's land and climate were changing, the ancestors of the dinosaurs were evolving, and many plants and animals were becoming extinct. Because these events took place, dinosaurs became rulers of the earth by the Jurassic Period.

At the beginning of the Triassic Period, all land was joined as a single large mass called Pangaea. It stretched nearly pole to pole. The only block of land not joined to Pangaea was southern China and southeast Asia, which collided with the Chinese mainland before the Late Triassic. Throughout the Triassic, Pangaea slowly moved north and turned clockwise. By the Middle Triassic, the continent was a crescent-shaped mass facing east and centered on the equator. The eastern side of Pangaea surrounded a large body of water, the Tethys Sea, which joined a single global ocean.

Large land masses are more sensitive than oceans to heating and cooling. During a hemisphere's summer, a large land mass warms the hemisphere. It then becomes the center of cooling during the hemisphere's winter. This produces air pressure changes, which result in strong seasons. Although scientists disagree about the exact climate, it seems the Triassic started out cool and dry and became warmer, with rainy summers and drier winters. This became a monsoon weather pattern, as in southeast Asia today.

This weather pattern affected the soil and land. Vertisols are fossil soils produced by a wet season followed by a dry season. This soil is found in Triassic formations. Red beds are also widespread in Triassic formations. Red beds get their color when iron in the soil oxidizes (rusts) because of warm, somewhat dry weather.

Triassic plants included ferns, conifers, and cycads. These plants would have needed warm, moist weather to survive. Throughout the Triassic, some plants were becoming extinct and others were evolving. The Late Triassic plant *Sanmiguelia* may be the ancestor of flowering plants, though it did not become established until the Early Cretaceous.

Dinosaurs did not appear until the Middle to Late Triassic. But many other animals lived in the Triassic world. The therapsids were mammallike reptiles that ruled the earth before dinosaurs. They included the labyrinthodonts, the late survivors of the early amphibians; procolophonids, the early plant-eating reptiles; dicynodonts, the turtlebilled plant-eaters; and cynodonts, the ancestors of mammals.

Left: Massospondylus, *prosauropods that lived during the Early Jurassic.*

Triassic Map

Lystrosaurus, a dog-size dicynodont, was the ruling animal at the beginning of the Triassic. Scientists have found its fossils on almost every continent of the world—Asia, Africa, South America, and Antarctica. There were no land or weather barriers to stop animals from roaming freely. Other therapsids were also present in the Early Triassic, including the cynodont *Thrinaxodon.*

Archosaurs first appeared in the Late Permian as a minor part of the fauna. Dinosaurs, crocodiles, and pterosaurs all descended from the earliest archosaurs. The crocodile-like proterosuchians were the first archosaurs, and they gave rise to many other groups, including the aquatic phytosaurs, the terrestrial carnivorous groups Erythrosuchidae and Rauisuchidas, and the herbivorous aetosaurs. *Proterosuchus,* which dates back to the early Triassic, was almost the size of a modern crocodile.

An Early Jurassic scene.

Postosuchus

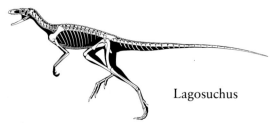
Lagosuchus

Euparkeria

Halfway through the Early Triassic, the *Lystrosaurus* fauna was replaced by other dicynodonts, cynodonts, and archosaurs. Important archosaurs that appeared were *Erythrosuchus,* a large meat-eater; and *Euparkeria,* a fast, small meat-eater. *Euparkeria* was important because it had features of later archosaurs; it stood more upright, it had armor, and it had no teeth on its palate. Also appearing around this time were the rhynchosaurs. This group of land herbivores were close relatives of the archosaurs and were among the most plentiful plant-eaters in the Middle and early Late Triassic.

The Middle Triassic is important as a time of transition. The archosaurs were becoming more important and more meat-eaters were emerging, including many kinds of small, crocodile-like archosaurs. Also showing up were the large, four-legged predators, the Prestosuchidae and Rauisuchidae, and the small land carnivore *Gracilisuchus.* All these were members of the line leading to crocodiles.

The ancestors of the dinosaurs were beginning to be important. *Lagosuchus, Pseudolagosuchus,* and *Lagerpeton* were tiny meat-eaters with long legs. They were close to the common ancestors of dinosaurs and pterosaurs, with ankles like later dinosaurs.

The earliest dinosaurs appeared in rocks that date to the late Middle Triassic or earliest Late Triassic. These were found in the Santa Maria Formation of Brazil and the slightly younger Ischigualasto Formation of Argentina. However, there are three-toed, dinosaurlike footprints from as early as the end of the Early Triassic.

The earliest dinosaurs were rare. The Middle to Late Triassic was a time dominated by rhynchosaurs. Big dicynodonts and medium to large cynodonts were in decline. The non-dinosaur archosaurs included the mostly meat-eating rauisuchids and proterochampsids; and the armored, plant-eating aetosaurs. A Late Triassic rauisuchid was *Postosuchus.* The earliest dinosaurs were *Staurikosaurus, Herrerasaurus,* and *Pisanosaurus.* Soon after, the herbivorous prosauropods and the carnivorous theropods appeared.

Halfway through the Late Triassic, a major change happened. New groups of phytosaurs and aetosaurs appeared, and a number of herbivore groups, including dicynodonts and rhynchosaurs, disappeared. Where this happened, theropod (meat-eating) dinosaurs appeared in larger numbers. Larger theropods were also emerging.

In the latest part of the Late Triassic Period, dinosaurs increased. In the latest Triassic beds in Europe, South America, and southern Africa, large prosauropods are the most plentiful dinosaur fossils uncovered. Other important animals at this time were primitive crocodilians, pterosaurs, and the first mammals.

At the end of the Triassic, a major extinction occurred. All archosaurs became extinct except for the dinosaurs, crocodilians, and pterosaurs. These extinctions probably happened because Pangaea was moving north and breaking apart, which caused the climate to change. Different dinosaurs then arose during the Early Jurassic, such as the two-crested theropod *Dilophosaurus. Scutellosaurus,* an armored ornithischian, and *Vulcanodon* and *Barapasaurus,* the first sauropods, also emerged.

In the Early Jurassic, except for the sauropods, few new major groups of dinosaurs appeared. Instead, the existing dinosaurs of this time mostly increased in number and diversity. They became, by the beginning of the Jurassic, the most important land animal.

ANCHISAURUS
(ank-ee-SORE-us)

Period:
Early Jurassic
Order, Suborder, Family:
Saurischia, Sauropodomorpha,
Anchisauridae
Location:
North America (United States)
Length:
6$^{1}/_{2}$ feet (2 meters)

Anchisaurus was one of the earliest North American dinosaurs described. The first partial skeleton was found in Connecticut in 1818 and was first thought to be human fossils. Scientists recognized it as a dinosaur in 1885. Its name means "near reptile," because its body was close to the ground.

Anchisaurus was different from most other prosauropods because its front and back feet were long and narrow. Peter Galton and Michael Cluver classified Anchisaurus and Thecodontosaurus as narrow-footed prosauropods, separating them from the prosauropods that had broader feet. Anchisaurus and Thecodontosaurus are among the smallest prosauropods, so the difference in foot shape may be because of their size.

The skull of Anchisaurus was lightly built and triangular when viewed from the side. Other prosauropods, such as Plateosaurus, had more rectangular skulls with flatter snouts. Anchisaurus also differs from other prosauropods because the jaw joint was level with the lower jaw, rather than below the tooth row. Anchisaurus had blunt, diamond-shaped teeth that were less tightly packed and fewer than in other prosauropods. All this shows that Anchisaurus probably ate soft, easily chewed plants.

Barapasaurus tagorsi

Anchisaurus polyzelus

BARAPASAURUS
(bah-RAP-ah-SORE-us)

Period:
Late Triassic
Order, Suborder, Family:
Saurischia, Sauropodomorpha,
Cetiosauridae
Location:
Asia (India)
Length:
49$^{1}/_{2}$ feet (15 meters)

Named for a word meaning "big leg" in a local dialect in central India, Barapasaurus is the oldest known sauropod dinosaur. Early Jurassic sauropods are rare. The sauropods may have evolved from a prosauropod ancestor. Barapasaurus proves that even the earliest sauropods were giants.

Barapasaurus lived at the same time as the last prosauropod dinosaurs. In some ways, Barapasaurus was similar to the prosauropods, but in other ways, it was quite advanced. But its vertebrae, pelvis, and large size prove it belongs to the sauropods. Barapasaurus was almost as large as Diplodocus (a Late Jurassic sauropod of North America). Barapasaurus was probably a plant-eater, using its long neck to gather leaves from treetops.

The only mounted dinosaur skeleton in India, where dinosaurs are rare, is Barapasaurus. The skeleton includes mostly leg bones and vertebrae. The skull was not found, but several teeth were found near the skeleton. The teeth were spoon-shaped; these may have been the front teeth that were used for cropping vegetation. The chewing teeth were likely larger and flattened for cutting or crushing food.

Relatives of Barapasaurus include Cetiosaurus from northern Africa and England, Patagosaurus and Volkheimeria from southern South America, *Amygdalodon* from Argentina, *Lapparentosaurus* from Madagascar, and possibly *Rhoetosaurus* from Australia. Descendants of *Barapasaurus* and its relatives dominated the Jurassic world.

COELOPHYSIS
(SEE-loh-FIE-sis)

Period:
Late Triassic
Order, Suborder, Family:
Saurischia, Theropoda, Podokesauridae
Location:
North America (United States)
Length:
10 feet (3 meters)

A mass of tangled bodies rolled with a flood, sliding over trees that had fallen into the muddy waters. The rains stopped and hundreds of carcasses of *Coelophysis,* the nimble predator of the Late Triassic, settled into the mud. Some skeletons were complete, some were torn apart, but all went to the bottom of the stream. Two hundred million years later, at Ghost Ranch in northern New Mexico, paleontologists unearthed a treasure trove of dinosaur skeletons. They were all from one group devastated by a flood in the Late Triassic. The animals here ranged from hatchlings to adults more than two meters long.

The body of *Coelophysis* was only a little larger than a turkey. It had a long slender tail and jaws filled with dozens of knife-edged teeth. *Coelophysis* was an unusual predator. It lived in large herds, something that does not happen in today's world. Although grazing animals such as wildebeest or caribou live in herds in our modern world, no predators live in large groups. Trampled areas around Ghost Ranch suggest that herds of *Coelophysis* migrated.

The animal's rear legs were strong and agile. It had feet with three long toes and one short one, and it was quick to leap away from larger predators, such as crocodilelike phytosaurs. The front legs of *Coelophysis* were small and probably were not used for walking. They were more likely used to gather food. Its head was large, with a pointed snout and large eyes. *Coelophysis* was a master of ambush. Perhaps a fish-eater, it seems that this 100-pound predator lived along streams, moving through ferns and horsetails, always on guard for its enemies. It also ate insects, lizardlike reptiles, and other small dinosaurs.

Besides the skeletons from Ghost Ranch, New Mexico, *Coelophysis* has also been found in the Painted Desert of Arizona. The petrified logs found there, many longer than 100 feet, show us what the forests looked like when these little dinosaurs ran about.

These are among the oldest, if not the oldest, dinosaurs in North America. *Coelophysis* is the oldest dinosaur in the world known from complete skeletons. The name *Coelophysis* means "hollow condition," referring to the hollow bones of the legs. They were built much like birds' bones for minimum weight and maximum strength. *Coelophysis bauri* is the only species known. *Coelurus* was an early name used for some of the original bones, which were mistakenly given several names.

In the rib cages of two adults from Ghost Ranch are the skeletons of young *Coelophysis.* They are too large and well developed to be unborn babies. This may have been cannibalism—one individual of a species eating another—and the prey was swallowed whole.

Relatives of *Coelophysis* include *Podokesaurus; Halticosaurus* and *Procompsognathus* from Germany; and *Syntarsus* from Zimbabwe and Arizona.

Unlike the giant predatory dinosaurs of later times, the Triassic theropod dinosaurs

were also prey. Their enemies included the enormous phytosaurs, which weighed a ton or more, and the active and powerful rauisuchid predators such as *Postosuchus.* These adversaries dominated the Triassic landscape, both on land and in the water.

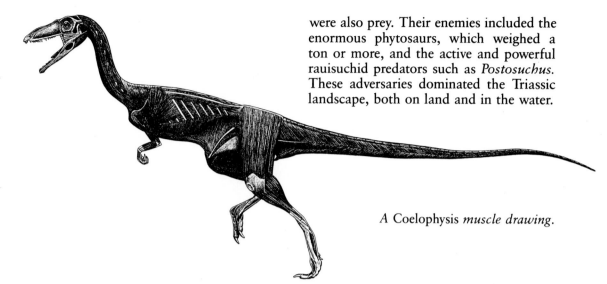

A Coelophysis muscle drawing.

Coelophysis

Two Coelophysis *in a Late Triassic landscape.*

53

DILOPHOSAURUS
(die-LOH-foh-SORE-us)

Period:
Early Jurassic
Order, Suborder, Family:
Saurischia, Theropoda, Podokesauridae
Location:
North America (United States)
Length:
20 feet (6 meters)

Dilophosaurus

The terror of the Early Jurassic, *Dilophosaurus* was one of the earliest large theropods. It weighed nearly 1,000 pounds and was the dominant predator of its time.

The teeth in the front of the snout were long and slender, probably for plucking and nipping at the flesh of its prey. The cheek teeth were long, pointed, and blade-shaped, typical of meat-eating dinosaurs. The lower jaw was slender, and the bones of the neck were not large. The muscles of the jaws and neck were not as powerful or as large as in later theropods. *Dilophosaurus* did not overpower its prey like its Late Jurassic relatives *Allosaurus* and *Ceratosaurus*. It slashed and tore at the flesh of its victim until it fell.

Balanced on its large hips, *Dilophosaurus* was fast and agile. The front legs were small and not often used for running. Three of the four fingers on the hands had claws that gripped and tore at the prey when it was feeding. The rear legs were long and made for running. The rear feet had three toes that were covered with claws. The muscular tail was as long as the front part of the body, and it helped balance the animal when it was moving.

Dilophosaurus had two parallel crests on the top of its head, from the tip of the snout to the top of the skull between the eyes. There was a thin bone in each crest. The animal's name means "two-ridged reptile," after these crests. Other theropods had horns and crests, but none were as prominent.

These crests made its head look rounder and larger; this may have helped it when competing for food or territory. Some paleontologists have suggested that this early theropod was social and that it settled disputes with rivals by displaying its crest, which may have shown the animal's social position. Perhaps the dominant males, with control of territory and females, had the largest and most colorful heads and crests. These crests would have also warned away challengers.

Before the skull of *Dilophosaurus* was discovered, this early theropod was confused with the European carnivore *Megalosaurus*. *Dilophosaurus* lived with the smaller theropods and the primitive ornithischian dinosaurs in the Kayenta Formation of Arizona. *Dilophosaurus* ate the large plant-eating prosauropod dinosaurs and any other prey it could capture.

Dilophosaurus wetherilli

EUSKELOSAURUS
(you-SKELL-oh-SORE-us)

Period:
Late Triassic
Order, Suborder, Family:
Saurischia, Sauropodomorpha,
Melanorosauridae
Location:
Africa (South Africa)
Length:
33 feet (10 meters)

Euskelosaurus was a prosauropod giant. Unfortunately, we do not have a complete skeleton—only limb bones and vertebrae. Thomas H. Huxley named it in 1866—its name means "true-limbed reptile."

Euskelosaurus had huge limbs. The length of the limbs, their massive build, and the size of the dinosaur support the idea that *Euskelosaurus* was among the most sauropodlike of the prosauropods. It was a massive animal that walked on all four legs (quadrapedal).

Its femur (the thigh bone) had a twisted shaft. Jacques van Heerden suggested that this twisting meant that the back legs of *Euskelosaurus* were "bow-legged." If van Heerden is correct, this would be unusual for a dinosaur. All other dinosaurs' thighs were directly under their bodies.

The habits of *Euskelosaurus* remain a mystery, because the head, hands, and feet are unknown. Based on the parts of the skeleton we have, it appears to have been a large, slow-moving plant-eater somewhat similar to *Apatosaurus*. However, we will not know for sure until scientists find better fossils of this dinosaur.

Euskelosaurus browni

Herrerasaurus ischigualastensis

HERRERASAURUS
(huh-RARE-uh-SORE-us)

Period:
Late Triassic
Family:
Herrerasauridae
Location:
South America (Argentina)
Length:
10 feet (3 meters)

This carnivore weighed perhaps 500 pounds and stood about four feet tall at the shoulders. *Herrerasaurus* was one of the dominant theropods of the Late Triassic of South America. The skull is unknown, but the other parts of the skeleton show that *Herrerasaurus* was a meat-eater that had muscular jaws, cutting teeth, and claws on the front feet. The pubis of *Herrerasaurus* is unusual; it looks much like the pelvis of later ornithischian dinosaurs. *Herrerasaurus* may be close to the ancestry of several major groups of dinosaurs.

Herrerasaurus lived among groves of ferns and tall conifer trees in a cool, moist habitat. It probably captured small animals by ambush and surprise. Its prey included rhynchosaurs, thecodont reptiles, and other early dinosaurs.

Herrerasaurus lived around 230 million years ago, when dinosaurs first appeared in the Triassic Period but were not yet dominant. These earliest dinosaurs were all small predators, like *Coelophysis* in North America. They competed with more powerful nondinosaur carnivores for food, including the rauisuchids, some of which were like huge crocodiles. Larger predators ate *Herrerasaurus* and other small dinosaurs.

Herrerasaurus represents the roots of dinosaur evolution. It cannot be classified as either a Saurischia or Ornithischia. This early and very primitive dinosaur had four toes on its back feet. This separates it from other meat-eating dinosaurs, which had three toes. It was advanced in other ways, however. Its pelvis and vertebrae (back bones) were similar to the advanced theropods of the Jurassic and the Cretaceous Periods.

Staurikosaurus, which some paleontologists place in the same family with *Herrerasaurus,* also had four toes on its back feet. *Herrerasaurus* was slightly more advanced in the hips, however, showing that it may be an ancestor that led to the prosauropod dinosaurs.

Herrerasaurus is known best from the Ischigualasto Formation in the Valle de la Luna (Valley of the Moon) National Park in San Juan, Argentina. A goat farmer, Victorino Herrera, found the skeleton and the dinosaur was named after him. The barren landscape has hills of red, purple, green, and tan shale. It is similar to the landscape in the Petrified Forest National Park in Arizona, where the Chinle Formation of about the same age has produced similar dinosaurs.

HETERODONTOSAURUS
(HET-ur-oh-DONT-oh-SORE-us)

Period:
Early Jurassic
Order, Suborder, Family:
Ornithischia, Ornithopoda,
Heterodontosauridae
Location:
Africa (South Africa)
Length:
3 feet (90 centimeters)

Heterodontosaurus was a small plant-eater that probably walked only on its back legs (bipedal). The front limbs were muscular, and the joints of the elbow and wrist show that it used its front limbs for grasping and not for walking. The fourth and fifth fingers were small and probably opposed the first three, forming a grasping hand for grabbing food.

The pelvis of *Heterodontosaurus* was long and narrow. The pubis was almost like those found in later ornithischians. The back legs were long, with the lower leg and foot longer than the thigh. The ankle bones and all but one of the bones in the foot fused (joined) together, as in birds. The joints of the knee and ankle only allowed forward and backward movement of the leg. These features support the idea that *Heterodontosaurus* could run quickly on its back legs. This would have helped it escape from carnivores.

The skull of *Heterodontosaurus* was about the size of a rabbit's. It had an unusual feature, for which it was named. Most dinosaurs had only one kind of tooth, but this dinosaur had three kinds of teeth. Its name means "different-toothed reptile." The front teeth were small and were on the sides of beaks on both the upper and lower jaws. These teeth were probably used to chop leaves and stems. The back teeth (cheek teeth) were tall and squared off, and the upper and lower teeth met at an angle

for grinding plants. A thick coat of enamel protected the teeth, so the animal could chew constantly. The teeth of *Heterodontosaurus* were more advanced than those of *Lesothosaurus*. But both dinosaurs' teeth were better suited to eating plants than the other plant-eaters at this time.

Heterodontosaurus also had large, paired tusks (the third type of tooth) that were in front of the cheek teeth. It probably used these teeth in feeding, but may have used them to attract females or to fight other males. The lower tusks were much larger than the uppers. Females may not have had these tusks.

Heterodontosaurus probably had fleshy cheeks. These would have kept food from falling out of the mouth during chewing. Similar cheeks were present in many other herbivorous dinosaurs, including most later ornithopods and many prosauropods.

The front and back limbs were similar to later ornithischians (except for the unusual joined ankle and foot bones). Also, the angled cheek teeth, the jaw, and the fleshy cheeks were all features of later ornithischians.

LESOTHOSAURUS
(lay-SOO-toh-SORE-us)

Period:
Early Jurassic
Order, Suborder, Family:
Ornithischia, Ornithopoda,
Fabrosauridae
Location:
Africa (South Africa)
Length:
3 1/2 feet (1 meter)

In a series of papers in the early 1970s, Tony Thulborn described the bone structure of the small ornithischian *Lesotho-*

Heterdontosaurus tucki

saurus, which he then called *Fabrosaurus*. Peter Galton renamed it *Lesothosaurus* ("Lesotho reptile," for the country where the first fossils were found).

Lesothosaurus was different from *Heterodontosaurus*, the other ornithischian that lived at the same time. It did not have the large tusks of *Heterodontosaurus*. The upper and lower teeth of *Lesothosaurus* were small and shaped like little arrowheads. Although its teeth did not form an angled grinding surface like those of *Heterodontosaurus*, the upper and lower teeth did interlock (occlude) and wear against each other when the jaws closed. This formed an efficient way to grind plants. It probably did not have a beak for cropping plants, although a small one might have been present in the lower jaw. *Lesothosaurus* probably did not have fleshy cheeks, or maybe it had very small ones.

The skeleton of *Lesothosaurus* was light; it had hollow limb bones and hollow spaces in the skull. The front limbs were small and were probably used for grasping. The hand had four well-developed fingers and a smaller fifth finger.

The back legs were adapted for running. The lower leg (shank) was longer than the thigh, and the long toe bones were arranged so that the long bones of the foot (metatarsals) were off the ground. *Lesothosaurus* did not have fused bones (bones that had joined together) in the ankle or foot. The fifth toe was very small and higher up on the foot, and the first toe was too short to reach the ground. *Lesothosaurus* was a quick runner.

The relatives of *Lesothosaurus* include the first ornithischian, *Pisanosaurus*, from Argentina. The little armored dinosaur of Arizona, *Scutellosaurus*, also may belong in this group.

Right: *A herd of* Lesothosaurus australis.

Lufengosaurus huenei

LUFENGOSAURUS
(loo-FUNG-oh-SORE-us)

Period:
Early Jurassic
Order, Suborder, Family:
Saurischia, Sauropodomorpha,
Plateosauridae
Location:
Asia (People's Republic of China)
Length:
20 feet (6 meters)

Lufengosaurus was a close relative of *Plateosaurus.* It was about the same size, but it lived earlier. There are many fossils of this dinosaur from the Lufeng basin of Yunnan Province in southwestern China. It

is one of several prosauropods known from the Early Jurassic Lufeng Formation, along with some early crocodiles, mammals, and therapsids.

Although there are complete skeletons of this dinosaur, it is not fully described. The skull of *Lufengosaurus* was long and flat, and it had a small bump on its snout just above the nostril. It had a long neck.

Its teeth were bladelike with crowns that were wider at the bottom. The teeth were widely spaced. Its diet is unknown. It probably ate plants, but its teeth were sharp and it may have also eaten small animals.

The front legs of *Lufengosaurus* were shorter than the powerful back legs. The animal walked on all fours, but probably

rose on its back legs to feed on tall plants. The hands of *Lufengosaurus* had a large thumb with a claw, used for getting food and maybe as a weapon.

A skeleton of *Lufengosaurus* was the first dinosaur mounted in the People's Republic of China. It appeared on a Chinese postal stamp when the skeleton went on display.

MASSOSPONDYLUS
(MASS-oh-SPON-die-luss)

Period:
Early Jurassic
Order, Suborder, Family:
Saurischia, Sauropodomorpha,
Plateosauridae
Location:
Africa (South Africa, Zimbabwe), North America (United States)
Length:
13 feet (4 meters)

Massospondylus was a medium-size prosauropod. Sir Richard Owen named the animal in 1854. Its name means "massive vertebrae." There are many skeletons of this

animal, including several good skulls from South Africa and one good skeleton from the Kayenta Formation of Arizona. The Kayenta skull is about 25 percent bigger than the biggest African specimen. Some of the smaller skulls from South Africa were likely juveniles. They had taller, narrower skulls with bigger eye sockets. This shows that the skull proportions changed as it grew.

The skull of *Massospondylus* was shallower and shorter than that of *Plateosaurus,* with more changes along the tooth row. The front teeth were round, but the back teeth were more oval. The lower tooth row was shorter than the upper. Because of this difference in jaw length, and the unusual wear on the front teeth of the upper jaws, *Massospondylus* might have had a small lower beak to cut vegetation. The teeth and jaws of *Massospondylus* were built for a diet of plants.

Several of the South African specimens of *Massospondylus* had rounded stones in or near their ribcages. These appear to have been used to grind food in the stomach, much like the gizzards of birds. Several sauropods had similar structures. These "stomach stones" were smooth and

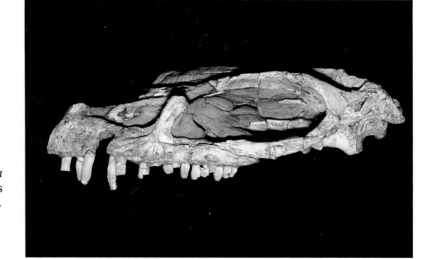

The top of a Massospondylus *skull.*

polished, as if by digestive acids or grinding against other stones and plant material.

The proportions of the skeleton of *Massospondylus* suggest that it, like *Plateosaurus,* could rear up and possibly walk on its hind legs. *Massospondylus* had an enlarged thumb claw that could have been used as a grooming tool or to dig or grasp food.

Many prosauropod dinosaurs have been found in the Late Triassic and Early Jurassic formations of Africa and North America. The *Massospondylus* from Arizona, however, provided the first proof of a prosauropod from both continents. The theropod *Syntarsus* and the early crocodilian *Protosuchus* were on both continents, as were some primitive mammals. This is evidence that climate and land barriers were absent up to the Early Jurassic. This suggests that many animals of the time could live all over the world.

MUSSAURUS
(MOOSE-sore-us)

Period:
Late Triassic
Order, Suborder, Family:
Saurischia, Sauropodomorpha, Plateosauridae
Location:
South America (Argentina)
Length:
Estimated 10 feet (3 meters)

In the mid-1970s, Jose Bonaparte led an expedition to the Late Triassic El Tranquilo Formation of southern Argentina. They made one of the most important Triassic dinosaur discoveries up to that time: a nest of tiny dinosaurs of a new prosauropod. Bonaparte and Martin Vince named it *Mussaurus* ("mouse reptile") in 1979.

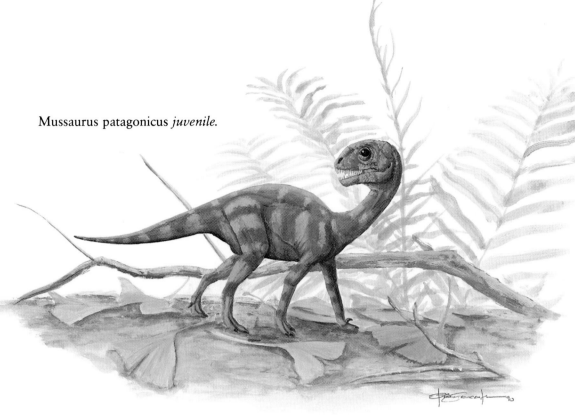

Mussaurus patagonicus *juvenile.*

Massospondylus

There was a nearly complete skeleton that was about six inches long without its tail. Although these specimens were all juveniles, *Mussaurus* is now very well known because the skeletons were complete. More recently, adult skeletons have been found in the same formation in Argentina.

Mussaurus was immediately recognizable as a prosauropod in the limb and pelvic area, although the hatchlings had short necks and high, short skulls with large orbits (eye sockets). The younger animals had different body proportions than did the older animals.

Bonaparte and Vince suggested that *Mussaurus* might be halfway between the prosauropods and sauropods, and might be closely related to the ancestry of the sauropods. It is also possible that many sauropod features in the juveniles might be only proportional differences in the skeleton between the juveniles and the adults. This question requires further study, and both the adult and hatchling skeletons will be studied in greater detail. *Mussaurus* may prove to be an important animal in finding the relationship between prosauropods and sauropods.

Mussaurus provided important information about dinosaur social behavior. The hatchlings and eggs in the nest show that these dinosaurs laid eggs. Several eggs in the nest show that prosauropods laid more than one egg at a time. Now that juveniles, immature specimens, and adults of *Mussaurus* are known, scientists can study proportion changes in the different-aged animals. This will give them information about growth rates and development of the prosauropod dinosaurs.

PLATEOSAURUS
(PLAT-ee-oh-SORE-us)

Period:
Late Triassic
Order, Suborder, Family:
Saurischia, Sauropodomorpha,
Plateosauridae
Location:
Europe (West Germany, East Germany,
France, Switzerland, England)
Length:
23 feet (7 meters)

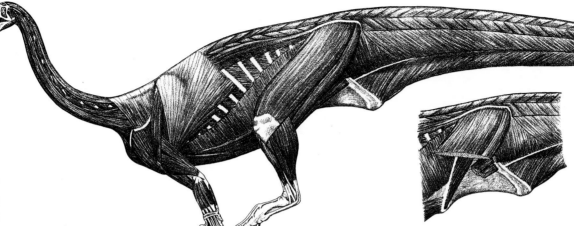

A muscle drawing of Plateosaurus
engelhardti *and a close-up of the hip region
showing underlying muscle.*

Plateosaurus is the best known of the early dinosaurs. It was among the largest of the Triassic dinosaurs, reaching an adult height of 15 feet when it stood on its back legs. An adult probably weighed close to a ton. It was the first Triassic dinosaur described. H. von Meyer named it in 1837; its name means "flat reptile."

Plateosaurus is the best-studied prosauropod dinosaur. The similarities between prosauropods and sauropods, their closest dinosaur relatives, are many. Both had massive trunks, long necks and tails, and small heads that were adapted to eating plants. However, adult prosauropods tended to be smaller. The smallest adult sauropods and the biggest prosauropods, such as *Melanorosaurus,* were about the same size.

One distinctive feature of *Plateosaurus* and of all prosauropods is their hands. They had small fingers and a huge thumb that had a large claw. This claw may have been used for plucking leaves from high branches, for digging roots, or for fighting. The front limbs were shorter than the back ones, but it walked on all four limbs.

The back legs of *Plateosaurus* were long and thick. Its legs were not made to run fast like *Coelophysis.* The feet of *Plateosaurus* had five toes, although the fifth (outer) toe was very small. The pelvis was short and massive, and the dinosaur had large, powerful leg muscles.

The prosauropods were unique among Triassic dinosaurs because they had long necks. This allowed them to reach leaves and branches high off the ground. *Plateosaurus* could reach even higher when it reared up on its back limbs, which it could have done while standing and maybe while walking.

The head of *Plateosaurus* was small. It was longer and flatter than the heads of the later sauropods. Its lower jaw curved down, as did the front of its snout; this made the animal look like it was smiling. It had simple, leaf-shaped teeth. They did not change shape from the front to the back of the jaw. Teeth in the upper jaw fitted between pairs of teeth in the lower jaw. This allowed it to chop the leaves as it ate. The jaws, muscles, and teeth of prosauropods were suited to a plant diet. *Plateosaurus* probably had fleshy cheeks. Dinosaurs may have stored food in these cheeks, and they kept food from falling out as the animal ate. To help its digestion, *Plateosaurus* may have had "gastroliths." These were stones in the stomach (swallowed by the dinosaur) that rubbed against one another and the food, slicing and grinding the leaves and plants.

Plateosaurus fed on high vegetation, such as the leaves of tree ferns. Prosauropods probably browsed in high tree branches much like sauropods did later in the Mesozoic and giraffes do today. A. W. Crompton and John Attridge noted that prosauropods were unique among Triassic herbivores because they had lightly built skulls, which suggests that they probably ate soft plants. To chew tougher branches and leaves, an animal's skull and jaw must be heavily built.

Dinosaurs did not become common until near the end of the Triassic. In Late Triassic European quarries, *Plateosaurus* is the most common vertebrate fossil. Michael Benton estimated that 75 percent of the skeletons from this age in West Germany belong to *Plateosaurus.*

In Halberstadt and Trossingen, West Germany, workers found mass graves of *Plateosaurus* and have removed dozens of skeletons from each. Trossingen contains one layer that has a herd of plateosaurs killed by a catastrophic event, possibly a flood. David Weishampel suggested that the reason *Plateosaurus* is so common in other layers of the quarry is because it was the most abundant animal at the time.

The sudden appearance and rise to dominance of *Plateosaurus* in the northern hemisphere, and other prosauropods elsewhere, is one of the most sudden and dramatic dinosaur success stories. Their great numbers could be because they were able to feed on high vegetation—this allowed them to find food that smaller herbivores could not reach.

Left: *A group of* Plateosaurus engelhardti.
Above: *A complete* Plateosaurus *skull.*

Riojasaurus incertus

RIOJASAURUS
(ree-OH-hah-SORE-us)

Period:
Late Triassic
Order, Suborder, Family:
Saurischia, Sauropodomorpha,
Melanorosauridae
Location:
South America (Argentina)
Length:
33 feet (10 meters)

Riojasaurus and the related South African genus *Melanorosaurus* are prosauropod giants. Both had a number of features in common with the sauropod dinosaurs. These include vertebrae with hollow spaces that made them lighter, and dense, massive limb bones.

Riojasaurus was a quadrupedal (it walked on all four legs) dinosaur; it could not rear up on its back legs like some of its relatives, such as *Plateosaurus*. Its long, massive body needed to be supported by all four limbs. The front limbs of *Riojasaurus* were nearly as long as its back limbs. It had four vertebrae connecting the pelvis to the trunk; most other small prosauropods had only three.

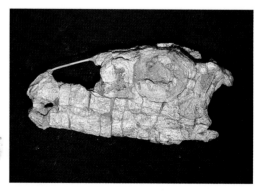

A skull of Riojasaurus.

Some scientists consider *Riojasaurus* and *Melanorosaurus* the closest relatives of the sauropods, because of their large size and some features of their limbs. Recently, however, Peter Galton and Paul Sereno have argued that the prosauropods and sauropods had a common ancestor sometime in the Triassic. If this is correct, the similarities probably are because both groups were large animals. More light will be shed on this question when newly discovered material of *Riojasaurus,* including at least one good skull, is described by scientists.

Riojasaurus was an early and short-lived prosauropod that lived at the end of the Late Triassic. In the Early Jurassic, smaller animals such as *Anchisaurus* become the dominant prosauropods, and the first sauropods, *Vulcanodon* and *Barapasaurus,* appeared.

Scelidosaurus harrisonii

SCELIDOSAURUS
(skee-LIE-doh-SORE-us)

Period:
Early Jurassic
Order, Suborder, Family:
Ornithischia, Thyreophora, Scelidosauridae
Location:
Europe (England)
Length:
13 feet (4 meters)

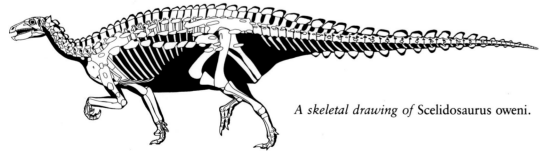

A skeletal drawing of Scelidosaurus oweni.

Scelidosaurus was first discovered in the middle of the 19th century in Early Jurassic rocks from southern England. Sir Richard Owen, creator of the name Dinosauria, described its remains. He named it *Scelidosaurus,* which means "limb reptile," referring to its large legs.

It was the earliest known ornithischian dinosaur and one of the most complete for its time. However, with the discovery of *Lesothosaurus* and *Heterodontosaurus* in the 1960s and 1970s, scientists know that *Scelidosaurus* is not the oldest ornithischian. But it still remains an important animal in the history of dinosaurs. It tells scientists much about the early evolution of ornithischians, particularly stegosaurs and ankylosaurs, the armored dinosaurs from later in the Mesozoic Era.

Scelidosaurus was a plant-eating dinosaur that grew to about 13 feet. It was a heavily built animal. The most unusual feature of *Scelidosaurus* was that it had many bony plates in the skin of its back and rib cage. These plates were not like the high, thin plates that extended from the backbone of stegosaurian dinosaurs. These plates were similar to the bony armor of ankylosaurs.

The large head of *Scelidosaurus* was equipped with somewhat simple, leaf-shaped teeth. From the teeth and the shape of the skeleton, scientists know that *Scelidosaurus* was a plant-eating animal. It likely ate a mixture of leaves of shrubs and low-lying branches, but may also have fed on succulent fruits and even eaten insects as a hatchling and juvenile.

The legs of *Scelidosaurus* were stout and the feet had four toes. The size and shape of the legs show that *Scelidosaurus* walked on all four legs. The tail of *Scelidosaurus* was long compared to most other ornithischian dinosaurs. The tail also had armor in the skin.

Recently, new discoveries of *Scelidosaurus* have been found from the area where the original fossils were unearthed. These include skull bones and the impressions of small, rounded scales in the skin. These skin impressions are rare fossils. They are helpful for scientists when they try to reconstruct the appearance of dinosaurs and to understand the biology of these extinct animals.

Scelidosaurus is one of the most primitive armored dinosaurs, along with its close relative *Scutellosaurus,* which also lived in the Early Jurassic. Both are early members of the group of dinosaurs that contains both stegosaurs and ankylosaurs (Thyreophora). *Scelidosaurus* is closely related to the Late Jurassic stegosaurs *Huayangosaurus* and *Stegosaurus*. It is also related to the Late Jurassic ankylosaur *Sarcolestes* and the Late Cretaceous ankylosaur *Shamosaurus*. *Lusitanosaurus* may also be related; it is known only from a fragment of the snout and was found in Late Jurassic rocks along the coast of Portugal.

SCUTELLOSAURUS
(skoo-TELL-oh-SORE-us)

Period:
Late Triassic
Order, Suborder, Family:
Ornithischia, Ornithopoda, Fabrosauridae
Location:
North America (United States)
Length:
4 feet (1.2 meters)

One of the earliest ornithischian dinosaurs, *Scutellosaurus* is unusual because it was a two-legged dinosaur with armor. While most armored dinosaurs were large quadrupeds (they walked on four legs), *Scutellosaurus* was small, about the size of a collie dog. The skull bones were slender, like other members of this family. The jaws were strong with powerful muscles. The animal had bladelike front teeth that were used for grabbing or nipping at plants. The teeth on the sides of the jaws were pointed, with tiny ridges on the sides that helped slice its food.

The front legs were strong for a biped. The front feet were also relatively large, showing that it often used its front legs for walking. Because of the bony armor, these little dinosaurs were heavy, so that movement on all fours was comfortable when they were resting or moving slowly. The tail was strong and probably useful not only when it was moving but also to defend itself against predators. The rear legs were

well suited for bipedal motion, and the extra long tail balanced the animal when it walked on its back legs.

The unusual feature of *Scutellosaurus,* or "shield reptile," is the presence of several hundred small bony plates (scutes) in the skin, probably covering the neck, back, ribs, and tail. These scutes were isolated and similar to the bony plates of alligators and crocodiles. In *Scutellosaurus* these plates were small; the largest was about the size of a quarter. Some flattened plates, though they were much smaller, were similar to the plates of *Ankylosaurus.*

Scutellosaurus had other plates that were tall and triangular, roughly similar to those of *Stegosaurus.* The function of the plates of *Scutellosaurus* was probably different from *Stegosaurus,* which was much larger and needed its plates to regulate its body heat. *Scutellosaurus* was small and did not need this. Instead, its plates probably protected its pelvic area, and the other armor probably protected its skin from coarse vegetation, much like modern-day armadillos.

Because of the armor and the overall form of the body, some paleontologists think *Scutellosaurus* was the ancestor of the later large armored dinosaurs, such as *Stegosaurus* and *Ankylosaurus.* In these Late Jurassic and Cretaceous species, the armor was heavy, so the animals always had to walk on all four feet. However, their front legs were short, showing the ancestry of the Early Jurassic dinosaurs that were small and bipedal.

A relative of *Scutellosaurus* was *Lesothosaurus* from South Africa, from approximately the same age. This little dinosaur lacked armor and had smaller front legs, showing that it more often used only its back legs to walk or run.

Right page: An Early Jurassic Scutellosaurus.

SELLOSAURUS
(SELL-oh-SORE-us)

Period:
Late Triassic
Order, Suborder, Family:
Saurischia, Sauropodomorpha, Plateosauridae
Location:
Europe (West Germany)
Height:
10 feet (3 meters)

Sellosaurus skeletons have been found in the middle Late Triassic beds in Nordwurttemberg, West Germany. These beds are slightly older than those where the skeletons of *Plateosaurus* were found. Although Frederich von Huene described *Sellosaurus* in 1907, confusion has surrounded the relationships of this dinosaur, *Plateosaurus,* and other members of the Plateosauridae. Using paleontological detective work, Peter Galton cleared up the mystery. By care-

ful comparisons, Galton has shown that *Sellosaurus* appeared first and was the only prosauropod in the middle Late Triassic. It was followed by but did not overlap in time with *Plateosaurus.*

Sellosaurus was similar to *Plateosaurus,* but smaller. Its teeth changed more from the front to the back of the jaw. This and other details of the skull may mean that *Sellosaurus* had a slightly different, softer plant diet than *Plateosaurus.* The two animals are similar in most details and are close relatives. An animal very much like *Sellosaurus* was probably the ancestor of *Plateosaurus.* The sharp contrast between the rarity of *Sellosaurus* and the extreme abundance of *Plateosaurus* is dramatic evidence of the sudden spread of prosauropods at the end of the Triassic and in the Early Jurassic.

Sellosaurus gracilis

A pair of Staurikosaurus.

are the earliest members of the Saurischia. Part of the uncertainty about the position of *Staurikosaurus* is because the skull is missing. *Staurikosaurus* and *Herrerasaurus* differ from other dinosaurs in the structure of their pelvis. Their lower legs and ankles are also different from the later dinosaurs.

Staurikosaurus fossils are not common, but they occur in formations where other land vertebrates, such as aetosaurs and rauisuchids, are common. The reason there are few *Staurikosaurus* fossils in these deposits could be because there were few animals; or perhaps they lived in areas where bones rarely fossilized, such as forests. It could also be a combination of both factors. Whatever the reason, there are few *Staurikosaurus* and *Herrerasaurus* fossils. Small theropod dinosaurs, such as *Coelophysis*, followed and perhaps replaced them by the end of the Triassic.

STAURIKOSAURUS
(store-ICK-oh-SORE-us)

Period:
Late Triassic
Family:
Staurikosauridae
Location:
South America (Brazil, Argentina)
Length:
6½ feet (2 meters)

Staurikosaurus is the earliest dinosaur known. The first skeleton came from the Santa Maria Formation of southern Brazil and dates back to the Late Triassic. Its name means "cross reptile," and it was named after a group of stars called the Southern Cross, which are best seen in the southern hemisphere.

Staurikosaurus was a bipedal (two-legged) dinosaur, although its back legs and pelvis were not well made for rapid motion. It had five fingers and five toes, which is a primitive feature. The third finger and toe were the longest. The teeth were curved backwards and serrated, like a steak knife. It was a meat-eater.

Edwin Colbert described *Staurikosaurus* in 1970. In 1987 Don Brinkman and Hans-Dieter Sues described a second skeleton from the slightly younger Ischigualasto Formation of Argentina. Workers have found fossil pieces in Late Triassic formations in the southwest United States and in the Elliot Formation of South Africa that may belong to this animal. One partial skeleton from the Petrified Forest National Park in Arizona, nicknamed Gertie, is being studied.

Paleontologists disagree on the relationship of *Staurikosaurus* and the closely related *Herrerasaurus*. These animals either represent primitive dinosaurs that share a common ancestry with all later dinosaurs or

SYNTARSUS
(sin-TAR-sus)

Period:
Early Jurassic
Order, Suborder, Family:
Saurischia, Theropoda, Podokesauridae
Location:
Africa (Zimbabwe), North America (United States)
Length:
10 feet (3 meters)

The agile and fleet-footed carnivore *Syntarsus* was a small predator. It strongly resembled *Coelophysis* from the Late Triassic of Arizona and New Mexico. The bones of the head and jaws were large compared to *Coelophysis*, and the neck was somewhat shorter. *Syntarsus* was sturdier and slightly larger than *Coelophysis*.

Syntarsus kayentakatae

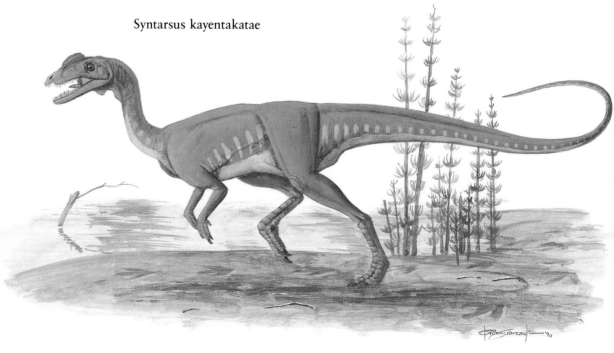

Its jaws had many small, bladelike, serrated teeth for slicing the flesh of its prey. *Syntarsus* probably ate other small reptiles and fish, and it lived along stream courses in herds. Like *Coelophysis,* a large number of *Syntarsus* remains were found in one area, suggesting that they were social animals.

The animal is named for its fused ankle, or tarsus, joint. Its name means "fused tarsus." This ankle gave it greater speed and endurance when running. It would have needed to run quickly to escape predators. The front legs were quite small and weak, while the rear legs were stout. The tail was large and probably stiff. The limbs' proportions suggest that *Syntarsus* may have moved by "saltation," or hopping, similar to rabbits or kangaroos. This hopping produces abrupt and unpredictable movements in order to escape predators.

The many skeletons from Zimbabwe have two body forms: males were smaller and more slender, while the females were robust and larger. There were many more females than males.

The bones of *Syntarsus* had so many bone cells and blood vessels that they resemble the bones of birds and mammals. This may mean that *Syntarsus* was a warm-blooded dinosaur.

It is difficult to pinpoint ancestral relationships, but a case may be made that *Coelophysis* is a close ancestor of *Syntarsus.* Changes in *Syntarsus* include fewer teeth; larger openings in the skull for larger and stronger jaw muscles; growth of small plates of bone between the teeth for more biting strength; smaller front limbs and weaker hands; stronger pelvis and bottom of the spine; and fusion of the ankle joints. *Syntarsus* became more powerful than *Coelophysis.* Similar trends happened to all the predatory dinosaurs that appeared in the Jurassic. This resulted in the development of the large and ferocious predators such as *Allosaurus* and its relatives millions of years later.

Yunnanosaurus huangi

YUNNANOSAURUS
(YU-nan-oh-SORE-us)

Period:
Early Jurassic
Order, Suborder, Family:
Saurischia, Sauropodomorpha,
Yunnanosauridae
Location:
Asia (People's Republic of China)
Length:
18-25 feet (5.5-7.5 meters)

Yunnanosaurus was a long-necked, four-legged plant-eater that lumbered through the fernlike vegetation of southern China. It had over 60 spoon-shaped teeth that sharpened themselves by wearing against each other as the animal fed. This was different from its prosauropod relatives, which had leaf-shaped teeth that wore away against the food that was being chewed. The advanced teeth of *Yunnanosaurus* were somewhat like those of the sauropods, the dominant plant-eaters of the Middle and Late Jurassic periods. The teeth of *Yunnanosaurus* probably evolved separately though, because the rest of its anatomy was not like the sauropods. One of the last of the prosauropods, *Yunnanosaurus* also had a skull that had a different shape than its earlier relatives.

Yunnanosaurus was named after the Yunnan Province in the People's Republic of China. In 1939, Young Chung Chien discovered several partial skeletons and Wang Tsun Yi excavated them. Young described *Yunnanosaurus huangi* in 1942; it was a smallish animal with a lightly built body. Nine years later, in 1951, he described a second species, *Yunnanosaurus robustus.* It was a larger, more heavily built animal. After further study of the fossils, it was found that the larger species is actually the adult of the smaller species.

The remains of as many as 20 individuals of various sizes have been unearthed in the Lufeng Formation in the People's Republic of China. After these skeletons have been studied and described, we should soon know more about this dinosaur.

CHAPTER 5

DINOSAURS TAKE OVER THE WORLD

The Middle and Late Jurassic Period

By the Middle and Late Jurassic, dinosaurs had taken over the world. There were herds of *Apatosaurus;* each adult was as large as five or six elephants. *Allosaurus,* a two-ton meat-eater, waited in the bushes for its next meal; it needed to eat often to fill its appetite. Bony plates protected slow, steady *Stegosaurus,* which had little fear of predators. The land quaked with dinosaur footsteps. Dinosaurs controlled this Jurassic world.

Pangaea continued to break apart in the Jurassic. It was splitting both north and south, and east and west. The land masses were beginning to resemble the shapes they have today. The Tethys Sea separated the southern land mass, called Gondwanaland, from the northern mass, called Laurasia. Laurasia consisted of North America, Europe, and Asia. Sometimes, probably because of sea level changes, it's likely there were land connections between Gondwanaland and Laurasia. Dinosaurs were very similar in North America and eastern Africa in the Late Jurassic. The Atlantic Ocean was still very narrow, and there was probably a land bridge that allowed the dinosaurs to migrate between the two continents.

The northern part of the Atlantic Ocean began to open during the Jurassic, and it separated Laurasia into eastern (Europe and Asia) and western (North America) land masses.

There were probably land bridges that connected these two land masses across the north when the sea level dropped. Antarctica gradually broke away from Gondwanaland and was over the South Pole by the Early Cretaceous. The continents were drifting apart at a rate of about a quarter of an inch to three inches a year (which is about as fast as a human fingernail grows).

All these changes in the continents changed the way the ocean waters flowed. Cold ocean currents in the southern hemisphere produced temperate climates in what is now South America, southern Africa, Antarctica, India (an island off eastern Africa), and Australia. The rest of the world was also warm and moist, and the Triassic deserts were shrinking and were gone by the Late Jurassic. There were no polar ice caps.

In this dry and semi-dry Jurassic landscape, conifers dominated wherever trees grew. Except for dinosaurs, the Jurassic plants and animals were much like those of earlier times. There were many ferns, tree ferns, cycads, ginkgos, and horsetails. Grasses had not yet evolved, but some ferns may have served as low ground cover.

Pterosaurs glided and flapped their way to feeding grounds. There were two types of pterosaurs, ones with tails

Left: Apatosaurus *was a sauropod that came to dominance in the Jurassic.*

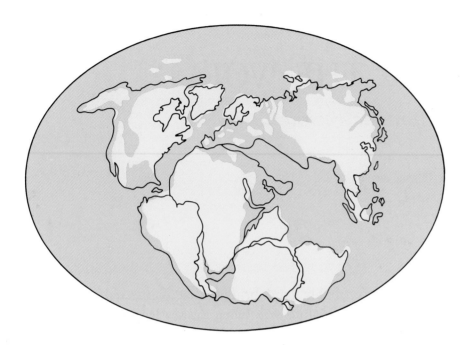

Jurassic Map

This landscape provided food, forage, and home for the dinosaurs. As the land became greener in the Late Jurassic, the sauropods gained the advantage. They reached from China to North America to Africa. From the earliest sauropods in the Early and Middle Jurassic, and the carnivores that evolved with them, arose the giants of the Late Jurassic. *Apatosaurus, Diplodocus, Brachiosaurus, Ultrasaurus, Supersaurus, Allosaurus,* and *Ceratosaurus* roamed the earth. Others, like the ornithopods *Stegosaurus* and *Camptosaurus,* survived the great deserts of the Middle Jurassic and added to the growing group of dinosaurs. Late Jurassic dinosaurs were spectacular. They exceeded the imagination in size and form.

The large plant-eaters such as *Apatosaurus* moved constantly, perhaps like elephants feeding almost around the clock. They probably destroyed plant life as they grazed through an

and ones without. The pterosaurs with tails did not last past the Late Jurassic; the pterosaurs without tails survived into the Cretaceous. Crocodiles, which replaced the phytosaurs of the Triassic, lurked in the undergrowth near water. Mammals, the descendants of the therapsids, were still running around. They were mostly shrewlike creatures that were four to five inches long, eating insects or chewing fruits and seeds. New insects were also evolving, including the ancestors of earwigs, flies, and bees, among others.

The mammallike reptiles that were so important in the Triassic were gone by the Middle Jurassic, as were the rauisuchids and other archosaurs. Late in the Jurassic, small lizards, frogs, and salamanders crawled around under the cover of plants. Turtles, though not large, had also appeared. In the seas, corals, clams, and snails flourished, as did sharks and the marine reptiles, including plesiosaurs and ichthyosaurs.

Above: *A* Ceratosaurus nasicornis *attacks two* Allosaurus fragilis. *Both animals were fierce predators during the Jurassic Period. Right:* Allosaurus *decides that* Camptosaurus *is its next meal.*

area, but at the same time they opened the ground to more sunlight for new growth. Migration of the sauropods was random and only loosely tied to a region. They may have had separate areas for laying eggs, where the young would hatch away from the adults. The large herds probably were mostly adults, with the adults protecting the young.

The large sauropods browsed at the tops of trees for food, where no other dinosaurs could reach. The smaller plant-eaters ate ground cover and shorter brush. Some, such as *Stegosaurus,* probably reared up on their hind legs to get higher brush. The small meat-eaters probably ate lizards and scavenged meals from other animals. Large meat-eaters would have eaten smaller dinosaurs and even attempted to kill a sauropod, perhaps a youngster that strayed from the herd.

Dinosaurs of the Late Jurassic in China showed general similarities of body to those in other parts of the world. There were sauropods, stegosaurs, carnosaurs, and coelurosaurs, but when we look carefully, we see that the Chinese forms were all unique. They were not found in Africa or North America. China seems to have been isolated from the rest of the world at this time.

Archaeopteryx flew from conifer tree to conifer tree. It was an ancestor of modern birds. A coelurosaur dinosaur of the Middle Jurassic may have been its ancestor.

More and more kinds of dinosaurs were evolving in the Middle and Late Jurassic Period, but the most important dinosaurs of this time were the sauropods. These immense creatures roamed the earth searching for food to sustain their enormous size. The earth did provide for them, though there are still some questions scientists have about their diets. These animals were the most successful dinosaurs, with their numbers growing rapidly. They were truly the masters of their universe.

Two camarasaurs with camptosaurs in the background. Far right: *A pair of nesting* Archaeopteryx.

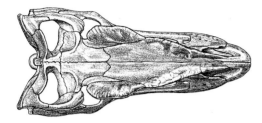

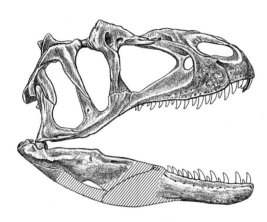

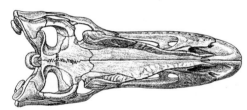

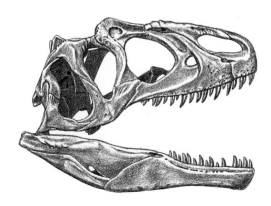

Top: *Skull drawings of* Allosaurus fragilis *(top) and* Allosaurus atrox *(bottom).* Left: Allosaurus atrox

ALLOSAURUS
(AL-oh-SORE-us)

Period:
Late Jurassic
Order, Suborder, Family:
Saurischia, Theropoda, Allosauridae
Location:
North America
Length:
35-40 feet (11-12 meters)

Allosaurus means "other reptile," a strange name for the most powerful, fearsome, and deadly dinosaur of the Late Jurassic. *Allosaurus* was the main enemy of the giant sauropods, including *Apatosaurus* and *Diplodocus,* even though the plant-eaters weighed much more than the two-ton predator. Until the tyrannosaurs appeared 50 million years later, *Allosaurus* and its relatives were the largest predators to roam the earth.

At the Cleveland-Lloyd Dinosaur Quarry in Utah, more than 10,000 bones have been excavated since 1927, and about half are *Allosaurus* bones. The number of *Allosaurus* bones is unusual, because there is usually about one predator for every ten plant-eaters. This was probably a predator trap, where a few animals that were prey got caught, maybe by tar, and then predators came to feed on the bodies. But they also got caught in the trap. None of the skeletons of *Allosaurus* are still connected. The skeletons were probably trampled and pushed around in this trap. Other animals, including the herbivores *Stegosaurus* and *Barosaurus,* were also found.

The allosaurs from this quarry include all ages. There were animals from only a little over a foot in length to those more than 40 feet long and weighing more than two tons. Other allosaurs were estimated at more than 49 feet long and weighed almost three tons. Two other predators at the Cleveland-Lloyd quarry were *Stokesosaurus* and *Marshosaurus;* both were small

and slender. A third predator found was *Ceratosaurus,* a medium-size theropod. All these animals were rare compared to *Allosaurus.*

The powerful skull of *Allosaurus* was the perfect meat-eating machine. The jaws were large and massive, with serrated teeth as well designed for cutting meat as a steak knife. It probably overpowered its prey and used its massive jaw muscles; its large, powerful neck and head; and its daggerlike teeth to kill and eat its prey. These predators were widespread. They left their broken teeth near the bodies of many animals, showing where they had been.

The front limbs of *Allosaurus* were short but strong, and the hands had three fingers each. Each finger had a sharply curved and pointed claw. It probably used its front limbs to capture prey and grab the flesh when feeding. The rear legs were large and powerful, built for both speed and agility.

Allosaurus probably ate any animal it could ambush or overpower. The tremendous size of the sauropods was probably an obstacle for even the largest *Allosaurus.* Like lions today, *Allosaurus* was probably opportunistic. It attacked old or weak animals when possible and stole carcasses from other predators.

The most common species is *Allosaurus fragilis.* A close relative of *Allosaurus* is *Acrocanthosaurus* from the Early Cretaceous in North America.

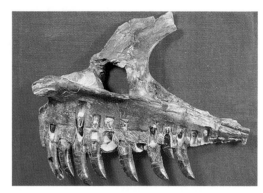

Top: *The top of an* Allosaurus *jaw found in the Morrison Formation in Utah.*
Bottom: *A muscle drawing of* Allosaurus fragilis *and a close-up of the underlying muscles of the hip (right).*

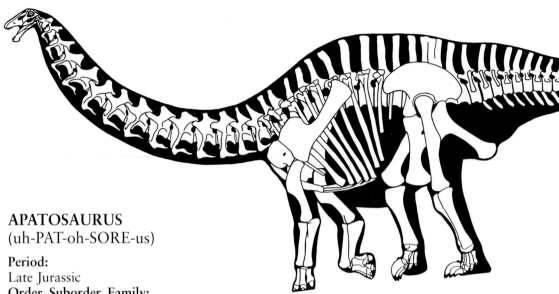

Skeletal drawing of Apatosaurus.

APATOSAURUS
(uh-PAT-oh-SORE-us)

Period:
Late Jurassic
Order, Suborder, Family:
Saurischia, Sauropodomorpha,
Diplodocidae
Location:
North America
Length:
70 feet (21 meters)

Apatosaurus moved constantly, feeding day and night. When they walked, the ground thundered, because each adult weighed as much as five adult elephants. The idea of a thundering walker gave *Brontosaurus* its name, which means "thunder lizard." The name *Apatosaurus* was used first for this dinosaur, so it is the correct name. But the literal meaning of its name, "deceitful reptile," is difficult to apply to this giant. With a shoulder height of 12 feet, a length of about 70 feet, and a weight of 30 tons, this peaceful herbivore could neither hide nor disappear into the background.

Like its close relatives *Diplodocus*, *Barosaurus*, and *Supersaurus*, this sauropod had a small head; a long, slender neck; and a deep, heavy midsection. It also had legs built like pillars and a long heavy tail that ended in a slender whip.

A few years ago, one of the most celebrated mistakes in science was found: the wrong head had been placed on the *Apatosaurus* skeleton in the Carnegie Museum of Natural History in Pittsburgh. A skull of *Camarasaurus*, which belongs to a different family, was put on the skeleton. The *Apatosaurus* was nearly complete when it was excavated except that it had no head. The best guess at the time was that its skull was like that of *Camarasaurus*, with a rounded and blunt profile, large crushing teeth, and powerful jaws. The scientists who discovered the mistake studied the quarry maps where all the bones were found and realized that the skull had slipped a few feet away from the neck before burial and preservation. The actual skull was at the Carnegie Museum. The skull of *Apatosaurus* turned out to look very much like that of Diplodocus, with a long slender profile and small delicate teeth in the front of the jaws.

The neck of *Apatosaurus* was small near the head, but the base of the neck near the body was huge, and the neck bones were long and massive. Despite its long neck, *Apatosaurus* had limited capability for rais-ing its head, which could probably not reach much higher than its shoulders.

The bones of the middle part of the body were huge. Its ribs were long and straight, and its vertebrae (bones of the spine) were huge but had hollow spaces that made them lighter but did not make them less strong. Its legs were straight and massive, like an elephant's, with short stubby toes. The toes of the front feet were blunt, except for the inner toe, which had a claw that pointed inward. The rear feet had three claws that looked a little like a cow's hooves.

Apatosaurus was taller at the hips than the shoulders; the height of a full-grown animal's hips was about 15 feet. Its hips were huge, and the hip sockets had to support the enormous stress of walking with such a heavy body. Its tail bones near the front of its tail were also huge, and all of the tail bones had tall spines where muscles attached for holding it off the ground. The tail probably weighed several tons, and it probably balanced the animal when it walked. The length of the tail, around 30 feet to the tip, helped distribute its weight.

Early paleontologists had many wrong ideas about *Apatosaurus*. Because of the animals' size, scientists thought they must have lived in water. The animals actually lived in semi-dry places. Their trackways show that they walked on land, and their skeletons show no adaptions for living in water.

For many years, artists and scientists drew *Apatosaurus* and its relatives with their tails dragging on the ground. But there is no evidence for this; there are no tail marks in sauropod trackways, and there was no wear or damage to the tail bones. Also, a two or three ton tail would have become tangled in plants or caught in cracks in the rocks if it was dragged. *Apatosaurus* carried its tail high off the ground, with the tail gracefully swaying to help the animal keep its balance.

Top: *A skeleton of the front foot of* Apatosaurus excelsus, *found in the Morrison Formation in Utah*. **Right:** Apatosaurus louisae

Another wrong idea came about because the skeleton was mounted wrong. *Apatosaurus* was put in a sprawling position, which would have meant that it waddled. Trackways prove that sauropods placed their feet almost perfectly under the center of their bodies when they walked. They probably walked as gracefully as elephants, and just as efficiently.

Apatosaurus, like the other sauropods, was a plant-eater. Paleontologists argue about how it could eat enough to keep a 30-ton body alive. The skull and jaws seem too small to keep enough food coming in. Also, the dominant plants of the time, the conifers, were not nutritious enough for these giants. One adaptation that aided their digestion was gastroliths or "stomach stones" that were in their digestive tracts. The dinosaurs swallowed small stones that then helped grind up the plants in their stomachs. Gastroliths are sometimes found in excavations of *Apatosaurus* and its relatives.

Adult apatosaurs had few enemies, but the younger animals were easy prey for giant predators such as *Allosaurus* and *Ceratosaurus*. The young probably stayed close to parents and other adults to protect them from attack. One set of dinosaur tracks in Texas seems to show that in a herd of sauropods traveling together, adults moved on the outside and the younger animals were in the center of the group.

Apatosaurus was one of the most common sauropods. Its remains have been found in Utah, Colorado, and Wyoming, but it may have lived farther south and farther north. Skeletons and restorations of *Apatosaurus* are among the most common museum exhibits, because only a few other dinosaurs were larger. It is the most studied sauropod.

Right: *An* Apatosaurus *and baby.*

ARCHAEOPTERYX
(AR-kee-OP-ter-iks)

Period:
Late Jurassic
Class, Subclass, Order, Family:
Aves, Archaeornithes,
Archaeopterygiformes, Archaeopterygidae
Location:
Europe (Germany)
Wingspread:
2 feet (60 centimeters)

Archaeopteryx lithographica is known from only six fossils—they may be the most famous fossils in the world. Its name means "ancient wing from the printing stone" because it was found in the limestone quarries in the Solnhofen region of southern Germany. Limestone has been used for decades to produce lithographs. Fossils found in this fine-grained Late Jurassic lagoon sediment are very well preserved. The fossils also include the rarest fossil find: feathers.

The skeleton of *Archaeopteryx* was so much like the small meat-eating dinosaurs that several specimens were catalogued as dinosaurs in museum collections. But after closer study, scientists discovered the faint impression of feathers. Because of the feathers, *Archaeopteryx* is usually classified as a primitive bird. But some paleontologists place *Archaeopteryx* with the dinosaurs.

Except for the feathers, *Archaeopteryx* is much like the tiny dinosaur *Compsognathus* and other small coelurosaurs. The biggest difference was that the long front legs of *Archaeopteryx* were modified for feathers. The three front toes of *Archaeopteryx* had claws, and the jaws had pointed teeth.

Archaeopteryx had a long stiff tail, like the tail of the small theropod dinosaurs; tail feathers were attached to it. In all other birds the tail bones are almost entirely lost. A stubby leftover tail, which is called the pygostyle, is where the tail feathers attach.

There is still much argument about the place of *Archaeopteryx* in evolution. The relationship to dinosaurs is strong, and *Archaeopteryx* could be the "missing link" between birds and the small carnivorous dinosaurs. This would mean that we see the descendants of dinosaurs every time we see a modern bird.

Three Ways to Fly

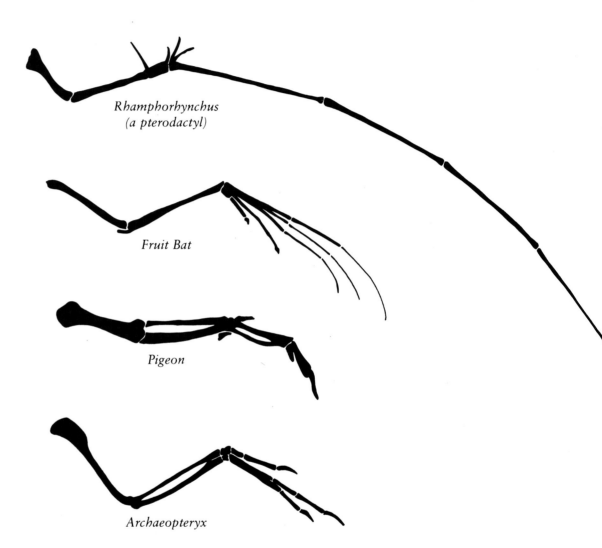

Rhamphorhynchus
(a pterodactyl)

Fruit Bat

Pigeon

Archaeopteryx

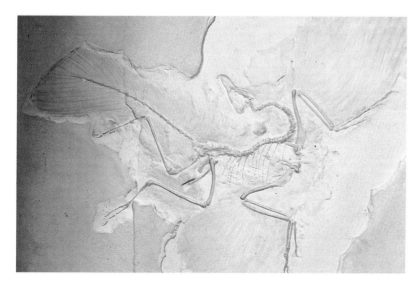

A detailed fossil of Archaeopteryx *that shows the outlines of feathers.*

Rhamphorhynchus *was the first flier. It had a much different arm structure than either birds or bats. Its wings were formed by a long fourth finger.* Archaeopteryx *was the second flier, and its wing was formed by the whole forearm. Also, some bones in the arm were fused together. Modern birds have similar wing structures (see Pigeon). Bats were the latest fliers, and their wing is formed by all the bones of the hand. All three groups of animals had a similar trait (the ability to fly) but they did not get the trait from a common ancestor. This is called convergent evolution.*

A Jurassic scene: A resting
Allosaurus *seems not to be
hungry, but it still watches two*
Camarasaurus *stroll by and
three* Diplodocus *drink.*
Stegosaurus *isn't bothered by*
Allosaurus; *it has its bony plates
and spines to protect it.*

BRACHIOSAURUS
(BRAK-ee-oh-SORE-us)

Period:
Late Jurassic
Order, Suborder, Family:
Saurischia, Sauropodomorpha,
Brachiosauridae
Location:
North America, Africa (Tanzania)
Length:
75 feet (23 meters)

Brachiosaurus, whose name means "arm reptile," was the giraffe dinosaur of the Jurassic. With its long neck (almost 30 feet long) and tall front legs, this giant sauropod could nip fresh shoots from the tops of trees more than 40 feet above the ground. If *Brachiosaurus* were alive today, it could peek into fourth story windows.

Other dinosaurs may be larger, such as *Antarctosaurus, Ultrasaurus,* and *Supersaurus,* or longer, such as "Seismosaurus," but this is the the largest sauropod known from nearly complete skeletons. So, for many paleontologists, this is the champion for size. Weighing 80 tons, about as much as 12 elephants, *Brachiosaurus* was a colossal dinosaur that had to feed constantly.

The front legs were taller than the back legs, and the tail was relatively short. *Brachiosaurus* was heavy in the front and light in the rear. The rib cage was enormous, but because the legs were so tall, the belly was so far off the ground that a *Stegosaurus* could walk underneath it.

The skull of *Brachiosaurus* was small, and the jaws were weak. Because the nostrils were high on the head, placed almost between the eyes, paleontologists at first thought *Brachiosaurus* lived in water and used its nostrils like a snorkel. Instead, *Brachiosaurus* lived on dry land or along shorelines. It probably did not often go into water where the muddy bottoms would have been slippery and dangerous.

The long neck and front legs resemble the body of a giraffe, and it is possible that *Brachiosaurus,* like giraffes in Africa today, stood guard in the Jurassic. While it was eating in the high trees, it would have watched for an *Allosaurus* sneaking in for an attack. Smaller and shorter herbivores such as *Apatosaurus* and *Stegosaurus* would have looked to *Brachiosaurus* for alarm signals.

Brachiosaurus adults were so enormous that they weighed as much as 40 times more than their principal enemy *Allosaurus.* Unless an adult was sick or wounded, it had little reason to worry about *Allosaurus,* but a young *Brachiosaurus* had no defense. When an adult signaled danger, the younger animals probably ran to the center of the herd for protection.

The excavation of *Brachiosaurus* in Tanzania, Africa, during the early part of the century involved hundreds of local workers who carried the enormous bones by hand for many miles to the seaport. They were then shipped to Germany, and the bones were mounted at the Humboldt Museum in East Berlin. This museum was designed to fit the skeleton of *Brachiosaurus.* That skeleton is still on display, and it is still the most impressive dinosaur mounted in the world. It is as staggering to visitors today as when it was unveiled many decades ago.

Unfortunately, only a few specimens of *Brachiosaurus* have been found in western North America. There may have been two species, one in the United States and one in eastern Africa, but they are so similar that their populations must have been connected before Pangaea broke apart. This is one of the largest ranges ever recorded for land animals.

Left: *A herd of* Brachiosaurus brancai.
Right: Camarasaurus

Allosaurus *watches* Camarasaurus *in the water.*

CAMARASAURUS
(CAM-er-uh-SORE-us)

Period:
Late Jurassic
Order, Suborder, Family:
Saurischia, Sauropodomorpha,
Camarasauridae
Location:
North America
Length:
60 feet (18 meters)

Camarasaurus was probably the most common sauropod dinosaur of the Late Jurassic Morrison Formation in North America. This large, 25-ton plant-eater was strong and massive, with powerful legs, a strong neck and tail, and a rounded head. Deep pockets or chambers in the vertebrae (bones of the spine) of *Camarasaurus* lightened the skeleton without giving up strength. It is also how the dinosaur got its name, which means "chambered reptile."

The most unusual features of *Camarasaurus* were on its head. The large jaw bones had strong jaw muscles, and the teeth were unusually large for a sauropod. They were as large as chisels, with sharp points that chopped the plants it ate. *Camarasaurus* probably fed on plants that were coarse and tough. Its relatives *Apatosaurus* and *Diplodocus,* with their small weak teeth, probably ate soft, tender plants.

With large eyes and nostrils, *Camarasaurus* was alert and active. Like other sauropods, it probably moved in herds. It lived in the arid and semi-arid open country of North America.

One *Camarasaurus* pelvis from the Cleveland-Lloyd Dinosaur Quarry in Utah has huge grooves in the bones where an *Allosaurus* tore into the flesh and gouged the bones. *Allosaurus* was its fiercest enemy, but an adult *Camarasaurus* was so much larger that it was seldom attacked. A complete skeleton of a juvenile *Camarasaurus* was excavated from Dinosaur National Monument in Utah. Such skeletons are rare. Perhaps young sauropods grew to adult size quickly, so there is little chance of finding them in the fossil record.

One interesting twist of fate for *Camarasaurus* was that its head was mistakenly placed on the skeleton of *Apatosaurus* at the Carnegie Museum of Natural History. The mistake was not fixed for 75 years.

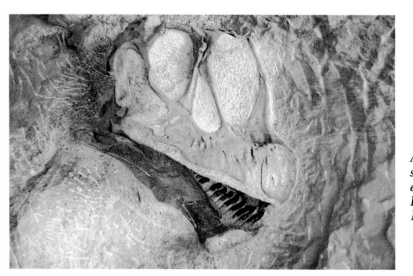

A Camarasaurus skull that is being excavated at Dinosaur National Monument.

CAMPTOSAURUS
(CAMP-toh-SORE-us)

Period:
Late Jurassic
Order, Suborder, Family:
Ornithischia, Ornithopoda,
Camptosauridae
Location:
North America, Europe
Length:
17 feet (5 meters)

Few plant-eating dinosaurs of the Late Jurassic were small. *Camptosaurus* was an exception; it reached an adult weight of no more than 1,000 pounds. This slender, graceful ornithischian stood around five feet tall at the hips. Some paleontologists compare *Camptosaurus* with a deer in today's forests. *Camptosaurus* browsed on low vegetation. The chisellike teeth on the sides of its jaws were strong and well suited for crushing tough plants. Instead of front teeth for nipping, the fronts of both jaws were covered with a beak.

The strong, agile rear legs were made for running. It needed to be able to escape from an *Allosaurus* that could easily overpower even the largest *Camptosaurus*. Its front legs were small but strong and were used for slow movement during feeding and grubbing around in the brush. It fed with its short front legs on the ground, and the tall hips and rounded curve of the tail gave *Camptosaurus* a curved or bent profile. This is why it got its name, which means "bent reptile."

This early herbivore is probably close to the ancestry of the family Iguanodontidae of the Cretaceous, which included the enormous *Iguanodon* and giant hadrosaurs such as *Parasaurolophus* and *Maiasaura*. Like its descendants, *Camptosaurus* lived in herds, which gave it protection from predators.

An *Allosaurus* (back) and *Camptosaurus* (front) are poised in combat at the Natural History Museum of Los Angeles County.

A skeletal drawing of Camptosaurus.

A Camptosaurus *and two dryosaurs.*

CERATOSAURUS
(seh-RAT-oh-SORE-us)

Period:
Late Jurassic
Order, Suborder, Family:
Saurischia, Theropoda, Ceratosauridae
Location:
North America, Africa (Tanzania)
Length:
20 feet (6 meters)

Ceratosaurus was the greatest rival of *Allosaurus*. *Ceratosaurus* had a fearsome appearance, with a prominent low, blade-like horn on its snout, knobs in front of its eyes, long daggerlike teeth with serrated edges that sliced through flesh, a huge head with powerful jaws, and a massive body. Its name means "horned dinosaur."

Ceratosaurus resembled *Allosaurus,* except that its front legs had four fingers rather than three. Each of the fingers and toes had curved claws that could tear flesh from a carcass or bring a victim to the ground with a single blow. Like *Allosaurus,* this meat-eater was an opportunist, probably taking smaller dinosaurs such as *Stegosaurus* or *Camptosaurus* when it could and scavenging on carcasses of the giant sauropods.

Ceratosaurus used its powerful legs and feet for running at high speeds. It could escape danger from other predators or attack its prey by overpowering it with a sudden burst of energy. The huge skull and mighty jaws surely delivered death blows to the victims.

The horns of *Ceratosaurus* may have been for display or for fighting other males of its kind, especially when competing for females. There were not as many ceratosaurs as allosaurs, and they were also not found in as many places. Perhaps *Ceratosaurus* ate only certain animals or needed to stay in one climate.

Two Ceratosaurus nasicornis *in battle.*

CETIOSAURUS
(SEE-tee-oh-SORE-us)

Period:
Middle Jurassic
Order, Suborder, Family:
Saurischia, Sauropodomorpha,
Cetiosauridae
Location:
Europe (England), Africa (Morocco)
Length:
60 feet (18 meters)

Cetiosaurus was a heavy sauropod. It looked much like *Diplodocus* and *Apatosaurus,* which may be its descendants. This is the best-known sauropod from England, where dinosaurs were first studied. Only the limbs, pelvis, and the greater part of the tail are known. The vertebrae are massive and do not have air pockets that reduce weight, as are found in most other sauropods. Like the legs of other sauropods, the limbs of *Cetiosaurus* were like pillars, and the tail was long and heavy. *Cetiosaurus* probably weighed up to 30 tons. It was one of the most primitive sauropods.

Cetiosaurus was described in 1841 and was the first sauropod dinosaur described. *Cetiosaurus,* which means "monster reptile" or "whale reptile," was the largest land animal known at the time, much larger than *Iguanodon* and other prehistoric reptiles. It was about the same size as the North Atlantic great whales. *Cetiosaurus* was thought to be a crocodile and was later confused with *Iguanodon,* an Early Cretaceous dinosaur.

Some paleontologists think another British sauropod, *Cetiosauriscus,* belongs to this genus. Bones in the tail of *Cetiosauriscus,* called "chevrons," resemble those of *Diplodocus.* If true, there is a close relationship between the families Cetiosauridae and Diplodocidae. This would show a connection between dinosaurs in Morocco, England, and North America during the Jurassic.

CHUNGKINGOSAURUS
(CHUNG-king-oh-SORE-us)

Period:
Late Jurassic
Order, Suborder, Family:
Ornithischia, Thyreophora,
Stegosauridae
Location:
Asia (People's Republic of China)
Length:
12 feet (4 meters)

At least five types of stegosaurs have been discovered in the Late Jurassic of China. More Late Jurassic stegosaurs have been found in China than anywhere else in the world. *Chungkingosaurus jiangbeiensis* was the smallest of these.

It was a spiky plant-eater with small, narrow, thickened plates arranged in two parallel rows along its back. The exact plate count is not known, but a specimen mounted at the Chongqing Municipal Museum has 14 pairs. That skeleton also has two pairs of tail spikes. Another *Chungkingosaurus,* perhaps a different species, has three pairs.

Workers unearthed *Chungkingosaurus* in 1977. Chinese paleontologists Dong Zhiming, Zhou Shiwu, and Chang Yihong described it in 1983. Other dinosaurs that were from the same age and found in the same place were the stegosaurs *Chialingosaurus* and *Tuojiangosaurus,* and the huge sauropods *Mamenchisaurus* and *Omeisaurus.* Other dinosaurs found from the same time were the giant meat-eaters *Yangchuanosaurus* and *Szechuanosaurus,* the small theropod *Sinocoelurus,* and the swift, small ornithopods *Gongbusaurus* and *Yandusaurus.*

Although these dinosaurs are different from those discovered by Marsh and Cope in the western United States, they do belong to the same families. The animals in the Late Jurassic in China were very similar to those found in North America.

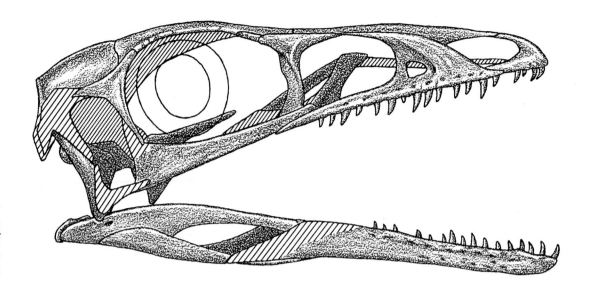

A skull drawing of Compsognathus.

COMPSOGNATHUS
(KOMP-sog-NAY-thus)

Period:
Late Jurassic
Order, Suborder, Family:
Saurischia, Theropoda,
Compsognathidae
Location:
Europe (Germany, France)
Length:
2 feet (60 centimeters)

Not all meat-eating dinosaurs were the gigantic brutes we imagine. Some were small and delicate. *Compsognathus* was one of the smallest known dinosaurs. It was a turkey-size predator that lived near water. This little animal ran birdlike on its back legs, chasing lizards and small mammals and attacking its prey with small, two-fingered hands and toothy jaws. Perhaps *Compsognathus* dined on *Archaeopteryx,* the oldest known bird.

German paleontologist Andreas Wagner described the first *Compsognathus* in 1861. Its name means "elegant jaw." A physician named Oberndorfer found it in lithographic limestone in a valley near the town of Kelheim. As happens with many small fossil vertebrates, sedimentary rock had squashed it flat. Its bones were too thin-walled to avoid being crushed when it was being fossilized. But nature preserved almost its entire skeleton, from the large head to more than halfway up the long, slender tail. Wagner did not identify *Compsognathus* as a dinosaur, probably because it did not fit his image of dinosaurs as huge and lumbering.

Several years later, Thomas Henry Huxley used *Compsognathus* as an example in his theory that present-day birds descended from "birdlike reptiles." As scientists studied the skeletons of other theropods, such as *Allosaurus* and *Ornithomimus,* it became clear that *Compsognathus* was a smaller relative of those dinosaurs.

In 1881, Othniel Marsh noticed that Wagner's specimen had something in its stomach and thought it might be an embryo. Franz Nopcsa in 1903 argued that the object was far too large to be an embryo and concluded that it was the remains of a lizard, the animal's last meal. Seventy-five years later, paleontologist John Ostrom identified the lizard as *Bavarisaurus*.

Compsognathus longipes is rare in museum collections. There is only one other specimen besides Wagner's, a skeleton about 50 percent larger that was discovered in lithographic limestone near Canjuers, France. A group of French paleontologists reported on this skeleton in 1972. They thought it belonged to a different species. They named this new species *Compsognathus corallestris*. It had flippers instead of hands and somewhat different skeletal proportions. Ostrom, however, showed that the "flipper imprint" in the specimen did not belong to the animal. He also showed that the differences between the specimen sizes were probably because one was younger. He considers the French skeleton a fully grown adult, while the German one was younger. Scientists now think both animals belong to the single species *Compsognathus longipes*.

Ostrom's 1978 study indicates that *Compsognathus* probably had two-fingered hands. This surprised many paleontologists, because all other known theropods except tyrannosaurids had hands with three or more fingers. Not everyone agrees that Ostrom's interpretation is correct. *Compsognathus* is different enough to be classified as the only member of its family, Compsognathidae.

A Compsognathus *chasing two* Archaeopteryx.

DACENTRURUS
(dah-sin-TRUE-rus)

Period:
Late Jurassic
Order, Suborder, Family:
Ornithischia, Thyreophora, Stegosauridae
Location:
Europe (England, Western Europe)
Length:
13 feet (4 meters)

Also known as "Omosaurus," *Dacentrurus* was an armored dinosaur related to *Stegosaurus*. *Dacentrurus* had a set of prominent spikes on its tail, a feature for which this dinosaur was named. Its name means "very spiny tail."

Like *Stegosaurus*, *Dacentrurus* had plates of bone on its back, but these were more like spikes then triangles. Spikes covered its hips and tail. In this way, *Dacentrurus* was closely related to the African stegosaur *Kentrosaurus*. *Dacentrurus* is not very well known. *Dacentrurus* was much smaller than *Stegosaurus*.

As typical for all stegosaurs, *Dacentrurus* was a plant-eater that fed on low-growing vegetation. Its plates and spines were probably its protection from predators. The real function of its armor, and the armor on all stegosaurs, is often a topic of discussion by paleontologists.

Dacentrurus armatus

DATOUSAURUS
(dah-too-SORE-us)

Period:
Middle Jurassic
Order, Suborder, Family:
Saurischia, Sauropodomorpha, Cetiosauridae
Location:
Asia (People's Republic of China)
Length:
50 feet (15 meters)

A rare Middle Jurassic sauropod from China, *Datousaurus* may have been an animal that traveled by itself and ate the leaves of the tallest plants in its environment. Its neck vertebrae were quite long, giving it a higher reach than *Shunosaurus*, an animal that lived at the same time.

The spines of some of the vertebrae at the base of its neck had a shallow channel for the attachment of muscles and ligaments that controlled the neck's movements. Its head was deep and boxlike. It looked a bit like the Late Jurassic North American sauropod *Camarasaurus*. *Datousaurus* may have been distantly related to *Camarasaurus*. Other features of its skeleton may mean that it was related to the diplodocid sauropods.

Only two incomplete skeletons of *Datousaurus bashanensis*, both headless, have been described since 1980. They were found in the Dashanpu Quarry, Sichuan Province. Since then, more material has been discovered. One skull probably belongs to *Datousaurus*, but scientists will not know until a skeleton is found with the head attached.

Datousaurus was larger than *Shunosaurus*, with larger, more spoon-shaped teeth. This may mean that *Datousaurus* ate different plants than *Shunosaurus*.

DIPLODOCUS
(die-PLOH-dah-kus)

Period:
Late Jurassic
Order, Suborder, Family:
Saurischia, Sauropodomorpha, Diplodocidae
Location:
North America (United States)
Length:
90 feet (27 meters)

Diplodocus got its name because of a feature of its vertebrae. Under each tail vertebra was a piece of bone (called a chevron) running forward as well as backward, so it was like a "double beam." *Diplodocus* was built like a giant suspension bridge set between four massive pillars. Unlike its heavier relatives *Apatosaurus* and *Barosaurus*, which lived in the same semi-arid places, *Diplodocus* was lightly built, with a long flexible neck and an even longer tail.

Datousaurus bashanensis

Diplodocus is the longest dinosaur known from complete skeletons. It weighed no more than 20 tons, half of what its larger relatives weighed. This gave *Diplodocus* an advantage in grace and agility when wandering over the landscape. Perhaps it could more easily avoid predators.

The head of *Diplodocus* was small and lightly built. It was long and slender, a little like the shape of a horse's head, and about the same size. But unlike a horse, *Diplodocus* had no teeth in the sides of the jaws. It had long slender teeth in the front of its mouth. Also, the jaw bones were small and the jaw muscles were weak; this shows that it ate soft plants, probably the freshest new growth at the tops of conifers and tree ferns, as well as ferns on the ground.

Clues as to how *Diplodocus* gathered food can be found in the skeleton. The neck was long, slender, and laterally flexible, allowing *Diplodocus* to graze across a broad arc without moving. However, its neck was relatively inflexible in a vertical plane; *Diplodocus* could not raise its head much higher than its shoulders. Gastroliths or stomach stones have been found with some sauropod skeletons. The gastroliths helped grind food in the stomach and thus aided digestion.

Early drawings of *Diplodocus* and *Apatosaurus* showed these dinosaurs as slow, plodding reptiles with a sprawling posture, dragging their tails over the ground. Trackways and their skeletons show that this is not correct. *Diplodocus* and its relatives walked with their feet directly beneath their bodies. They also kept their tails off the ground, which balanced their bodies as they walked.

Skeletons of *Diplodocus* discovered by Earl Douglass in eastern Utah in the 1890s became sensational news. It was larger and more impressive than any other dinosaur in North America, except *Apatosaurus*. The mounted skeleton in the Carnegie Museum of Natural History in Pittsburgh was named "Dippy." It became an instant celebrity.

Diplodocus has been on display in more places in the world than any other sauropod. Early in this century, Andrew Carnegie sent casts of the complete skeleton from the Carnegie Museum to the most important museums in Europe.

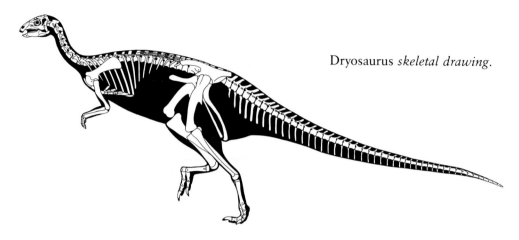

Dryosaurus skeletal drawing.

DRYOSAURUS
(DRY-oh-SORE-us)

Period:
Late Jurassic
Order, Suborder, Family:
Ornithischia, Ornithopoda, Dryosauridae
Location:
North America, Africa (Tanzania)
Length:
10-13 feet (3-4 meters)

Dryosaurus is the most important member of the family Dryosauridae. This is a group of small plant-eating dinosaurs from the Late Jurassic and Early Cretaceous of North America, eastern Africa, and Europe.

Dryosaurus had long, powerful back legs. Its foot was slim and had three toes. Its arms were strong and had five-fingered hands; the animal probably used its hands to grasp leaves and branches when feeding. Its stiff tail balanced the body while it was standing or running across the countryside.

Dryosaurus had no teeth at the front of its mouth. It used its horny beak to nip plants from the ground, shrubs, and low-level branches. *Dryosaurus* had chewing teeth, located toward the back of the jaws, which ground up leaves and shoots before the animal swallowed them.

Workers found *Dryosaurus* in Late Jurassic rocks in the western United States. Also, a spectacular fossil site of the same age is in Tanzania, Africa. W. Janensch from Berlin, Germany, collected hundreds of *Dryosaurus* bones from Tanzania in the early part of the 20th century. Many of these fossils were young, even hatchling, dryosaurs. This will tell scientists a great deal about how these dinosaurs grew up.

Othniel Charles Marsh coined the name *Dryosaurus* in 1894. The name means "oak reptile." *Dryosaurus*, along with its close relative *Valdosaurus*, was one of the earliest members of a large group of important ornithopods known as iguanodontians. Other members of this group included *Tenontosaurus*, *Camptosaurus*, and the later iguanodontids and hadrosaurids.

Fossil teeth of **Diplodocus** *found at Dinosaur National Monument.*

Right: *Two dryosaurs.*

A few Pleurocoelus *on a Jurassic beach. Paleontologists once thought sauropods lived in water, but they did not. They probably enjoyed a swim on a warm day, just as elephants today do.*

EUHELOPUS
(you-HEL-oh-pus)

Period:
Late Jurassic
Order, Suborder, Family:
Saurischia, Sauropodomorpha,
Euhelopodidae
Location:
Asia (People's Republic of China)
Length:
50 feet (15 meters)

Euhelopus was a large sauropod from China. It was much like *Camarasaurus* from the Late Jurassic of North America, but it was long and slender, with extra vertebrae in the neck and trunk. The skull of *Euhelopus* had a long snout region, quite unlike the short, blunt head of *Camarasaurus*. Unfortunately no teeth were found with the skull.

Euhelopus is known from a partial skeleton, including most of the neck and body vertebrae. The neck and body were long because of the extra vertebrae. It probably weighed around 15-20 tons. With its long, slender neck, *Euhelopus* may have looked like *Brachiosaurus*. It also probably reached high into treetops for food.

Originally named *Helopus*, a name that had been used before, it was renamed *Euhelopus* in 1956. Its name means "true marsh foot." Because of its unusual combination of features, *Euhelopus* is sometimes classified in a separate family, but it seems it was closely related to the *Camarasauridae* because of its vertebrae.

Euhelopus *skeletal drawing.*

Euhelopus zdanskyi

HUAYANGOSAURUS
(hoy-YANG-oh-SORE-us)

Period:
Middle Jurassic
Order, Suborder, Family:
Ornithischia, Thyreophora,
Huayangosauridae
Location:
Asia (People's Republic of China)
Length:
15 feet (4.5 meters)

For many decades, scientists only guessed at the origin and history of the stegosaurs, which seemed to appear suddenly in the fossil record. They give little hint of where they came from or how they came to be. With the discovery in 1977 of a new Middle Jurassic dinosaur location in China, however, the mystery started to clear up.

At the Dashanpu Quarry in Zigong, China, a group of paleontology students excavated the skeleton of a 40-foot-long sauropod dinosaur that was later named *Shunosaurus*. By 1979, as the dig progressed, the students found many more *Shunosaurus* bones. They also found skeletons of several other kinds of dinosaurs that lived at the same time as *Shunosaurus*. Among these were the remains of 12 bodies of a new kind of stegosaur. This dinosaur was many millions of years older than any stegosaur known. In 1982, a group of Chinese paleontologists named it *Huayangosaurus taibaii*.

Huayangosaurus had many primitive features. For example, its skull had a small opening in front of each eye, and there was another small opening in each half of the lower jaw. Both of these openings closed off in later stegosaurs. At the front of its snout, *Huayangosaurus* had 14 teeth (seven on each side). Later stegosaurs did not have these teeth. *Huayangosaurus* had long front limbs—three-quarters longer than the back limbs. Later stegosaurs had

forelimbs that were much shorter. Finally, the armor plates that ran in two rows along the back of *Huayangosaurus* were more narrow and much thicker than the plates on the backs of its later relatives. All these features are clues to the stegosaurs' place in the dinosaur family tree.

We know of only one other dinosaur that may be related to *Huayangosaurus*. In the late 1940s, a partial left lower jaw bone that was later named *Tatisaurus oehleri* was found. This small jaw, more than 200 million years old, resembled the jaw of an ankylosaur. But that was 50 million years

older than any ankylosaur known in 1965, so it was tentatively classified as a hypsilophodontid. Recently, a Chinese paleontologist noted that the *Tatisaurus* jaw looked very much like the jaw of *Huayangosaurus*. He has proposed that the dinosaurs be grouped together in a separate stegosaur subfamily, the Huayangosaurinae. More research may show that this subfamily bridges the gap between the stegosaurs and the ankylosaurs.

Huayangosaurus lived in a land of lakes, rivers, and lush vegetation. By looking at its teeth, scientists can tell it was a plant-eater. Its spiky, upstanding armor plates and shoulder spines could have protected it from predators, but they could also have been for show, perhaps to attract a mate. They may also have been used to regulate its body temperature. The plates seem too thick, however, to have been very good for this. Certainly, the animal's tail spikes would have kept its enemies away.

Huayangosaurus taibaii

Kentrosaurus

KENTROSAURUS
(KEN-troh-SORE-us)

Period:
Late Jurassic
Order, Suborder, Family:
Ornithischia, Thyreophora, Stegosauridae
Location:
Africa (Tanzania)
Length:
10 feet (3 meters)

Kentrosaurus was only about half as large as its relative *Stegosaurus*. *Kentrosaurus* had spikes over its back, hips, and tail. It was an unusual stegosaur because it had an extra pair of spines that stuck out sideways and backward over its hips. It had large triangular plates of bone on its shoulders. The spikes discouraged predators. Its tail spines were long and pointed. *Kentrosaurus* got its name, "prickly reptile," because of its spikes.

This small stegosaur stood about three feet tall at the hips. Because of its short front legs and short neck, it could only eat the lowest shrubs and plants. Occasionally, *Kentrosaurus* may have leaned backward and stood on its back legs, supported partially by its tail, to reach for taller plants.

Kentrosaurus lived with *Brachiosaurus* in eastern Africa. Both were probably troubled by large, powerful predators, such as *Allosaurus*. The armor of *Kentrosaurus* only partly protected its body; its sides and underbelly were left uncovered. Kentrosaurus may have had some other ways to protect itself that paleontologists have not yet discovered.

Other stegosaurs of the Late Jurassic, including *Dacentrurus* in western Europe, *Stegosaurus* in North America, and *Tuojiangosaurus* in China, were closely related. Land connections in the Jurassic may have let the stegosaur ancestors travel around the northern continents.

MAMENCHISAURUS
(mah-MEN-chee-SORE-us)

Period:
Late Jurassic
Order, Suborder, Family:
Saurischia, Sauropodomorpha,
Euhelopodidae
Location:
Asia (People's Republic of China)
Length:
72 feet (22 meters)

The slender and almost delicate proportions of this sauropod are an architectural wonder. It had extra vertebrae (bones in the spine) in its neck and its vertebrae were longer than usual; this gave *Mamenchisaurus* an almost impossibly long neck of about 33 feet. Add the shoulder height of about 11 feet, and *Mamenchisaurus* could

reach around 44 feet off the ground. It would have been tall enough to peek into fourth story windows.

Dinosaurs have been associated with dragons for a long time. *Mamenchisaurus* was discovered at a collection site for "dragon bones" that were ground up and sold in drug stores. This site in China is called Mamenchi. "Chi" means brook, and "Mamen" was the name of the brook; so *Mamenchisaurus* means "reptile from the brook named Mamen."

Mamenchisaurus is the largest sauropod known from China and nearly half its length was its neck. The front limbs and skull were not found, but the rest of the skeleton was complete. This plant-eater weighed between 40 and 50 tons and was 72 feet long. The legs and tail of *Mamenchisaurus* were light and slender compared to other sauropods; it was probably agile

and graceful when it walked. It may have wandered in herds like other sauropods, always feeding and protecting the young animals from meat-eating dinosaurs waiting to attack.

Many features of *Mamenchisaurus* resemble *Diplodocus* and other members of the family *Diplodocidae*. This shows a close relationship between the North American-European sauropod dinosaurs and the Chinese sauropods in the Late Jurassic. There was probably a land connection between Europe, North America, and China in the Late Jurassic that allowed the dinosaurs to migrate.

Replicas of the original skeleton have been shown in many museums around the world. Other dinosaurs from China have been excavated in recent years, and several projects have led to an exchange of information between museums in China, Canada, and the United States.

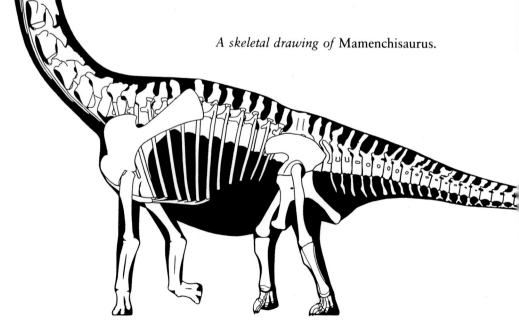

A skeletal drawing of Mamenchisaurus.

A Kentrosaurus *skeleton on display.*

Megalosaurus tanneri

MEGALOSAURUS
(MEG-ah-loh-SORE-us)

Period:
Middle Jurassic
Order, Suborder, Family:
Saurischia, Theropoda, Megalosauridae
Location:
Europe (England)
Length:
30 feet (9 meters)

Megalosaurus was the first dinosaur to be described as a reptile. The bones were discovered at Stonesfield in Oxfordshire, England. The fossils included parts of a back leg, hip bones, a shoulder blade, and a lower jaw. James Parkinson named it *Megalosaurus*, which means "great lizard." Dinosaurs were not known then, and scientists thought it was a giant lizard.

For many years, scientists identified nearly every scrap of any large theropod fossil in England or Europe as *Megalosaurus*. Even recently, specimens from the United States and Australia were called *Megalosaurus*. For this reason, scientists refer to *Megalosaurus* as the "waste basket" genus. Also, the family Megalosauridae has been the "waste basket" family because scientists included dinosaurs as different as *Tyrannosaurus*, *Allosaurus*, and *Dilophosaurus*. Scientists have sorted out many of the fossils that were incorrectly called *Megalosaurus* or put in Megalosauridae, and placed them in the correct genus and family. There is still much work for scientists to do before they correct everything.

Despite the mistakes, *Megalosaurus* is still an important dinosaur, though it is not well known. Most of the bones of the original specimen are important, particularly the jaw and hip bones. These bones show that it was a large theropod, weighing over one ton. The large, serrated teeth in the robust jaw bone show it was a powerful predator. Like most modern meat-eating

animals, it probably ate any animal it could catch.

The Late Jurassic theropod *Torvosaurus* could be a North American relative of *Megalosaurus*. However, even though there are enough similarities to group them in the same family, there are enough differences that they probably do not belong in the same genus.

OMEISAURUS
(OH-mee-SORE-us)

Period:
Late Jurassic
Order, Suborder, Family:
Saurischia, Sauropodomorpha, Euhelopodidae
Location:
Asia (People's Republic of China)
Length:
35-67 feet (10.5-20 meters)

Most of the sauropods known from the Late Jurassic of China had extraordinarily long necks. Not only did their necks have several more vertebrae than the sauropods of North America and Africa, the vertebrae themselves were larger and longer.

Herds of *Omeisaurus* roamed along Jurassic river banks, feeding on low, shrubby ferns and seed ferns. Like most sauropods, *Omeisaurus* mostly inhabited open areas rather than grazing in forests as was previously believed.

Omeisaurus was the most common Late Jurassic Chinese sauropod. Workers have found many skeletons, some nearly complete, and several skulls of this dinosaur since it was first described and named in 1939. It was named after the sacred mountain Omeishan, located near where the first skeleton was excavated. Most skeletons were unearthed in the 1970s and 1980s as part of the "great Chinese dinosaur rush."

Chinese paleontologists have identified five different species of *Omeisaurus*. These include *O. junghsiensis*, *O. changshouensis*, *O. fuxiensis*, *O. tianfuensis*, and *O. luoquanensis*. Scientists named all of the species after the locations where workers dug up the skeletons. More detailed studies may show that some of these species belong in a

A front and side skeletal drawing of Omeisaurus tianfuensis.

different genus or that some species may need to be combined. Scientists first classified the smallest species, the 35-foot-long *Omeisaurus fuxiensis,* in a separate genus, *Zigongosaurus.* The Middle Jurassic species that may be the ancestor of the other four species is *O. luoquanensis.*

Omeisaurus had 17 neck vertebrae. The longest neck belonged to *O. tianfuensis;* its neck was about 30 feet long. A 67-foot-long mounted skeleton of *O. tianfuensis* is on display at the Zigong Museum. Only the neck of *Mamenchisaurus hochuanensis,* with 19 neck vertebrae, was longer. *Mamenchisaurus* was a close relative of *Omeisaurus.* The neck of *Omeisaurus* seems too long when compared with its body; it does not seem balanced. But its vertebrae had thin walls and large holes, making them light. Groups of muscles and long, delicate ribs attached to each vertebra so that *Omeisaurus* could control its neck.

Omeisaurus had a deep, blunt head and spoon-shaped teeth for eating plants. Its skull resembles the skull of *Camarasaurus.* For this reason, scientists classified *Omeisaurus* as a camarasaurid sauropod. Now that there are more skeletons, Chinese paleontologists group *Omeisaurus* with *Euhelopus* and *Mamenchisaurus* in the family Euhelopodidae. Other paleontologists believe that it belongs with *Shunosaurus* in the more primitive family Cetiosauridae.

Their huge size probably protected most sauropods from attack by predatory dinosaurs, but *Omeisaurus* may have had something else to protect it. In the late 1980s, paleontologists working on the Middle Jurassic sauropod *Shunosaurus* discovered that its tail ended in a large bony club, like that of the ankylosaurids. Workers found more tail clubs, of a different shape, in the same locations as *Omeisaurus.* Some Chinese paleontologists think they may belong to *Omeisaurus.* But an *Omeisaurus* skeleton with the tail club attached must be found for scientists to be sure.

Omeisaurus tianfuensis

ORNITHOLESTES
(OR-nith-oh-LEST-ees)

Period:
Late Jurassic
Order, Suborder, Family:
Saurischia, Theropoda, Coeluridae
Location:
North America (United States)
Length:
6 1/2 feet (2 meters)

A crew from the American Museum of Natural History found the first remains of *Ornitholestes* (or "bird robber") at Bone Cabin Quarry near Medicine Bow, Wyoming, in 1900. It consisted of a skull and partial skeleton. This is the same quarry where workers found *Apatosaurus,* now mounted in the American Museum of Natural History.

H. F. Osborn briefly described *Ornitholestes* in 1903. In that paper, he also grouped a partial hand from the same quarry, but not the same animal, in the same genus. The skull is complete, though badly crushed. Serrated teeth line the jaws. The first tooth in the upper jaw is the largest. *Ornitholestes* may have had a small horn over its nose, but scientists are not sure.

The hands are not complete. If the partial hand of the other animal belongs to the same genus, the first finger was short, and the second and third fingers were much longer. *Ornitholestes* may have captured and held its prey with its hands. All the fingers had sharp curved claws. The animal probably weighed about 35 pounds.

For many years, scientists thought *Ornitholestes* and *Coelurus* were the same genus. In 1980, however, John Ostrom showed that they are not the same. Since the discovery of *Ornitholestes* in 1900, workers have not found additional skeletons of this animal. It seems *Ornitholestes* was a rare member of its fauna or it was rarely preserved.

Ornitholestes hermanni

OTHNIELIA
(oth-NEE-lee-ah)

Period:
Late Jurassic
Order, Suborder, and Family:
Ornithischia, Ornithopoda,
Hypsilophodontidae
Location:
North America
Length:
10 feet (3 meters)

Othnielia rex

Othnielia is a recently named dinosaur. Peter Galton named it in 1977 and described the animal in 1983. The name Othnielia is in honor of Othniel Charles Marsh, an early American paleontologist. Of Late Jurassic age, Othnielia is not a well-known hypsilophodontid dinosaur. The only material we know about is three or four skeletons and some pieces of skull and teeth. Unfortunately, no full skull has been found for Othnielia, but there is still much information that scientists can piece together.

From the teeth of Othnielia, we know that it probably ate leaves, succulent plants, and possibly insects. Its close relatives lived in the Early and Late Cretaceous, among them Zephyrosaurus, Thescelosaurus, and Orodromeus. These animals also fed on low-growing plants such as shrubs.

The limbs of Othnielia show that it would have been a good runner. This speed was useful when Othnielia needed to escape from predators such as Ornitholestes, Coelurus, and Allosaurus. Speed would have been needed to catch insects.

During the Late Jurassic, Othnielia was part of a fauna of plant-eating dinosaurs in western North America, including Camptosaurus, Dryosaurus, and Stegosaurus. Othnielia also lived at the same time as the sauropods Apatosaurus and Diplodocus.

PATAGOSAURUS
(pah-TAG-oh-SORE-us)

Period:
Middle Jurassic
Order, Suborder, Family:
Saurischia, Sauropodomorpha,
Cetiosauridae
Location:
South America (Argentina)
Length:
50 feet (15 meters)

Older than the Late Jurassic dinosaurs of North America, *Patagosaurus* is one of only two sauropods known from the Middle Jurassic of South America. The other sauropod is *Volkheimeria,* which is a member of the same family as *Patagosaurus.* A *Patagosaurus* skeleton was found in Patagonia, Argentina, in rocks about 15 million years older than those where the North American sauropods were found.

Patagosaurus is known from a nearly complete skeleton, except for the skull. It resembled the English sauropod *Cetiosaurus,* but its hips and vertebrae were different. *Patagosaurus* was a medium-size sauropod that weighed about 15 tons. In some ways it resembled the North American sauropod *Haplocanthosaurus,* but it was somewhat more primitive. *Patagosaurus* and its relatives may be the direct ancestors of some of the Late Jurassic sauropods. There may have been land connections that allowed the sauropods to travel between South America, western Europe, and Africa. Members of the same family have been found in all these different places.

Patagosaurus ate plants, and its enemies were the theropod dinosaurs. *Piatnitzkysaurus,* a theropod found at the same time and in the same location as *Patagosaurus* and *Volkheimeria,* was as large as *Allosaurus* and a menace to most plant-eaters.

Patagosaurus fariasi

105

Camarasaurus *was usually safe from predators because of its large size, but this predator is taking advantage of an already dead* Camarasaurus.

107

SEISMOSAURUS
(SIZE-moh-SORE-us)

Period:
Late Jurassic
Order, Suborder, Family:
Saurischia, Sauropodomorpha,
Diplodocidae
Location:
North America (United States)
Length:
120-140 feet (36-42.5 meters)

Nearly half as long as a football field, *Seismosaurus* is possibly the largest dinosaur from North America. The single skeleton of this genus was excavated in central New Mexico. It was given its name because of its great size—"earth shaker reptile."

This giant sauropod reached an estimated length of 120-140 feet. If this is correct, it is the record length for a dinosaur. The skeleton is mostly joined (articulated) and consists of the front half of the tail, the pelvis and sacrum, and the vertebrae in the rib-bearing region. In future excavations, paleontologists hope to recover the front legs, neck, and skull. Some paleontologists feel that the partial *Sesismosaurus* skeleton simply represents a particularly large specimen of Diplodocus.

Like other diplodocids, *Seismosaurus* probably had a long slender neck, large bulky body, short front legs, tall rear legs, and long heavy tail. "Stomach stones," or gastroliths, have been found with the skeleton. It is one of the few articulated (joined) sauropod skeletons that had gastroliths in place when it was excavated.

SHUNOSAURUS
(SHOE-noh-SORE-us)

Period:
Middle Jurassic
Order, Suborder, Family:
Saurischia, Sauropodomorpha,
Euhelopodidae
Location:
Asia (People's Republic of China)
Length:
40 feet (12 meters)

The dominant plant-eater of Middle Jurassic China, *Shunosaurus* may have roamed in large herds. With its long, thick neck it could feed on plants and leaves high above the ground that most other herbivores could not reach. Its large body, weighing about one ton, made it almost safe from attack by predators, such as the theropod *Gasosaurus*. The tail of *Shunosaurus* ended in a large bony club with two pairs of short spikes. It used its tail as a weapon to scare away predators.

Shunosaurus lii, the only species known for the genus, was discovered in 1979 by paleontology students working in the Lower Shaximiao Formation in the Sichuan Province. It was named after the area it was found in; *Shuo* is a Chinese word that means Sichuan. Since then, more than 20 nearly complete *Shunosaurus* skeletons, including five good skulls, have been excavated. *Shunosaurus* is now one of the best-known sauropods.

Shunosaurus was a member of the Euhelopodidae, a diverse family of sauropods that seems to have been geographically restricted to Asia. Although the neck of *Shunosaurus* was long, it was not as long as the necks of the Late Jurassic sauropods

A "Seismosaurus" and three allosaurs in the background.

of China and North America. The skull of *Shunosaurus* shows that it may be near the ancestry of some of the long-necked euhelopodids, such as *Mamenchisaurus* and *Omeisaurus* (which may also have had a tail club). It was also related to *Datousaurus*. As one of the most primitive of the euhelopodids, *Shunosaurus* may have been close to the ancestry of many different sauropod families, such as the Camarasauridae (with which it shares a short, blunt skull) and the Diplodocidae (with which it shares slender teeth, tall spines on the tail vertebrae, and a few "double beam" chevron bones on the tail).

Dinosaur-bearing Middle Jurassic rocks are rare, so there is a gap in our understanding of dinosaur evolution. To date, the remains of more than 100 dinosaurs have been unearthed from the Dashanpu Quarry. The name "*Shunosaurus* fauna" is used for that group of Middle Jurassic Chinese animals. Animals of the *Shunosaurus* fauna have also been found in Tibet and in northern China. These dinosaurs were widespread. Once they are all described, the dinosaurs of the *Shunosaurus* fauna will help fill in some gaps in our knowledge of dinosaur evolution.

Shunosaurus lii

109

STEGOSAURUS
(STEG-oh-SORE-us)

Period:
Late Jurassic
Order, Suborder, Family:
Ornithischia, Thyreophora, Stegosauridae
Location:
North America
Length:
20-24 feet (6-7 meters)

No dinosaur has been the subject of as much controversy as *Stegosaurus,* the armored dinosaur of the Late Jurassic. For more than a hundred years, this strange plant-eater has baffled paleontologists and captured the imagination of the public. Nothing interesting about this dinosaur is very typical.

For example, few ornithischian dinosaurs were quadrupedal (walked on four legs), fewer were armored, and no dinosaur besides *Stegosaurus* and its relatives had huge plates of bone arranged in rows along their backs. Pointed spines on its tail gave the rear end of *Stegosaurus* more protection than its front end. Its name comes from this armor; *Stegosaurus* means "covered reptile."

Stegosaurus weighed more than two tons. This plant-eater had few competitors in the Jurassic. *Stegosaurus* preferred food that was near the ground. It was not an agile animal, so it could not compete with other herbivores for leaves and twigs higher off the ground. Perhaps *Stegosaurus* was hidden by low plants, hiding in the cycads and tree ferns from the giant predators *Allosaurus* and *Ceratosaurus.*

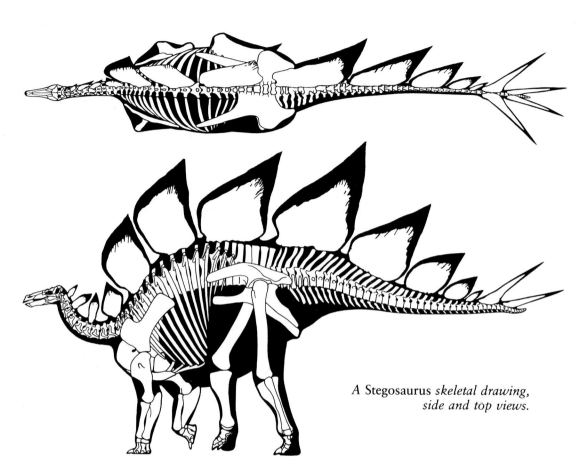

A Stegosaurus *skeletal drawing, side and top views.*

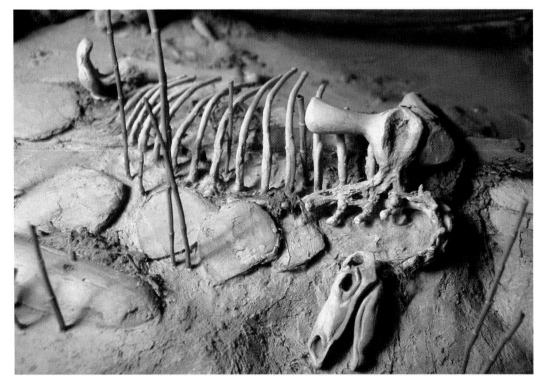

A Stegosaurus *skeleton on a sandbar.*

Stegosaurus was tallest at the hips, which were about ten feet high. The largest bony plates were just behind the hips and added another three feet to its height. This exaggerated its profile, which curved steeply downward both in the front and back. From the side, a predator would have a hard time deciding which end was the head and which was the tail.

The head was small, with weak jaws. The fronts of the jaws were toothless; it had a beak that chopped vegetation. On the sides of its jaws, *Stegosaurus* had dozens of leaf-shaped teeth with grooves for crushing food.

Some writers thought *Stegosaurus* was stupid, because it had a small head and brain. This idea seems to be the beginning of the belief that all dinosaurs were dim-witted, slow, and stupid. Because *Stegosaurus* had a small brain, some scientists believed it had a secondary brain in its hip region. The brain of *Stegosaurus* was just the right size for its body and lifestyle. After all, stegosaurs lived for millions of years. The enlargement in the hip region was not brain tissue, but a complex nerve center called the "sacral plexus." It was a secondary control center for the spinal cord. *Stegosaurus* may have lacked intelligence, but not all dinosaurs were stupid. Most others had larger brains and were possibly capable of more complex mental processing.

Right: Stegosaurus *flees from* Allosaurus.

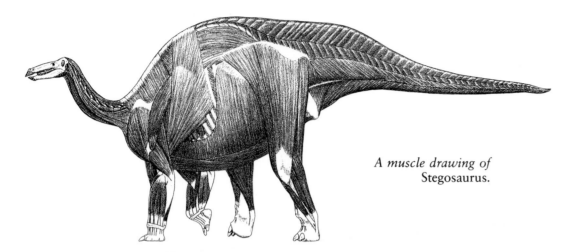

A muscle drawing of Stegosaurus.

The front legs of *Stegosaurus* were only half as long as the heavy rear legs, but they were stout and well suited for carrying the weight of the front of the body. The feet were short and stubby, with four blunt toes on the front feet and three toes on the rear feet. The difference in size between the front legs and rear legs shows the bipedal (two-legged) ancestry of *Stegosaurus*. Because of the evolutionary development of its heavy armor, it could no longer walk on two legs.

A double row of flat triangular plates of bone extended from its neck to its tail, which at the tip was armed with two to four pairs of pointed spikes. The plates were several inches thick at the base where they attached to the body, but they were thin and narrow at the tips. Also, smaller knobs and plates in the skin strengthened and protected the flanks and legs.

Scientists have often wondered why these animals had bony plates. The plates were covered with skin that had many blood vessels in it. The blood would have released heat if the animal was too warm and taken heat from the sun to warm the animal if it was cold. Others argue that the plates were for protection from predators or from coarse vegetation, much as the bony armor of armadillos protects them from predators and plants that would

pierce their skin. Some scientists think that the plates were for display in combat or when faced with an enemy. These plates made them look twice as large as they were. Perhaps all these ideas are correct.

Another old argument is how the plates were arranged on the animal's body. The plates of several skeletons seem to be staggered and project upward from the backbone; it is possible that this is because of changes that happened after the animal died. So some paleontologists have restored *Stegosaurus* with the plates covering the sides of the body for protection from predators such as *Allosaurus,* but this leaves the lower parts of the body unprotected. The staggered rather than paired plates is also difficult to explain, and it was recently proposed that the plates of *Stegosaurus* were arranged in a single row along its back. But no complete animal has yet been discovered to resolve these different interpretations.

Stegosaurus has been found only in western North America, but close relatives such as *Kentrosaurus* from Tanzania and *Tuojiangosaurus* from China show a worldwide distribution of this family. Stegosaurs became extinct in North America at the end of the Jurassic, but they survived in other places until late in the Cretaceous Period.

Stegosaurus

SUPERSAURUS
(SUE-per-SORE-us)

Period:
Late Jurassic
Order, Suborder, Family:
Saurischia, Sauropodomorpha,
Diplodocidae
Location:
North America (United States)
Length:
100 feet (30 meters)

Supersaurus deserves its name, "super reptile." A relative of *Apatosaurus* and *Diplodocus,* this enormous plant-eater was rare in the Late Jurassic. *Supersaurus* is known from a single shoulder bone (the scapulacoracoid), which is nearly eight feet

long. Only the scapulacoracoid of *Ultrasaurus* is as long or longer.

Other bones from the same site, the Dry Mesa Quarry in southern Colorado, have also been identified as *Supersaurus.* These include a separated ischium (one of the bones of the pelvis), a complete sacrum and pelvis, a separate tail vertebra, and a section of 12 articulated (joined) tail vertebrae.

If restorations of *Supersaurus* are correct, this sauropod was at least 100 feet in length and stood more than 18 feet tall at the shoulder. Stretching the neck up into the trees for soft young shoots, *Supersaurus* could reach 50 feet above the ground, or about the height of fifth story windows. *Brachiosaurus* could reach around 40 feet above the ground. The size

Supersaurus vivianae

of *Supersaurus* is difficult to estimate because only the two scapulacoracoids definitely belong to this genus; the other bones are not positively from *Supersaurus* so they cannot be used to figure sizes.

The long shoulder bones of *Supersaurus* are surprising, because other members of the family Diplodocidae have short front legs and long rear legs, unlike the giraffe dinosaurs of the family Brachiosauridae where long scapulacoracoids and long front legs are typical. By comparing proportions of the scapulacoracoid of *Supersaurus* with those of other members in the family Diplodocidae (such as *Diplodocus* or *Apatosaurus*), scientists have concluded that this giant sauropod was a record-breaker for length and mass. Only "Seismosaurus" may have been longer.

Supersaurus, like other giant sauropods of the Late Jurassic, was so large that even the largest predatory dinosaur, *Allosaurus,* was little threat. But the carnivores were always ready to attack weak or sick animals, or to separate young sauropods from their herds.

The feeding habits of *Supersaurus* were probably like those of other sauropods. They ate leaves and shoots from treetops and ferns from the ground, and they fed almost constantly. Adults must have eaten hundreds of pounds each day. Gastroliths (or "stomach stones") may have helped grind the plants and leaves in the stomach.

Supersaurus is a puzzle that can only be solved by more excavations at the Dry Mesa Quarry. More than a dozen dinosaurs are known from the quarry, each having several hundred bones per animal. With such a mix-up of bones, many years of excavation and careful study will be necessary to resolve the identity of this colossal dinosaur.

Supersaurus

TUOJIANGOSAURUS
(toh-HWANG-oh-SORE-us)

Period:
Late Jurassic
Order, Suborder, Family:
Ornithischia, Thyreophora,
Stegosauridae
Location:
Asia (People's Republic of China)
Length:
20 feet (6 meters)

The banks of a quiet, slow-moving Late Jurassic stream are lined with low, fernlike vegetation, and tall araucaria trees are in the background. A flock of leathery-winged, loud pterosaurs flaps by. The distant sound of ponderous footsteps gets closer. A bulky, rhino-size beast with a brightly colored zigzag of plates and spikes along its back and tail comes into view. Every few seconds it pauses to snip off a succulent cycad or a low fern with its horny beak, then moves on, mashing other plants underfoot. Its head is close to the ground where the thickest vegetation grows. For such a huge body, about 2,500 pounds, it had a small head. Its back curved up over hips higher than a man is tall. Many narrow paired triangular plates exaggerated the animal's arching profile. At the end of its tail were four sharp spines.

The slow-moving, peaceful life of *Tuojiangosaurus* was sometimes interrupted by battles with predators such as *Yangchuanosaurus* and *Szechuanosaurus.* It would also battle with another male *Tuojiangosaurus* for females.

Stegosaurs such as *Tuojiangosaurus* may not have had bony spikes and plates when they hatched. The armor may have developed slowly, growing fastest as the animal reached maturity. Different genera and species probably had different arrangements of plates and spines. This may have helped animals from the same species recognize each other.

Tuojiangosaurus multispinus probably had 17 pairs of thick, narrow, pointed plates. The last two pairs were thin cone-shaped spines at the end of its tail. The plates were low and bulbous on the neck and grew taller along the back toward the hips, then became shorter down the tail. There was also a large, platelike spine above each shoulder.

The fossils of two *Tuojiangosaurus* animals were found in the mid-1970s from the Wujiaba Quarry in the Shangshaximiao Formation near the Tuojiang, a river in the Sichuan Basin. One animal, the first almost complete stegosaur skeleton found in China, was mounted there in early 1977. The other specimen was only a set of five vertebrae. The skeleton of a third animal was discovered later but has not yet been prepared.

Plant-eating dinosaurs that lived at the same time as *Tuojiangosaurus* included its cousin stegosaurs *Chialingosaurus* and *Chungkingosaurus,* the sauropods *Omeisaurus* and *Mamenchisaurus,* and the small ornithopods *Gongbusaurus* and *Yandusaurus.*

Tuojiangosaurus *skeleton at the Natural History Museum in London.*

Tuojiangosaurus multispinus

115

ULTRASAURUS
(UL-tra-SORE-us)

Period:
Late Jurassic
Order, Suborder, Family:
Saurischia, Sauropodomorpha,
Brachiosauridae
Location:
North America (United States)
Length:
90 feet (27 meters)

Ultrasaurus was enormous, which is how it got its name, "ultra reptile." It could be the largest dinosaur known. *Ultrasaurus* could have peered into fifth and sixth story windows. Walking in a line, only two or three could have fit in a city block, and they were so large that they would have had difficulty turning around except in an intersection.

Like *Supersaurus,* which also came from the Dry Mesa Quarry in southern Colorado, *Ultrasaurus* is known only from one bone, a vertebra from the rib region of the body. Other bones from the quarry may also belong to *Ultrasaurus,* but scientists are not yet positive. The other bones include a shoulder bone (the scapulacoracoid), a vertebra from the neck, and several vertebrae from the tail.

The scapulacoracoid is about nine feet long and is slightly larger than the scapulacoracoids of *Supersaurus.* It is much more like the shoulder bones of the brachiosaurs. Also, the vertebra from the rib region looks like those of *Brachiosaurus,* although it may be somewhat larger. *Ultrasaurus* belongs in the same family as *Brachiosaurus,* and its body shape resembles that of the brachiosaurs more than other sauropods.

The tall front legs of *Ultrasaurus* reached a height at the shoulder of perhaps 25 feet, and the long, massive neck could have reached nearly 60 feet above the ground. It had proportions like a giraffe;

the front legs were taller than the rear legs and the greatest mass of the body was in the front. The tail was small and short compared to the tails of the diplodocids. The length of *Ultrasaurus* was probably close to 90 feet, nearly as long as *Supersaurus.* However, because it was a heavy-bodied brachiosaur, *Ultrasaurus* was twice as heavy as the other giant sauropods.

Ultrasaurus was a plant-eater, like all sauropods. It ate leaves and needles of conifers and tree ferns and any other plant it could reach. With such a large body, weighing more than 80 tons, *Ultrasaurus* fed almost constantly, probably always moving to search for food. Herds of *Ultra-saurus* must have devastated every forest they entered.

The main enemy of *Ultrasaurus* was the two-ton predator *Allosaurus* and its relatives such as *Ceratosaurus,* which were no match for these 80-ton giants. However, packs of *Allosaurus* could have followed the herds, bothering single animals or babies, or waiting for a sick animal to fall. Like elephants today, though, a healthy adult *Ultrasaurus* was seldom bothered by predators.

Until more bones from the Dry Mesa Quarry are excavated and identified positively as *Ultrasaurus,* this poorly known sauropod will be a puzzle for scientists.

The scapula of Ultrasaurus *being excavated.*

Jim Jensen lays alongside the nine-foot-long scapula (shoulder blade) of Ultrasaurus.

Left: Ultrasaurus *was much taller than any of its relative sauropods.* Top: *Half of a scapula (shoulder blade) of* Ultrasaurus *is lifted by a crane.*

XUANHANOSAURUS
(zoo-ahn-HAN-oh-SORE-us)

Period:
Middle Jurassic
Order, Suborder, Family:
Saurischia, Theropoda, Unknown
Location:
Asia (People's Republic of China)
Length:
20 feet (6 meters)

Only the front limb and six primitive-looking vertebrae of this dinosaur have been discovered. But they are so different from other theropods that in 1984 Chinese paleontologist Dong Zhiming named a new genus and species, *Xuanhanosaurus qilixiaensis,* for them.

Named after Xuanhan County in the Sichuan Basin where it was found, this theropod lived at the same time as the better-known theropod *Gasosaurus,* the stegosaur *Huayangosaurus,* and the sauropods *Shunosaurus* and *Datousaurus.* Dong at first classified *Xuanhanosaurus* in the family Megalosauridae, but paleontologists now believe it requires its own family.

The arm of *Xuanhanosaurus* was about the same size as the arm of the later theropod *Allosaurus,* but it was more robustly built. The first two fingers were large and thick and had prominent claws. The third finger was slender and it also probably had a claw, but it was not found with the skeleton. A fourth finger was only a single small bone that was most likely imbedded in the palm of the hand and not visible in the living animal. It did not have a grasping hand. The shoulder bones and the breastbone were large, which suggests that *Xuanhanosaurus* sometimes used its arms for walking.

Scientists are hoping to find more fossils of *Xuanhanosaurus* so they have more information to study. More fossils may also give clues as to which family this unusual dinosaur belongs to.

Yandusaurus

YANDUSAURUS
(YAN-doo-SORE-us)

Period:
Middle Jurassic
Order, Suborder, Family:
Ornithischia, Ornithopoda, Hypsilophodontidae
Location:
Asia (People's Republic of China)
Length:
6¹/₂ feet (2 meters)

Yandusaurus, a name meaning "reptile from Yandu," is a very important animal in the history of hypsilophodontid dinosaurs. In the late 1970s and early 1980s, workers found it in the Sichuan Province in the People's Republic of China.

Paleontologists are studying several articulated (the bones are joined) skeletons and skulls of *Yandusaurus.* It is the earliest known hypsilophodontid and was found in Middle Jurassic rocks. All other hypsilophodontids are from the Late Jurassic, Early Cretaceous, and Late Cretaceous.

This small animal had a short snout, and the back of the skull was high and wide. The spaces for the eyes were large, which might mean that *Yandusaurus* had good eyesight. It had many small triangular teeth in its jaws. The teeth had ridges on their surfaces, which were similar to the teeth of *Thescelosaurus, Parksosaurus,* and *Zephyrosaurus.* The teeth and jaws show that *Yandusaurus* was a successful plant-eater. It may have also eaten slow-moving insects.

Its neck was long and the body somewhat thinly built. The front limbs were strong with large hands with claws. Scientists do not know whether the hands were able to grasp.

The back limbs were very long and athletic, much like its close relative *Orodromeus.* Its legs were built for running fast. This running ability must have been how *Yandusaurus* was able to escape its fierce predators, such as *Szechuanosaurus* and *Yangchuanosaurus.* The feet of *Yandusaurus* also had claws.

The base of the tail is present in only one specimen. The long tail may have acted as a balance for the body while the animal was running. All other ornithopods used their tails for balance. Scientists hope to find more specimens to study.

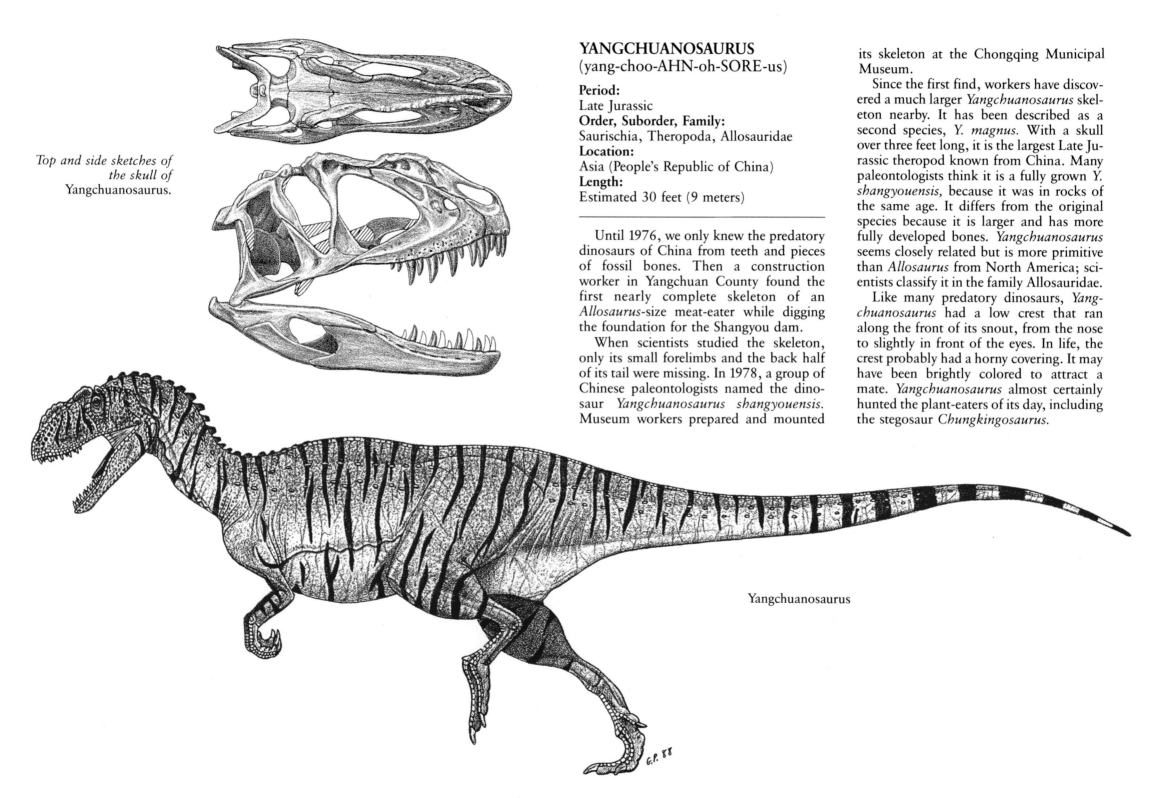

Top and side sketches of the skull of Yangchuanosaurus.

YANGCHUANOSAURUS
(yang-choo-AHN-oh-SORE-us)

Period:
Late Jurassic
Order, Suborder, Family:
Saurischia, Theropoda, Allosauridae
Location:
Asia (People's Republic of China)
Length:
Estimated 30 feet (9 meters)

Until 1976, we only knew the predatory dinosaurs of China from teeth and pieces of fossil bones. Then a construction worker in Yangchuan County found the first nearly complete skeleton of an *Allosaurus*-size meat-eater while digging the foundation for the Shangyou dam.

When scientists studied the skeleton, only its small forelimbs and the back half of its tail were missing. In 1978, a group of Chinese paleontologists named the dinosaur *Yangchuanosaurus shangyouensis*. Museum workers prepared and mounted its skeleton at the Chongqing Municipal Museum.

Since the first find, workers have discovered a much larger *Yangchuanosaurus* skeleton nearby. It has been described as a second species, *Y. magnus*. With a skull over three feet long, it is the largest Late Jurassic theropod known from China. Many paleontologists think it is a fully grown *Y. shangyouensis*, because it was in rocks of the same age. It differs from the original species because it is larger and has more fully developed bones. *Yangchuanosaurus* seems closely related but is more primitive than *Allosaurus* from North America; scientists classify it in the family Allosauridae.

Like many predatory dinosaurs, *Yangchuanosaurus* had a low crest that ran along the front of its snout, from the nose to slightly in front of the eyes. In life, the crest probably had a horny covering. It may have been brightly colored to attract a mate. *Yangchuanosaurus* almost certainly hunted the plant-eaters of its day, including the stegosaur *Chungkingosaurus*.

Yangchuanosaurus

CHAPTER 6

DINOSAURS BUILD THEIR EMPIRE

The Early Cretaceous Period

The earth was still in the process of change as the early Cretaceous began. The land masses were drifting and the climates were changing. These changes affected the plant and animal worlds. Dinosaurs were becoming more plentiful and many more types were evolving. Some of the more fanciful dinosaurs with unusual crests and frills appeared. In contrast to earlier periods, dinosaurs at this time were different in different areas. Dinosaurs in Africa developed sails, while their relatives in the northern hemisphere did not have them.

When the Early Cretaceous Period began 144 million years ago, the huge land mass known as Pangaea had already started to separate. Laurasia (present-day North America, Europe, and Asia) was almost completely separated from Gondwanaland (present-day South America, Africa, India, Antarctica, and Australia). Antarctica and Australia were separated from Africa and moved southeast across the Indian Ocean. India headed northeast. Africa was separated from South America, which became an island continent. Only Eurasia stayed attached to North America during the Early Cretaceous. Rifts in the Tethys Sea grew during this period.

The Early Cretaceous world was very warm. There were wet and dry seasons rather than summer and winter. Most areas of the world were covered by tropical and semitropical jungles. The low-growing plants were ferns and fernlike vegetation. Plants of medium height were the cycads and their relatives. Treelike plants over 60 feet tall were mostly tropical conifers, ginkgos, and czekanowskian trees (an extinct group of trees with long, needlelike leaves). Fast-growing angiosperms—flowering plants—appeared for the first time.

Surprisingly modern-looking frogs, salamanders, turtles, and crocodiles lived in the rivers and lakes. Snakes had only begun to evolve, but there were many lizards, along with primitive furry mammals. All these animals provided food for small predatory dinosaurs. The long-tailed pterosaurs from the Jurassic were replaced by short-tailed ones, including *Anhanguera, Tropeognathus,* and *Tupuxuara.*

As Laurasia and Gondwanaland broke into smaller continents, dinosaurs on the separated continents evolved differently. England and Belgium contain the best-studied Early Cretaceous rocks. The most famous herbivore of this time was *Iguanodon.* The remains of its smaller, speedier relatives *Hypsilophodon, Valdosaurus,* and *Vectisaurus* are more scarce. All these ornithopod dinosaurs were closely related to the Jurassic dinosaurs *Othnielia, Dryosaurus,* and *Camptosaurus.*

Left: Sauropelta, *an Early Cretaceous armored dinosaur.*

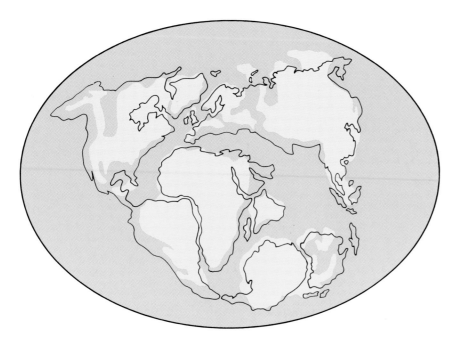

Early Cretaceous Map

Other plant-eaters from this area include the sauropod *Pelorosaurus,* with a long, slender upper-arm bone; it seems to have been a brachiosaurid. *Craterosaurus* is the only known stegosaur; the ankylosaur *Hylaeosaurus* seems to have been quite a bit more abundant than *Craterosaurus.* Armored dinosaurs were short and probably ate lower-growing plants. The small herbivore *Stenopelix* also lived during this period. It was possibly the earliest known ceratopsian. *Yaverlandia* is thought to be a very early pachycephalosaur.

Since North America was still joined to Europe (via Greenland), it had dinosaurs quite similar to those of Europe. *Iguanodon* is known from the Early Cretaceous rocks of the western United States. *Hypsilophodon* was also present. Huge sauropods were in decline; the stegosaurs were almost completely gone. They were replaced by ankylosaurs such as *Hoplitosaurus* from South Dakota and *Silvisaurus* from Kansas. Large predators, including *Acrocanthosaurus,* were also present.

Wyoming and Montana have the best-known North American Early Cretaceous dinosaur fauna. The bulky ornithopod *Tenontosaurus* is the best-known herbivore. It seems to have been hunted by packs of *Deinonychus,* a wolf-size predator famous for its sickle-shaped claws. Also found were the small predator *Microvenator,* the spiky armored *Sauropelta,* and the hypsilophodontid *Zephyrosaurus.*

Large ornithopods were not common in the Early Cretaceous of eastern Asia. The iguanodontid *Probactrosaurus* is thought to be close to the ancestry of the duckbilled dinosaurs. Of roughly the same age was a massive, large-nosed iguanodontid, *Iguanodon orientalis.* One common herbivore in Asia was *Psittacosaurus;* it was a small bipedal dinosaur. Armored plant-eaters were also common. One of the last stegosaurs, *Wuerhosaurus,* was a 25-foot-long plant-eater.

Preying upon these herbivores were large and small theropods. *Kelmayisaurus* was a megalosaurid that probably ate the armored *Wuerhosaurus. Chilantaisaurus maortuensis* could easily have held a struggling *Probactrosaurus* in the grip of its powerful front limbs.

Dinosaurs from the Early Cretaceous of Gondwanaland are less well known than those of Laurasia and show some intriguing and unexpected differences. Sauropods remained prominent in the southern hemisphere despite their drastic decline in the northern hemisphere. Large ornithopods were more scarce than their northern relatives; small ornithopods were common. Theropods in the South were often from families different from those in the North.

Dinosaurs from northern Africa had sails on their backs, including *Ouranosaurus* (an iguanodontid), *Rebbachisaurus* (a sauropod), and *Spinosaurus* (a theropod). With their wide surface area, these sails would have helped the animals keep cool, particularly if they stood in the shade with breezes blowing by.

Most of Australia's known dinosaurs are from the Early Cretaceous. Because Australia was within the Antarctic Circle, some of its dinosaurs show adaptations to life in seasonal dark-

Reconstruction of prehistoric animals at Crystal Palace Park in Sydenham, England, prepared by Waterhouse Hawkins.

ness with small size and large eyes. Large Early Cretaceous Australian dinosaurs included the sauropod *Austrosaurus,* the plant-eater *Muttaburrasaurus,* and the large meat-eater *Rapator.* Smaller dinosaurs included the hypsilophodontids *Leaellynasaura, Atlascopcosaurus,* and *Fulgurotherium;* the theropod *Kakuru;* and the armored *Minmi.* All these dinosaurs are much different than their relatives on other continents.

In the early Cretaceous, many new dinosaurs appeared. They also greatly increased in number. During this period, dinosaurs not only maintained but also expanded their "empire."

ACROCANTHOSAURUS
(AK-roh-KANTH-oh-SORE-us)

Period:
Early Cretaceous
Order, Suborder, Family:
Saurischia, Theropoda, Megalosauridae
Location:
North America
Length:
25 feet (7.5 meters)

Until recently, *Acrocanthosaurus* was not well known. In some ways it looked like many other meat-eating dinosaurs. It had a large head, many sharp teeth, short arms, powerful back legs, and a long slender tail that balanced its body when it ran. But *Acrocanthosaurus* had one feature that made it look very different; it had a tall "sail" along its neck, back, and tail. The sail was formed by very tall spines on the bones of the spine (vertebrae). Some of these spines were over a foot tall; the spines of *Tyrannosaurus* were only half that tall.

Scientists have debated why *Acrocanthosaurus* had a sail along its back. Some think it released heat when the animal was too hot. It was probably used for display to make the animal look bigger when it faced rivals for territories or mates. This is much like a house cat fluffing up its fur and arching its back to make itself look bigger.

No complete skeleton of *Acrocanthosaurus* has been found. Instead, paleontologists have built the dinosaur from parts of three skeletons. One skeleton had a three-foot-long skull. An adult *Acrocanthosaurus* was about ten feet tall at the hips and weighed between two and three tons.

Scientists have found footprints probably made by *Acrocanthosaurus* in several places in Texas. In one place, it looks like an *Acrocanthosaurus* stalked a large sauropod across a mud flat. When the sauropod footprints changed direction, so did those of *Acrocanthosaurus*. The outcome of the chase is not known; the end of the trackway has never been found.

There are other tall-spined meat-eating dinosaurs from Europe and Africa, but paleontologists do not know how *Acrocanthosaurus* is related to them. *Altispinax* had spines almost three feet tall and *Spinosaurus* had spines six feet tall.

Acrocanthosaurus atokensis

BARYONYX
(BEAR-ee-ON-icks)

Period:
Early Cretaceous
Order, Suborder, Family:
Saurischia, Theropoda, Spinosauridae
Location:
Europe (England), Africa (Niger)
Length:
31 feet (9.4 meters)

Baryonyx was found in 1983 by an amateur fossil collector in Surrey, England. He discovered a large claw that was nearly a foot long, and the animal was named for this fossil. Its name means "heavy claw." Paleontologists from the British Museum of Natural History went to the clay pit where the first fossil was found, and they discovered almost all of the skeleton. At first, scientists thought *Baryonyx* was unique and should be placed in its own family, the Baryonychidae. Now it seems that it is related to *Spinosaurus,* and so it is placed in the family Spinosauridae. *Baryonyx* is the most complete theropod dinosaur skeleton ever found in England.

The body and back legs of *Baryonyx* were much like those of other theropods, but not much else was the same. Unlike most theropods, its arms were long and heavily built. Also, the claws of the hands, especially the claw of the inside finger, were very heavily built. The length and robustness of the arm may mean that *Baryonyx* walked on all four limbs some of the time. If true, this is the only known theropod that did so.

The skull was more surprising than the arms. Most theropods had skulls that were a little longer than they were high, and they usually had 16 teeth in each side of the jaw. *Baryonyx,* however, had a very long, low

Right: Baryonyx walkeri

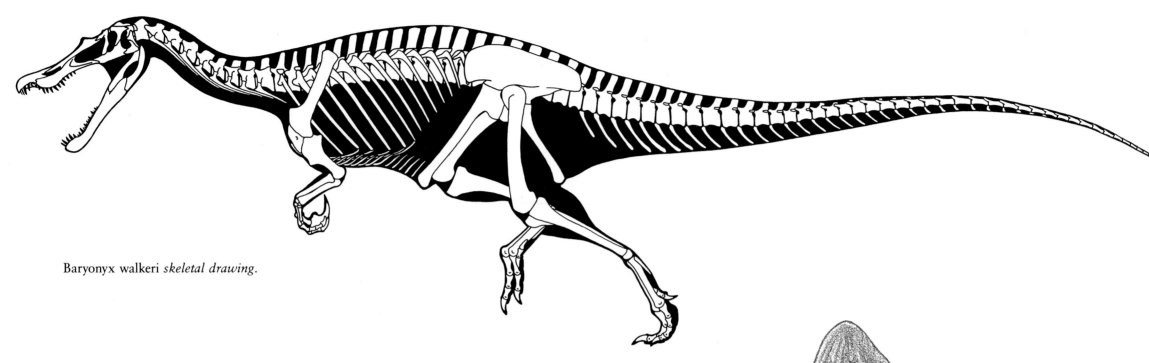

Baryonyx walkeri *skeletal drawing.*

skull. The lower jaw was slender and had 32 teeth. While most theropods had a "U" or "V" shaped snout (when viewed from above or below), the snout of *Baryonyx* was spoon-shaped. The shape of the snout and the very small serrations on the teeth were more like a fish-eating crocodile than most dinosaurs. Another strange feature of *Baryonyx* is that the nasal openings were behind the snout, rather than near its tip as in other theropods. *Baryonyx* also had a long neck, unlike most other large, meat-eating dinosaurs. From these features, scientists think *Baryonyx* probably was a fish-eater. It may have wandered along river banks, stretching its long neck out over the water and using its large claws to catch fish that swam by.

In several ways, *Baryonyx* was similar to primitive Early Jurassic dinosaurs such as *Dilophosaurus.* When all the bones of this unusual dinosaur are ready to be studied (it takes several years to prepare a large dinosaur), they will show more about its life and ancestry.

CARNOTAURUS
(CAR-noh-TORE-us)

Period:
Early Cretaceous
Order, Suborder, Family:
Saurischia, Theropoda, Abelisauridae
Location:
South America (Argentina)
Size:
21 feet (6.5 meters)

This recently described genus was an unusual theropod. *Carnotaurus* (its name means "meat bull") is known from a single, nearly complete skeleton that had skin impressions over much of the skull and body. It was so complete because it was preserved in a large concretion (a lump of rock that is harder than the rock around it) that protected the bones and skin impressions. It was found in Early Cretaceous rocks in the Patagonia region of Argentina.

Its skull had stout horns above its very small eye sockets. Its bladelike, serrated

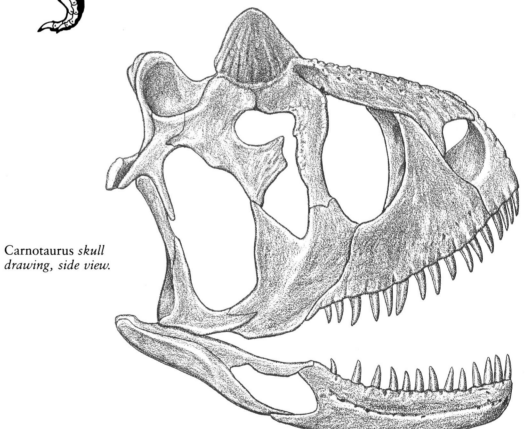

Carnotaurus *skull drawing, side view.*

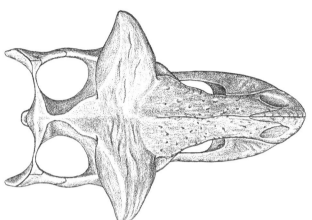

Left: Carnotaurus *skull drawing, top view.* Right: Carnotaurus sastrei

teeth were much like those of other theropods. The arms of *Carnotaurus* were short for its body size, but unlike *Tyrannosaurus* with its slender arm bones, the arms of *Carnotaurus* were stout. Its arms were so short that it almost looked like the hands were attached to the upper arm bone (the humerus). The bones in the back and tail (vertebrae) were also unusual; they look a little like the wings of a fantasy spaceship.

The most exciting feature of this animal is its skin. It is more common to find skin impressions of hadrosaurs (duckbilled dinosaurs); theropod skin impressions are rare. The skin impressions of *Carnotaurus* show that its skin was made of many low, disklike scales with larger semiconical scales in rows along its sides. Like the skin of all known dinosaurs, these scales did not overlap like scales on some lizards and snakes.

Carnotaurus and other South American Cretaceous dinosaurs were much different from related animals in other areas of the world, even North America. This group of animals supports the theory that during the Cretaceous Period South America was isolated from the rest of the world, so the animals evolved differently. The unusual and exciting Cretaceous dinosaurs of South America are just beginning to be worked on and will reveal a great deal of information in the near future.

DEINONYCHUS
(die-NON-ick-us)

Period:
Early Cretaceous
Order, Suborder, Family:
Saurischia, Theropoda, Dromaeosauridae
Location:
North America (United States)
Size:
8-10 feet (2.5-3 meters)

At least three nearly complete skeletons of this fierce, small theropod were discovered in southern Montana in 1964. *Deinonychus* is the best-known member of the family Dromaeosauridae.

John Ostrom studied this dinosaur. Before his research, theropods were divided into two major groups: Carnosauria and Coelurosauria. He showed that *Deinonychus* had features of both groups. This helped convince other paleontologists that this division was incorrect. Also, several features of *Deinonychus* are also found in birds. Several paleontologists now think that *Deinonychus* and other members of its family, the Dromaeosauridae, are more closely related to birds than are any known dinosaurs.

Though *Deinonychus* was small compared to *Tyrannosaurus* or *Allosaurus,* it was an agile theropod capable of deadly attacks. *Deinonychus* had a large head with sharp teeth that pointed back. Its teeth were well suited to biting off pieces of flesh and keeping smaller prey from escaping its jaws. Its arms were long, and like most theropods, it had three fingers on each hand. Each of its fingers ended in a well-developed claw. The fingers could move, which means *Deinonychus* used its hands to attack and eat its prey.

The thigh bone (femur) of *Deinonychus* was shorter than the shin bones (tibia and fi-

Left: Deinonychus

bula), which means the animal was a fast runner. Like other theropods and birds, the back foot was tridactyl, meaning that it walked on only three toes (the three middle toes). But *Deinonychus* had something completely different from other dinosaurs—a claw on the second toe that was very large, sharply pointed, and strongly curved. It is this "terrible claw" that the genus is named after. Similar claws are found only on other members of the family Dromaeosauridae, which includes *Dromaeosaurus, Velociraptor,* and *Hulsanpes* (a Mongolian specimen known only from fragmentary material). Studies of the sharp clawed second toe show that the claw was not used while walking but was carried off the ground in a raised position. Walking on the toe would have worn down the sharp tip.

Another interesting feature of this genus and the family Dromaeosauridae are thin rods of bone along the sides of the tail vertebrae (bones of the spine). These rods stiffen the back of the tail while allowing

some flexibility. The part of the tail nearest the body does not have these stiffening rods so it can still move. This allowed the tail to be used as a balancing device. Just as the tight rope walker shifts his balance stick from side to side to keep his balance, *Deinonychus* could swing its tail from side to side and up and down.

Deinonychus may have hunted in packs; the remains of several animals were found with the plant-eating *Tenontosaurus.* During an attack, *Deinonychus* may have grasped its prey with its jaws and hands while kicking the victim's underbelly with the large, knifelike claw. If *Deinonychus* did hunt in packs, several animals may have brought down prey much larger than themselves.

Skeletal reconstruction of Deinonychus *attacking* Tenontosaurus.

Deinonychus *attacking* Tenontosaurus.

©'85 Walters

HYPSILOPHODON
(HYP-sih-LOH-foh-don)

Period:
Early Cretaceous
Order, Suborder, Family:
Ornithischia, Ornithopoda,
Hypsilophodontidae
Location:
Europe (England)
Length:
7 ¹/₂ feet (2.3 meters)

Hypsilophodon was the first small ornithopod dinosaur studied by paleontologists. It is also the best-known member of
the family Hypsilophodontidae. The first
remains of *Hypsilophodon* were discovered
in 1849 from Early Cretaceous rocks on
the Isle of Wight, England. It was first described as a juvenile *Iguanodon* by Dr. Gideon Mantell and later by Sir Richard
Owen. But more fossils convinced Thomas
H. Huxley that it was a new dinosaur. He
named it *Hypsilophodon*, which means
"high-ridged tooth."

Hypsilophodon was long-legged, swift,
and agile. Its short arms and five-fingered
hands were not used for running, but probably were used to grasp, much like other
hypsilophodontids. The long tail, which
was stiffened by bony tendons, was a balance for the front of the body.

Scientists once thought *Hypsilophodon*
lived in trees. This curious idea came from
some of the early studies of the animal,
based on its fingers and toes. Particular attention was paid to how similar *Hypsilophodon* was to the present-day tree
kangaroo of Australia. For example, it was
said that the claws were highly curved, the
toes were very long, the arm was moveable
at the shoulder, and the first toe of the foot
may have been able to grasp branches. It
took nearly 100 years for scientists to take

Left: Hypsilophodon *nesting area.*

Hypsilophodon out of the trees. Many of
those features were incorrect. The big toe
probably could not grasp, the claws were
not strongly curved, and it had little movement at the shoulder. Finally, the long toes
worked with the long legs to make *Hypsilophodon* a very fast runner.

Hypsilophodon, together with about
seven other small ornithopods, form the
family Hypsilophodontidae. This group
was very successful, both in how long it
lived and in its geographic range. The earliest hypsilophodontids are known from the
Middle Jurassic, such as *Yandusaurus,* and
the family continues to the end of the Cretaceous. Most of these animals were found
in Europe, North America, and eastern
Asia, but others have been discovered in
parts of Africa, South America, and Australia.

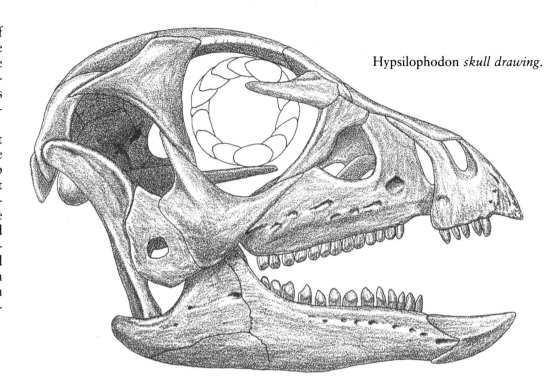

Hypsilophodon *skull drawing.*

*Top, side, front (left), and rear (right)
skeletal drawings of* Hypsilophodon.

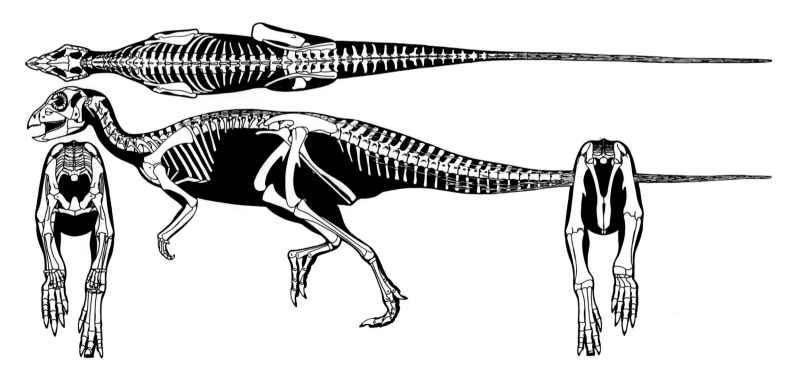

IGUANODON
(ih-GWAN-oh-DON)

Period:
Early Cretaceous
Order, Suborder, Family:
Ornithischia, Ornithopoda,
Iguanodontidae
Location:
Europe (England, France, West Germany,
Belgium, Spain), North America (United
States)
Length:
33 feet (10 meters)

When Sir Richard Owen coined the term Dinosauria in 1841, he included only three animals: *Megalosaurus, Hylaeosaurus,* and *Iguanodon. Iguanodon* was first known only from several teeth, which were found by Mary Ann Mantell in England. The animal was later described and named by her husband Dr. Gideon Mantell in 1825. It got its name, "iguana tooth," because its tooth looked like the teeth of an iguana. Later (in the 1870s), many complete skeletons of adults and younger animals were found. From all this material, we know a great deal about the behavior, anatomy, and evolution of this important dinosaur.

Iguanodon was a large ornithopod. It walked on its stocky back legs, but the largest animals often walked on all four legs. The front legs were strongly built and the hands specially constructed. Like the toes of the back feet, the fingers had blunt hooves, much like those of today's cows and horses. The outer finger was small and could have been used to grasp, much like our thumb. The large *Iguanodon* thumb, however, was sharp and like a spike. Scientists are not sure what this spiked thumb was for. It may have been used during sparring matches, perhaps between rival males competing for females, territory, or resources, or it may also have been used as a weapon.

As in other ornithopods, the front half of the body was balanced by the long, rigid tail, reinforced by bony tendons. This balance was needed when the animal walked on its back legs. Also, the bony tendons kept the tail from dragging on the ground.

Iguanodon was a plant-eater. The front end of the snout was blunt and had no teeth. Instead, it had a horny covering and was used to crop leaves, shoots, and small branches. Once *Iguanodon* had gotten food into its mouth, the many broad teeth in the back of the jaw tore apart the plants. Muscular cheeks kept food from falling out of the sides of its mouth.

Groups of nearly complete *Iguanodon* skeletons jumbled into piles have been found in Belgium and West Germany. These groups of animals may be the remains of small herds of *Iguanodon* caught by a flash flood or while trying to cross a flooded river.

Although *Iguanodon* has been found in many places in Europe, the newest member of the genus was discovered in South Dakota. This species is probably the most primitive.

Iguanodon is the best-known member of the family Iguanodontidae. Another member is *Ouranosaurus,* from Niger in western Africa. A possible relative was *Craspedodon,* known only from three teeth from the Late Cretaceous of Belgium.

Iguanodon *skeletal drawing.*

Iguanodon mantelli

Right: Iguanodons *making a trackway in northeast New Mexico.*

Muttaburrasaurus langdoni

MUTTABURRASAURUS
(MUTT-ah-BURR-ah-SORE-us)

Period:
Early Cretaceous
Order, Suborder, Family:
Ornithischia, Ornithopoda,
Iguanodontidae
Location:
Australia
Length:
23 feet (7 meters)

The "reptile from Muttaburra," *Muttaburrasaurus* is one of the recently discovered ornithopods from Australia, and it is one of the best known from there. There are only a few incomplete skeletons and skulls. It was a large animal, only slightly smaller than *Iguanodon* from Europe and nearly the size of *Ouranosaurus* from western Africa. These two animals were probably closely related to *Muttaburrasaurus*.

Muttaburrasaurus lived during the Early Cretaceous in western Australia. It probably walked and ran on its back legs, but rested on all fours. A complete hand has not been found, so it is not known whether it had a thumb spike like *Ouranosaurus* and *Iguanodon*. Further discoveries will tell us more about this important part of the *Muttaburrasaurus* skeleton.

The broad head of *Muttaburrasaurus* looked like many other large ornithopods of its time. It did, however, have a large hooked arch over the snout, unlike any other large ornithopods except the hooknosed hadrosaurids. The fronts of the jaws were toothless and had a horny covering, much like turtles and birds. This beak was used to tear leaves and fruits from shrubs and low tree branches. The backs of the jaws were lined with many large teeth to tear apart food. The stomach of *Muttaburrasaurus* seems to have been large; it probably needed a large gut to digest a diet of plants.

Muttaburrasaurus and its relatives *Iguanodon*, *Ouranosaurus*, and *Probactrosaurus* show that these large ornithopods were worldwide. They are best known from the Early Cretaceous, before duckbilled dinosaurs appeared. When the duckbilled dinosaurs arose, there was a decline in all other ornithopods, among them *Muttaburrasaurus*.

OURANOSAURUS
(oo-RAN-oh-SORE-us)

Period:
Early Cretaceous
Order, Suborder, and Family:
Ornithischia, Ornithopoda,
Iguanodontidae
Location:
Africa (Niger)
Length:
23 feet (7 meters)

Ouranosaurus is one of the most puzzling large ornithopods of the Cretaceous. Discovered in 1966 in Niger, Africa, this new dinosaur was first named and studied in 1976. Its name means "brave reptile."

In many ways, *Ouranosaurus* looked about the same as other ornithopods. It was a large and powerfully built animal that mostly walked on its stocky back legs. The front legs were smaller than the back legs but were strongly built. The toes of the hands and feet had blunt hooves. *Ouranosaurus* may have used all four legs to walk slowly or to rest. It probably used only its back legs for rapid running. Like its relatives *Iguanodon* and *Camptosaurus*, its hand had a sharp thumb spike that would have been a dangerous weapon against any predators.

What is puzzling about *Ouranosaurus* is its very different head and skeleton. Its head was very large and its jaws were long. There was room for massive jaw muscles for chewing. The front of the snout was flat and

Ouranosaurus nigeriensis

broad and was probably covered by a horny beak. The nostrils were somewhat back from what is seen in *Iguanodon* and *Muttaburrasaurus*. *Ouranosaurus* looked a little like the hadrosaurid *Edmontosaurus* from the Late Cretaceous in Canada.

Above the eyes along the top of the snout was a pair of low, broad bumps. Only *Ouranosaurus* had these, and they may have been used for display, much like the small horns of some antelopes. A male *Ouranosaurus* might have used the bumps during head-butting contests, perhaps to defend his territory, or the bumps may have been important for its own family group or species to recognize each other.

Ouranosaurus had many features in common with *Iguanodon*. The jaws of *Ouranosaurus* had many teeth, which were similar to the teeth of *Iguanodon*. *Ouranosaurus* was probably the main plant-eater of its time in what is now western Africa. *Ouranosaurus* used an interesting, somewhat complex skull motion of the upper jaws. It produced sideways movement during chewing. This way of chewing, also found in hypsilophodontids and hadrosaurids, may have made these animals the most successful plant-eaters of the Mesozoic Era.

Perhaps the most puzzling thing about *Ouranosaurus* is the large sail on its back. The sail was formed by the long spines on the vertebrae (bones of the spine). How this sail functioned has been somewhat perplexing. Since *Ouranosaurus* lived in a somewhat warm and dry climate, the sail may have helped it live in this harsh habitat. The skin around the sail may have had many blood vessels that would have released heat on hot days and captured heat on colder days.

Several nearly complete skeletons of *Ouranosaurus* have been found in Niger and surrounding areas in Africa. *Ouranosaurus* is closely related to *Iguanodon* and the more primitive hadrosaurid *Telmatosaurus*.

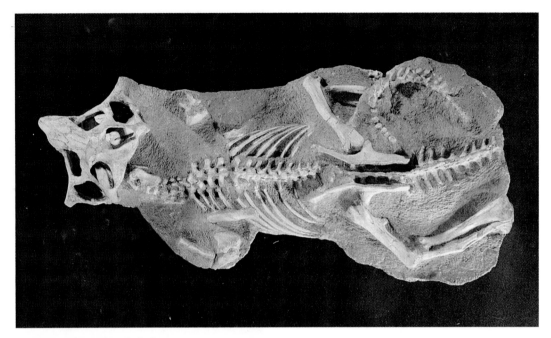

Psittacosaurus *fossil skeleton.*

PSITTACOSAURUS
(sie-TACK-oh-SORE-us)

Period:
Early Cretaceous
Order, Suborder, Family:
Ornithischia, Ceratopsia, Psittacosauridae
Location:
Asia (Mongolian People's Republic, People's Republic of China, Siberia)
Length:
6 1/2 feet (2 meters)

Psittacosaurus was one of the smallest and most primitive members of the Ceratopsia. It was found in rock that is thought to be Early Cretaceous (the exact age is not known). *Psittacosaurus* is the earliest known ceratopsian.

Psittacosaurus was first discovered in Outer Mongolia in 1922. Henry Osborn named the first specimen *Psittacosaurus mongoliensis* and gave a second specimen the name *Protiguanodon mongoliense*. Later, paleontologists realized that *Protiguanodon* and *Psittacosaurus* were the same animal. Additional *Psittacosaurus* specimens have since been found in China as well, and a number of species have been added.

This small dinosaur did not look much like its later relatives. It had short arms and long grasping hands, and it walked bipedally (on two legs). It also had a small head without a neck frill or horns. But like all later ceratopsians, it had a high palate (the bone in roof of the mouth), flared cheek bones, and a deep face with a parrotlike beak. This beak is how it got its name, which means "parrot reptile." Although *Psittacosaurus* did not have a neck frill, it had a small, shelflike edge on the back of its skull. This may have been the beginning of a frill. *Psittacosaurus* had no horns or large frill for protection; it probably escaped predators by running quickly.

Although the skull of *Psittacosaurus* shares many features with later ceratopsians, its skeleton looks like the bipedal ornithischian dinosaurs, such as *Fabrosaurus* or *Hypsilophodon*. Osborn at first thought *Psittacosaurus* was an ornithopod dinosaur. If the skeleton had been found without the skull, we would not know that it was a ceratopsian.

Two of the specimens of *Psittacosaurus* were tiny juveniles; they are among the smallest known dinosaurs. These juveniles were smaller than a robin. One tiny, nearly perfectly preserved skull is only about an inch long and would fit into a teaspoon. The teeth of the small *Psittacosaurus* specimens were slightly worn, which means they had already been feeding on tough plant material. A newly hatched *Psittacosaurus* would have been even smaller.

Psittacosaurus is the only known member of the family Psittacosauridae. Its closest relatives were the protoceratopsid dinosaurs *Protoceratops, Bagaceratops, Microceratops, Montanaceratops,* and *Leptoceratops.* Although it is the earliest and most primitive ceratopsian, it is not known if *Psittacosaurus* was the direct ancestor of the protoceratopsians.

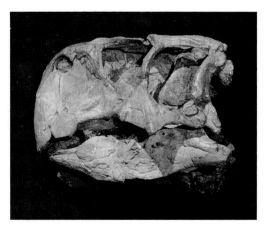

Psittacosaurus *skull.*

SAUROPELTA
(SORE-oh-PEL-tuh)

Period:
Early Cretaceous
Order, Suborder, Family:
Ornithischia, Thyreophora,
Nodosauridae
Location:
North America (United States)
Length:
17 feet (5 meters)

One of the best-known ankylosaurs, *Sauropelta* is known from several partial skeletons. These are important because much of the armor was in its natural position. From these, it has been possible to make the most accurate skeletal reconstructions and life restorations of any known ankylosaur.

Like all members of the family Nodosauridae, *Sauropelta* had a long, tapering tail without the bone-club of the members of the family Ankylosauridae. The neck of *Sauropelta* had long bone spikes projecting up and out; such spikes are not found in ankylosaurids. These spikes would have protected the neck from the bite of its pred-

ators, including *Acrocanthosaurus*. Perhaps more importantly, they would have made the animal look bigger and more dangerous. Bluffing would have allowed an animal to avoid a fight.

The armor of *Sauropelta,* and all ankylosaurs, formed in the skin, just like it does in modern alligators, crocodiles, and certain lizards. It got its name from this feature; its name means "lizard skin." The armor of *Sauropelta* consisted of rows of oval plates across the neck, back, and tail; spines and spikes along the sides; and large circular plates over the hips. Tiny, irregular pieces of armor filled the gaps between the larger plates. Even the skull had armor, with the plates tightly joined to the outer surface of the skull and jaws. This occurs in all nodosaurids and ankylosaurids, and is unique among the dinosaurs.

Sauropelta was different from many ankylosaurs because it had two types of teeth. Small pegs lined the upper front of the mouth, while leaf-shaped teeth lined both the upper and lower cheek region. The shape of the cheek teeth and their pattern of wear show that *Sauropelta* ate soft plants.

Some scientists think *Sauropelta* lived in herds, because at least five animals were

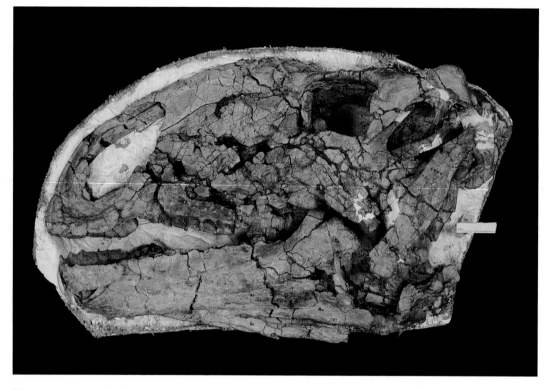

Tenontosaurus *skull.*

Tenontosaurus

found in one fossil quarry. Other animals that lived alongside *Sauropelta* were a large sauropod, possibly *Pleurocoelus;* the ornithopod *Tenontosaurus;* a large carnivore, which might be *Acrocanthosaurus;* and packs of the sickled-clawed *Deinonychus.*

TENONTOSAURUS
(teh-NON-toh-SORE-us)

Period:
Early Cretaceous
Order, Suborder, and Family:
Ornithischia, Ornithopoda,
Hypsilophodontidae
Location:
North America (United States)
Length:
22 feet (6.5 meters)

Tenontosaurus tilletti was a medium-size ornithopod dinosaur from Montana and Wyoming. Barnum Brown of the American Museum of Natural History discovered the first *Tenontosaurus* skeleton in Montana in 1903. Since then, several dozen partial to complete skeletons of *Tenontosaurus* have been found, as well as parts of many more. These skeletons range in size from very small juveniles to almost 22-foot-long adults.

Some of the skeletons of the younger animals were found jumbled together in groups—three in one group and four in another. The group of four was found with an adult *Tenontosaurus.* These *Tenontosaurus* juveniles may have gathered in groups or stayed in family groups after they hatched, possibly for protection from predators.

Tenontosaurus had an extremely long, deep tail that was stiffened by "ossified tendons"—tendons that turned to bone. Since *Tenontosaurus* walked mostly on its back legs, these ossified tendons probably helped hold its tail out straight to balance the front of its body. It is these stiffened tendons that gave the dinosaur its name: *tenon* is the Greek word for "sinew" or "tendon." About two-thirds of the entire length of *Tenontosaurus* was tail. Ossified tendons were also present along its back and over its hips. Even though it probably did most of its walking and running on its back legs, *Tenontosaurus* also had very strong front legs with short, wide front feet. It probably used them to walk quadrupedally (on all four limbs) to browse on low vegetation.

Tenontosaurus had a long, flexible neck. The front of its mouth had no teeth; it had a horny beak for biting off plants. Rows of strong, tightly fitted teeth ground up even tough plants.

At the time *Tenontosaurus* lived, the weather was quite warm and seasonal, with some rain. Plants like cycads, ferns, and conifers were common, and the flowering plants were just beginning to evolve. While browsing for food, *Tenontosaurus* probably had to keep watch for the small, fast carnivorous dinosaur *Deinonychus*. We know that *Deinonychus* preyed on *Tenontosaurus* because their broken teeth have been found with some *Tenontosaurus* skeletons. Some paleontologists believe that *Deinonychus* may have hunted *Tenontosaurus* in packs.

Other animals that lived alongside *Tenontosaurus* included the ankylosaur *Sauropelta,* the coelurid *Microvenator,* and the hypsilophodontid *Zephyrosaurus.* *Tenontosaurus* seems to have been most closely related to the iguanodontids *Dryosaurus, Iguanodon,* and *Camptosaurus.* *Tenontosaurus* was also distantly related to the smaller hypsilophodontids, such as *Hypsilophodon.*

Wuerhosaurus homheni

WUERHOSAURUS
(woo-AIR-oh-SORE-us)

Period:
Early Cretaceous
Order, Suborder, Family:
Ornithischia, Thyreophora, Stegosauridae
Location:
Asia (People's Republic of China)
Length:
20 feet (6 meters)

As far as paleontologists know, stegosaurs almost became extinct at the close of the Jurassic Period. Very few lived during the Cretaceous Period. *Craterosaurus,* known only from a piece of a vertebra, is from the Early Cretaceous of Great Britain. Another stegosaurian, *Dravidosaurus,* is known from remains from the Late Cretaceous of India. The undescribed stegosaurian "Monkonosaurus" from Tibet may also be of Early Cretaceous age. But the best-documented Early Cretaceous stegosaur is *Wuerhosaurus.*

Presently the latest known Chinese stegosaurian, *Wuerhosaurus homheni* is based on a fragmentary skeleton lacking the skull and on three tail vertebrae of a second animal, all found in the Tugulo Formations near the northwestern part of the Junggar Basin. It was described by Dong Zhiming in 1973. Two armor plates found with the skeleton are thin, long, low, and somewhat semicircular. They are quite different from the tall, triangular plates of other stegosaurians.

Its body was broad, as shown by its wide pelvic bones, and its front limbs were quite short. Although the back limbs have not been found, the shortness of the front limbs shows that the animal had an arch in its back—perhaps even more curved than in *Stegosaurus.* Comparing bones with those of other stegosaurs shows that *Wuerhosaurus* was most closely related to *Stegosaurus,* which is the only stegosaur that had an alternating arrangement of armor plates. Some Chinese paleontologists think *Wuerhosaurus* may have had alternating plates, but since only two plates were found with the skeleton, there is not enough material to be certain.

Tenontosaurus *browses as the*
theropod Microvenator *watches.*

CHAPTER 7

DINOSAURS ADVANCE AND RULE THE WORLD

The Late Cretaceous Period

During the Late Cretaceous, land and seas continued to change and move. The climate of the world changed toward cooler and more seasonal weather. New types of plants and animals were appearing. An amazing collection of dinosaurs had evolved. Some had become advanced, even caring for their young. Dinosaurs, at first plentiful, disappeared from the earth by the end of the period.

The continents continued to separate during the Late Cretaceous. North and South America moved west into the Pacific Ocean, and the North and South Atlantic Oceans widened. India continued to move north toward Asia. Still joined together, Australia and Antarctica journeyed away from Africa, going beyond the South Pole.

A shallow sea covered North America's middle. About halfway through the Late Cretaceous, Alaska butted up against Siberia. Eastern Asia and western North America were a single land mass called Beringia. The North American part of Beringia was tropical and swampy. The Asian section was dryer. The link from Eurasia to North America began to break. South America remained isolated throughout most of the Late Cretaceous. Australia and Antarctica remained joined around the South Pole, and Eurasia and Africa never drifted far apart.

Flowering plants spread rapidly throughout the northern hemisphere in the early Late Cretaceous, appearing first as small weeds. They quickly became the most important land plants. They provided a dense clutter of leaves, stems, and branches. In drier areas, flowering plants became underbrush. Able to grow rapidly after being eaten or trampled, flowering plants fed a larger number of animals.

During the early Late Cretaceous, the climate was warm. As the period came to a close, the average climate became cooler, but it was still much warmer than today. By the end of the period, the tropics were only in areas near the equator. The climate in the farther northern and southern hemispheres (and polar regions) became temperate and more seasonal, with cool winters and warm summers. Forests in the temperate zones became less tropical, with magnolias, sassafras, redwoods, and willow trees plentiful.

Dinosaurs remained the main large land animals. Smaller land animals included turtles, crocodiles, snakes, lizards, frogs, and salamanders. Mammals remained small, but mammals that gave birth to live young appeared for the first time.

Almost all Late Cretaceous flying birds were tiny. But pterosaurs became the largest flying creatures ever known. Ich-

Left: *The tyrannosaur* Daspletosaurus.

thyosaurs became extinct, and mosasaurs became the main marine predators. These evolved from small-to-medium-size monitor lizards. They shared the seas with plesiosaurs.

As many dinosaur species are known from the Late Cretaceous as are known from all the other periods together. In North America, the duckbilled hadrosaurs diversified into nearly two dozen known types, including *Brachylophosaurus, Prosaurolophus,* and *Saurolophus.* The horned ceratopsians divided into at least a dozen varieties, including the most famous, *Triceratops.*

Although the hadrosaurids are best known for their broad, horny, ducklike beaks, they are also famous for the different shaped crests on their heads. Perhaps used for vocalizing, the crests may also have identified male and female animals during mating season. Horns and frills evolved for the same reason in ceratopsians, with horns also used for combat and defense.

Plant-eaters were eaten by fierce tyrannosaurids. Most of those known from North America were 25 to 35 feet long, such as *Albertosaurus.* But the latest Late Cretaceous saw one of the smallest, *Nanotyrannus,* about 18 feet long, and the largest, *Tyrannosaurus,* 40 feet long. Ankylosaurs and nodosaurs were heavily armored plant-eaters that did not need the protection of a herd to avoid being eaten.

There were many small predators in North America. Among these were *Aublysodon, Chirostenotes,* and *Troodon.* They ate the small plant-eating dinosaurs, such the hypsilophodontids (*Orodromeus, Parksosaurus,* and *Thescelosaurus*), the small protoceratopsids (*Leptoceratops* and *Montanoceratops*), and the smaller dome-headed dinosaurs (*Stegoceras* and *Stygimoloch*). The swift, ostrichlike ornithomimids outran their predators.

Eastern Asia—especially Mongolia—was an abundant source of dinosaur species. Tyrannosaurids from Asia were smaller and more primitive than their North American relatives. Dome-headed dinosaurs from Mongolia were much different from those in North America. The only armored dinosaurs from Asia were ankylosaurids, such as *Talarurus* and

Late Cretaceous Map

Tarchia. At least three types of sauropods survived in Mongolia to the latest Late Cretaceous: *Nemegtosaurus, Opisthocoelicaudia,* and *Quaesitosaurus.*

The most interesting dinosaurs discovered in Mongolia and China are the segnosaurs. Wide-bodied herbivores with powerful claws, *Erlikosaurus, Segnosaurus,* and *Therizinosaurus* are known from nowhere else in the world. Another interesting Asian group was the oviraptorids, including *Conchoraptor* and *Oviraptor.*

Small predators closely related to those in western North America abounded in eastern Asia. These included the sickle-clawed dromaeosaurids *Adasaurus, Hulsanpes,* and *Velociraptor.* Other small predators were the troodontid *Saurornithoides* and *Elmisaurus,* which was found in both Mongolia and Canada. *Shanshanosaurus* from China may have been related to North America's *Aublysodon.* Ostrich-dinosaurs were quite unusual in Mongolia. Some were more primitive than their American relatives, while others were quite advanced, such as *Anserimimus* and the huge *Gallimimus.*

Europe was covered by a continental sea that divided it up into islands. This led to the evolution of dwarf dinosaurs known as "island endemics." *Struthiosaurus* was a miniature nodosaurid; *Magyarosaurus* and *Hypselosaurus* were small titanosaurids; and *Rhabdodon* and *Craspedodon* were small iguanodontids. Only *Telmatosaurus,* a primitive hadrosaurid, was about "normal" size.

The Gondwanaland continents had different Late Cretaceous dinosaurs. Almost all the Late Cretaceous Gondwana-land sauropods were titanosaurids. They were found mainly in South America, Africa, India, and Madagascar. Some titanosaurids were small, about 35 to 40 feet long, with ankylosaurlike armor scutes (plates) on their backs. Others were larger, such as *Argyrosaurus.*

The Late Cretaceous ended about 65 million years ago. All dinosaurs, mosasaurs, plesiosaurs, and pterosaurs vanished from the face of the earth. Furthermore, it seems that this extinction happened at almost the same time on all continents, in both northern and southern hemispheres. The rule of the dinosaurs ended with the end of the Mesozoic Era.

A Late Cretaceous scene, with (from left to right) a crested Kritosaurus, *an armored* Edmontonia, *a pair of crested hypacrosaurs, a fierce* Tyrannosaurus rex, *the single-horned* Monoclonius, *and a herd of* Chasmosaurus.

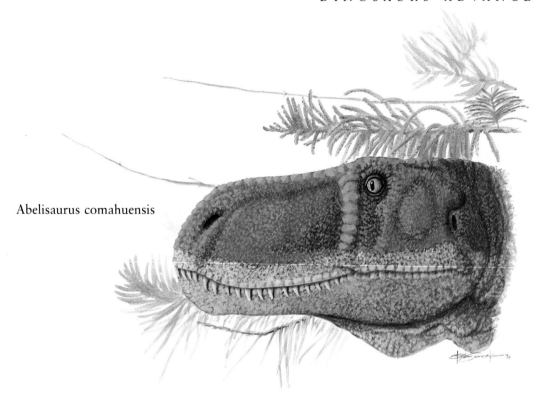

Abelisaurus comahuensis

ALBERTOSAURUS
(al-BUR-toh-SORE-us)

Period:
Late Cretaceous
Order, Suborder, Family:
Saurischia, Theropoda,
Tyrannosauridae
Location:
North America
Length:
30 feet (9 meters)

Albertosaurus was an older "cousin" to the better-known *Tyrannosaurus*. In many ways the two were similar: the head was large compared to the body, the tiny forearms had only two fingers each, and the long tail balanced the body over two powerful back legs. But the eyes of *Tyrannosaurus* looked forward and those of *Albertosaurus* looked more toward the sides. This suggests that *Albertosaurus* did not judge distances as well, so that when it hunted, it probably did not leap onto its prey.

Stealth, power, and speed were its biggest assets. With its long, powerful rear

Albertosaurus *skeleton.*

ABELISAURUS
(AH-bell-ih-SORE-us)

Period:
Late Cretaceous
Order, Suborder, Family:
Saurischia, Theropoda, Abelisauridae
Location:
South America (Argentina)
Length:
25-30 feet (7.5-9 meters)

During the Cretaceous, dinosaurs that lived in the southern hemisphere were much different from their northern-hemisphere relatives. This was the result of the separation of the northern and southern land masses that began in the Jurassic Period. The recently discovered large theropod *Abelisaurus comahuensis,* from Patagonia, Argentina, looked a little like *Albertosaurus* from Alberta, Canada, particularly in its size and lifestyle. But parts of its skull led two Argentinian paleontologists to put it in its own family, the Abelisauridae. They think it was more closely

related to the theropod *Ceratosaurus* from the Jurassic Period.

Only the skull of *Abelisaurus* has been found, but its body proportions were probably similar to other large theropods with the same size skulls (three feet long). *Carnotaurus* had slender legs with the front shorter than the back. Since *Carnotaurus* probably was an early abelisaurid, scientists suppose that *Abelisaurus* also had short front limbs and slender legs. Other details of its body are unknown.

The discovery of *Abelisaurus* is important because it shed light on many different southern-hemisphere theropods that are known only from fragmentary and puzzling material. These remains were difficult to identify and were occasionally used to suggest that Late Cretaceous tyrannosaurids from the northern hemisphere were in the southern hemisphere. Now that good abelisaurid material has been discovered and described, scientists have learned that many of those remains were abelisaurids. The possibility of southern-hemisphere tyrannosaurids is less likely.

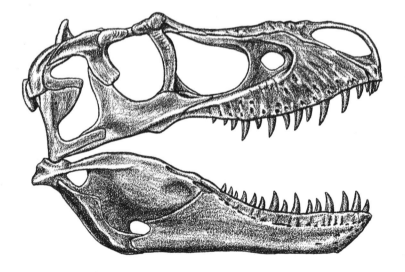

Left: Albertosaurus libratus *skull drawing.*
Right: Albertosaurus *bothering a herd of* Styracosaurus.

Two albertosaurs attacking a herd of **Monoclonius.**

ANCHICERATOPS
(ANK-ee-SAIR-ah-tops)

Period:
Late Cretaceous
Order, Suborder, Family:
Ornithischia, Marginocephalia,
Ceratopsidae
Location:
North America (Canada)
Length:
20 feet (6 meters)

Anchiceratops was discovered along the Red Deer River in Alberta in 1912 by an expedition from the American Museum of Natural History led by Barnum Brown. They found the back part of a skull that had a new kind of neck frill. Brown named it *Anchiceratops ornatus,* the "close-horned reptile." In 1924, Charles Sternberg collected a nearly complete skull of *Anchiceratops,* which provided the information missing on the first skull. Sternberg noted that this skull was slightly different from the first one, so he designated it a new species, *Anchiceratops longirostris.* Paleontologists are not sure if there is more than one species of *Anchiceratops.* More specimens have since been found, with a nearly complete skeleton that is at the National Museum of Canada.

The most distinctive features of *Anchiceratops* are in its unusual neck frill. The frill is moderately long and rectangular with small, oval fenestrae (openings). The edge of the frill is thick just behind the brow horns. On the back of the frill are six large epoccipitals (bony knobs around the frill) that were expanded into short, triangular, backward-pointing spikes. Also on the frill are two short spikes that curve up and out.

Anchiceratops had a short nasal horn, a very long nose, and two moderate-size brow horns. Its skeleton shows it had a very short tail, but otherwise it looked much like other ceratopsids.

Anchiceratops lived at the same time as its close relative *Arrhinoceratops.* It was also closely related to *Torosaurus, Chasmosaurus, Pentaceratops,* and *Triceratops.*

legs, *Albertosaurus* could outrun its prey or ambush a heavy herbivore that stood alone and unprotected. The rear legs could deliver crushing blows, knocking the prey off balance. It delivered deadly wounds with its claws. The light build and long legs show that it was fast and graceful. It may have been able to run 25-30 miles per hour.

The head of *Albertosaurus* had two small, blunt horns, just in front of the eyes. These may have been for show, much like the comb on a chicken today. It is possible that the male had brightly colored skin covering the horns to attract the female during mating season. It would be like birds today, with the males brightly colored to attract females.

Fossil remains of *Albertosaurus* are common, especially teeth, which often broke when it was feeding. Several species are recognized: *Albertosaurus sarcophagus* and *Albertosaurus libratus* are the most common. *Albertosaurus lancensis* has been recently renamed *Nanotyrannus.* Some paleontologists think the theropod dinosaur *Alectrosaurus olseni* from Mongolia is a species of *Albertosaurus.* If this is correct, *Albertosaurus* lived in both North America and Asia. *Albertosaurus* may have hunted in packs.

Albertosaurus libratus
skeleton.

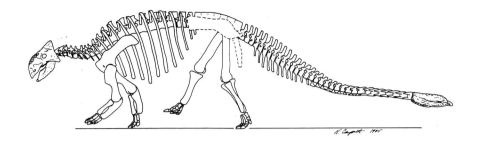

Left: Ankylosaurus *skeletal drawing*.
Below: Ankylosaurus

ANKYLOSAURUS
(an-KEE-loh-SORE-us)

Period:
Late Cretaceous
Order, Suborder, Family:
Ornithischia, Thyreophora,
Ankylosauridae
Location:
North America
Length:
23 feet (7 meters)

Next to *Tyrannosaurus* and *Triceratops*, *Ankylosaurus* is one of the best-known dinosaurs. Therefore, it may come as a surprise that this dinosaur is known only from three partial skeletons, none of which has been fully described. Its popularity mostly comes from a fanciful life-size restoration made for the 1964 New York World's Fair.

Through the studies of Walter Coombs, we now know that *Ankylosaurus* and all members of the family Ankylosauridae did not have spines and spikes projecting from the body as shown in the World's Fair restoration. Such spines and spikes only occur in the other ankylosaur family, Nodosauridae (see *Sauropelta*). Furthermore, there is no basis for showing keeled (ridged) rectangular plates in even rows across the body. Keeled plates have been found with the *Ankylosaurus* specimens, but these are different sizes and shapes. We don't know the arrangement of the plates on the body because no specimen has been found with the plates preserved as they were in life.

The arrangement of plates is known for the nodosaurids *Sauropelta* and *Edmontonia* and the ankylosaurid *Saichania*. These specimens are important because they provide the only proof of how the armor looked in various species of ankylosaurs. The shape and arrangement of the armor is different on all three animals.

Like most armored dinosaurs, *Ankylosaurus* had bone plates fused (joined) to the outside of the skull and jaws. But unlike *Sauropelta* where there were many large plates, *Ankylosaurus* had many small plates. *Ankylosaurus* also differs from *Sauropelta* in having horns in the upper and lower corners of the skull behind the eyes. Why *Ankylosaurus,* and all ankylosaurids, developed these horns is not understood. They may have used them to fight among themselves. The animals would have stood side-by-side and swung their heads into the other's body. Such a blow would be painful but not fatal.

Ankylosaurus had a large bone club on the end of its tail. All members of its family had these clubs, and the lack of a club characterizes the other ankylosaur family, the Nodosauridae. The shape of the club is different for each member of the family. The club of *Ankylosaurus* was wide and long, but not very tall. The club in all the ankylosaurids was made of large armor plates fused together at the end of the tail. The bones of the tail were modified for swinging the club; they interlocked to form a "handle" to the club. This allowed *Ankylosaurus* to put force into the swing.

A Cretaceous landscape of modern-day Montana. Flowering plants, called angiosperms, had evolved in the Cretaceous. They began as weeds by marshes and swamps. This development probably led to Late Cretaceous plant-eaters becoming varied and abundant.

ANSERIMIMUS
(AN-sair-ah-MIME-us)

Period:
Late Cretaceous
Order, Suborder, Family:
Saurischia, Theropoda, Ornithomimidae
Location:
Asia (Mongolian People's Republic)
Length:
10 feet (3 meters)

All known ornithomimids, or "ostrich dinosaurs," were similar and can be told apart only by minor details. They all have names that end in *-mimus* (meaning "mimic" or "imitator"). The root of the name comes from the names of birds or other flying creatures. The ornithomimid *Anserimimus planinychus,* described by Mongolian paleontologist Rinchen Barsbold in 1988, has the name "goose mimic." Its species name means "flat-clawed," for the flattened claws on its hands. These claws distinguish it from other ornithomimids.

Anserimimus is known from a single headless partial skeleton; mainly the arms and feet were preserved. This skeleton was found in the Nemegt Formation of Bugeen-Tsav, Mongolia. It had more powerful front limbs than other ornithomimids. The three-fingered hands, like those of most other ornithomimids, could weakly grasp objects. The arms, hands, and spadelike finger claws seem built for rooting through loosely packed soil or plant matter—possibly for finding nests of dinosaur eggs.

ANTARCTOSAURUS
(ant-ARK-toh-SORE-us)

Period:
Late Cretaceous
Order, Suborder, Family:
Saurischia, Sauropodomorpha, Titanosauridae
Location:
South America (Argentina, Brazil, Uruguay)
Length:
Estimated 80-100 feet (24-30 meters)

With a thigh bone (femur) over seven and a half feet long, longer than any other femur known, *Antarctosaurus* was a sauropod of spectacular proportions. Like other members of the Late Cretaceous family Titanosauridae, it had massive hips, tall rear legs, front legs nearly as tall as the rear, a long tail, and a long neck.

Antarctosaurus had a very small head, even for a sauropod. It was a plant-eater that had weak, peglike teeth. None of the preserved skeletons of *Antarctosaurus* are complete, so there is still much to learn about this animal.

Some paleontologists calculate that, based on the length of the limb bones, *Antarctosaurus* may have been larger than *Brachiosaurus brancai*, which is the largest dinosaur known from complete skeletons. But the two are not closely related; *Brachiosaurus* belongs to a different family and lived only in the Jurassic Period. *Antarctosaurus* was the largest dinosaur of the Late Cretaceous. It may have weighed as much as 80 to 100 tons and stood as tall as 15 feet at the shoulders.

Its name means "Antarctic reptile." It was found in South America, which in the Late Cretaceous was not far from the Antarctic Circle. Fragmentary remains from India have been found that may belong to *Antarctosaurus*, but scientists have not yet proved they belong to the same animal. A relative, *Titanosaurus*, has been found in India and Argentina. This may mean that Gondwanaland may have still had land connections at that time.

Antarctosaurus wichmannianus

ARALOSAURUS
(ah-RAL-oh-SORE-us)

Period:
Late Cretaceous
Order, Suborder, Family:
Ornithischia, Ornithopoda,
Hadrosauridae
Location:
Asia (U.S.S.R.)
Length:
Unknown

Aralosaurus is from Kazakhstan in the Soviet Union. It is known only from a nearly complete skull that is missing the front of the snout and all of the lower jaw, but no skeleton. This Late Cretaceous duckbilled dinosaur, whose name means "reptile from the Aral region," had a strongly hooked nasal arch in front of the eyes. This hook is more strongly developed than in any other hadrosaurid, including close relative *Gryposaurus*. *Hadrosaurus* may also have had an arched snout, but this part of the skeleton was not preserved. The hook of *Aralosaurus* was not only high, but also wide from side to side. The nostril openings beneath the arch were large.

The upper jaw of *Aralosaurus* was strongly built and relatively high. Like other duckbilled dinosaurs, it had many teeth for grinding plant food. *Aralosaurus* seems to have had as many as 30 tooth rows, with several teeth per row in each upper jaw. This arrangement was called the dental battery. The back of the skull was very high and wide. This suggests that there must have been long, massive muscles for chewing food.

Aralosaurus was first named and described in 1968. Since then, very little has been written about dinosaurs from this area of the world. Perhaps future efforts will tell us more about *Aralosaurus,* its anatomy, and its evolution.

ARGYROSAURUS
(ar-GUY-roh-SORE-us)

Period:
Late Cretaceous
Order, Suborder, Family:
Saurischia, Sauropodomorpha,
Titanosauridae
Location:
South America (Argentina)
Length:
65-70 feet (20-21 meters)

In 1893, British paleontologist Richard Lydekker published the first description of sauropod dinosaurs from South America that had been unearthed in Patagonia, Argentina. Lydekker named two new South American species of *Titanosaurus,* and a new titanosaurid, *Argyrosaurus superbus* or "superb Argentine lizard." All that was found were the bones of a left front limb more than nine feet long, and a few bones that may belong to the same animal. *Argyrosaurus* was a large titanosaurid. If it had the same proportions as other titanosaurids, it would have been 65 to 70 feet long. It would have been as long as *Apatosaurus* but with a bulkier body, shorter neck, and much shorter tail.

The titanosaurids of South America are being restudied by paleontologist Jaime Powell. His results have not been published, but he has found that the front limbs of *Argyrosaurus* were different from those of India's *Titanosaurus* and Argentina's *Saltasaurus* and *Laplatasaurus*.

Even if it needs to be placed in another family, its lifestyle was much like that of its better-known sauropod relatives. It wandered in herds across South America, using its long neck to reach high into the treetops for leaves and branches. *Argyrosaurus* probably spent most of its waking hours searching for food.

Aralosaurus tuberiferus

ARRHINOCERATOPS
(ar-RINE-oh-SAIR-ah-tops)

Period:
Late Cretaceous
Order, Suborder, Family:
Ornithischia, Marginocephalia,
Ceratopsidae
Location:
North America (Canada)
Length:
20 feet (6 meters)

Arrhinoceratops is a rare ceratopsian known from only one skull that lacks a lower jaw. This single specimen was found in 1923 along the Red Deer River of Alberta by an expedition from the University of Toronto. William A. Parks named this dinosaur *Arrhinoceratops brachyops,* meaning "no nose-horn face," in 1925. This name is incorrect; *Arrhinoceratops* did have a short, blunt nasal horn.

Arrhinoceratops had a short, deep, wide face with large nostrils. Its two brow horns were moderately long, very pointed, and curved forward. The neck frill was broad with small, oval fenestrae (openings), and was rounded. Much of the skull of *Arrhinoceratops* was slightly crushed and dis-

torted, making it difficult to understand the pattern of the skull bones. Paleontologists don't know what the rest of its body looked like.

Arrhinoceratops lived at the same time as its close relative *Anchiceratops.* It was also closely related to *Torosaurus, Chasmosaurus, Pentaceratops,* and *Triceratops.*

Arrhinoceratops brachyops

Arrhinoceratops brachyops *skull.*

These duckbilled dinosaurs, named Saurolophus, *enjoy the shade and water on a warm Late Cretaceous day.*

Aublysodon

AVACERATOPS
(AYV-ah-SAIR-ah-tops)

Period:
Late Cretaceous
Order, Suborder, Family:
Ornithischia, Marginocephalia, Ceratopsidae
Location:
North America (United States)
Length:
7¹/₂ feet (2.3 meters)

Avaceratops lammersi was a small ceratopsid known from a single skeleton found in the Judith River Formation of Montana in 1981. The bones of *Avaceratops* were scattered in a fossil stream. After death, the animal was probably washed down the stream and buried in a sand bar. This little dinosaur was named by Peter Dodson, in honor of Ava Cole. Her husband Eddy found the skeleton. The species is named for the Lammers family, who own the ranch where *Avaceratops* was found. Its skeleton is on display at the Academy of Natural Sciences in Philadelphia.

Avaceratops was only about seven and a half feet long, and some paleontologists believe it may have been a juvenile. Others think it was an adult, and that *Avaceratops* may have been a small ceratopsid. Although only slightly larger than *Protoceratops*, *Avaceratops* appears to have had a moderately heavy build like its larger ceratopsid relatives. Unfortunately, many of the pieces of the skeleton are missing.

Avaceratops had a short, deep snout and a thick, powerful lower jaw. The neck frill appears to have been solid. Since the top of the skull is missing, it is not known what kind of horns it had, or if it had any. Most of its closest relatives, including *Centrosaurus, Styracosaurus,* and *Brachyceratops,* had a large nasal horn and no brow horns, so *Avaceratops* may have looked similar.

Because of its small size, *Avaceratops* probably ate low vegetation, which would have been mostly angiosperms (the flowering plants). Many other animals lived alongside *Avaceratops,* including hadrosaurs, pachycephalosaurs, ankylosaurs, hypsilophodontids, dromaeosaurs, crocodilians, turtles, champsosaurs, and small mammals.

AUBLYSODON
(oh-BLISS-oh-don)

Period:
Late Cretaceous
Order, Suborder, Family:
Saurischia, Theropoda, Unknown
Location:
North America (United States)
Length:
Unknown

This carnivorous dinosaur was named more than one hundred years ago for an unusual tooth found in the Judith River Badlands of northern Montana. When it was discovered, much of the West was still wild.

Since its discovery, many paleontologists have offered different opinions about the tooth. Most accept the genus *Aublysodon*, although reluctantly. The reason is that during the early days of paleontology, many names of dinosaurs were given to very scrappy material. Some have argued that the single tooth, although unusual, might belong to a dinosaur already known.

The mystery was finally solved recently when a partial skull was found in Montana. The skull shows a long, low snout and an unusual step in the lower jaw. Unfortunately, so little is known of this animal that we don't know its size or weight. We do know that *Aublysodon* was widespread; its unusual teeth have been found in many states.

Avaceratops

154

AVIMIMUS
(AYV-ee-MIME-us)

Period:
Late Cretaceous
Order, Suborder, Family:
Saurischia, Theropoda, Avimimidae
Location:
Asia (Mongolian People's Republic)
Length:
5 feet (1.5 meters)

Avimimus ("bird mimic") was a small, lightly built theropod from the Upper Cretaceous Djadokhta Formation of Mongolia. The original specimens were collected by Soviet scientists, and several partial skeletons and skulls have since been found. The most complete skeleton is a partial skull, vertebrae from the neck and back regions, an incomplete arm, most of both back legs and feet, and part of the pelvis.

The skull was short and birdlike; it was toothless and had a beak and a long neck. The bones that surrounded and protected the brain were large, showing it may have had a large brain. The hole in the back of the skull where the spinal cord was, called the foramen magnum, is very large for a dinosaur of this size. But the occipital condyle (the bump of bone on the back of the skull that connects the skull to the neck vertebrae) is very small, showing the skull was light for its size.

The ulna (the largest of the two forearm bones) had a ridge similar to rows of bumps on the ulna of modern birds. These bumps are where the quills of large flight feathers attach. Seriozha Kurzanov claimed that this is evidence that *Avimimus* had feathers. The original skeleton was missing a tail, which led Kurzanov to speculate that *Avimimus* did not have a tail. Since then, however, tail vertebrae have been found with other fossils. The back legs of *Avimimus* were long in relation to its thigh bones, showing it was a fast runner. Kurzanov believes that the many birdlike features in the skull and arm of *Avimimus* show it was capable of weak flight. This would have made it a feathered, flying theropod dinosaur that developed separately from true birds. Most paleontologists, however, do not agree.

Kurzanov thinks this animal fed mainly on insects. Others have suggested it was herbivorous. More information is needed to determine the exact nature of this unusual dinosaur, its habits, and its relationship to other dinosaurs.

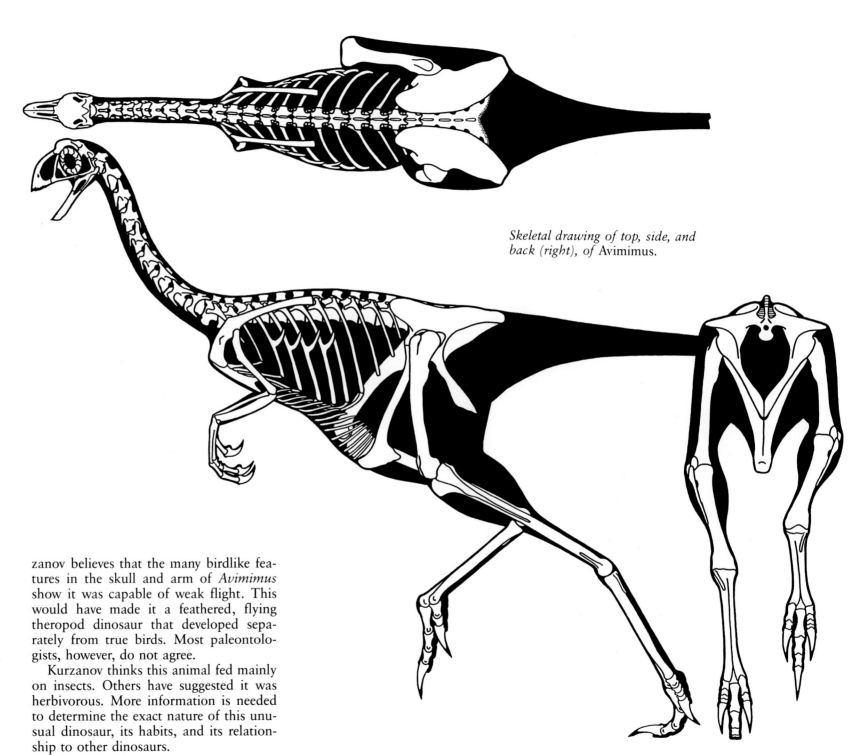

Skeletal drawing of top, side, and back (right), of Avimimus.

Bactrosaurus johnsoni

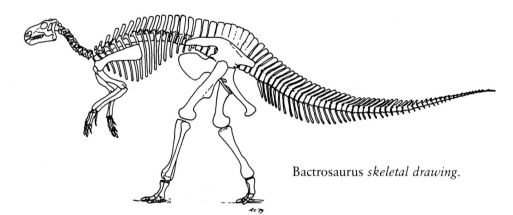

Bactrosaurus *skeletal drawing.*

BACTROSAURUS
(BACK-troh-SORE-us)

Period:
Late Cretaceous
Order, Suborder, Family:
Ornithischia, Ornithopoda,
Hadrosauridae
Location:
Asia (People's Republic of China)
Length:
20 feet (6 meters)

Very little is known about the earliest hadrosaurids (duckbilled dinosaurs). The best known of the earliest are *Gilmoreosaurus* and *Bactrosaurus* from the Inner Gobi Desert of the People's Republic of China. The rocks from which these two hadrosaurids were found are dated as early Late Cretaceous, but they may be somewhat later than that. Further research in the field and in the laboratory now being done in China, Canada, and the United States will provide more information.

Bactrosaurus ("reptile from Bactria") is known from many skull and skeletal pieces, but not a complete skeleton. Many of these bones are from juveniles and perhaps hatchlings, while others are from small adults. The pelvis, the limbs, and most of the important parts of the head, including the jaws with teeth, are known for *Bactrosaurus.*

For a long time, it was thought that *Bactrosaurus* was different from all other lambeosaurine hadrosaurids because it did not have a crest. That would have made it an unusual lambeosaurine. But recent work on both *Bactrosaurus* and *Gilmoreosaurus* has finally sorted out what bones go with which animal. This helped identify parts of the base of a crest—similar to the kind found on its close relative *Parasaurolophus.*

BAGACERATOPS
(BAG-ah-SAIR-ah-tops)

Period:
Late Cretaceous
Order, Suborder, Family:
Ornithischia, Marginocephalia,
Protoceratopsidae
Location:
Asia (Mongolian People's Republic)
Length:
5 feet (1.5 meters)

Bagaceratops rozhdestvenskyi was a small protoceratopsian with a big name: "baga" is the Mongolian word for "small," "ceratops" means "horned face," and the species name is in honor of Russian paleontologist A. K. Rozhdestvensky. *Baga-ceratops* was discovered in the Gobi Desert of Mongolia in the early 1970s by the Joint Polish-Mongolian Paleontological Expeditions. Specimens of *Bagaceratops* are at the Paleobiological Institute in Warsaw.

Bagaceratops was one of the smallest and most primitive of the known protoceratopsid dinosaurs. Very little is known about the skeleton of *Bagaceratops,* as only a few fragments were found. It was probably similar to that of *Protoceratops.* However, paleontologists did find partial to nearly complete skulls of both juveniles and adults. One of the tiny juvenile skulls is only about the size of a golf ball. The skull of *Bagaceratops* had a short, low snout that was topped by a nasal "boss," or bump, rather than a horn. The neck frill was triangular and very short, and it had

Bagaceratops rozhdestvenskyi

no openings (fenestrae). It had only ten grinding teeth in each jaw, and no teeth in its beak. One unusual feature of *Bagaceratops* was a large opening on each side of its snout.

Other animals that lived with *Bagaceratops* included the carnivorous dinosaurs *Velociraptor* and *Oviraptor,* as well as ankylosaurs, lizards, and small mammals.

BRACHYCERATOPS
(BRAK-ee-SAIR-ah-tops)

Period:
Late Cretaceous
Order, Suborder, Family:
Ornithischia, Marginocephalia, Ceratopsidae
Location:
North America (Canada, United States)
Length:
5 feet (1.5 meters)

Brachyceratops montanensis was found in 1913 by paleontologist Charles W. Gilmore on the Blackfeet Indian Reservation in Montana. He found parts of at least five animals of the same size, all jumbled together. In this mix of *Brachyceratops* bones was a single incomplete and disarticulated (not attached) skull. These fossils are now at the Smithsonian Institution. Although a few other bones of *Brachyceratops* have since been found, it remains a rare ceratopsian.

Because *Brachyceratops* was so small, and the skull Gilmore found was in pieces, many paleontologists believe that these *Brachyceratops* specimens were juveniles. Some paleontologists thought that *Brachyceratops* might be a young *Monoclonius,*

but this has not been proven. It is probable that *Brachyceratops* is a separate genus. Gilmore's discovery of these five small animals together is very unusual. If these animals were juveniles, as seems likely, they may have been nest mates.

Brachyceratops had a low, thick nasal horn; small bumps over the eyes (but no real brow horns); and a moderate-size neck frill. Since some pieces of the frill are missing, it isn't known if it was fenestrated (had openings). Since it may have been a juvenile, we don't know how large it may have been as an adult. *Brachyceratops* was a centrosaurine ceratopsid; its closest relatives were *Avaceratops, Centrosaurus, Monoclonius, Styracosaurus,* and *Pachyrhinosaurus.*

BRACHYLOPHOSAURUS
(BRAK-ee-LOAF-oh-SORE-us)

Period:
Late Cretaceous
Order, Suborder, Family:
Ornithischia, Ornithopoda, Hadrosauridae
Location:
North America (Canada, United States)
Length:
30 feet (9 meters)

One of the most unusual duckbilled dinosaurs in the Late Cretaceous was *Brachylophosaurus* ("short-ridged reptile"). This hadrosaurid was discovered and named by Charles Sternberg of Ottawa, Canada, in 1953. In some ways it was similar to other hadrosaurids; it had many functional and replacement teeth and a flaring, ducklike snout. But *Brachylophosaurus* had a broad, flat, shieldlike crest on top of its head, directly above its eyes. This bony crest is unlike any other crest of any hadrosaurid.

Most crests of hadrosaurids, from simple arches and bumps seen in hadrosaurines to the elaborate hollow crests found in lambeosaurines, may be related to how the animal behaved. They might have been used in contests of strength to defend territory or females, or used for display to avoid contests of strength. *Brachylophosaurus* seems to have engaged in head-to-head pushing matches or outright butting. This behavior fits with what is known about other hadrosaurids.

The upper beak of *Brachylophosaurus* was larger and broader than in other duckbilled dinosaurs that lived at the same time. The upper beak also turned down where the horny covering was attached. The lower jaw had a predentary bone that was covered by a horny beak. Like other large ornithopods, it used this horny beak to nip foliage from low-standing boughs and shrubs.

Brachyceratops

©'85 Walters

Brachylophosaurus canadensis

Brachylophosaurus had many teeth behind its beak for chewing plant food. Like other hadrosaurids (and many ornithopods), chewing was done by an unusual movement of the upper jaws with the large jaw muscles at the back of the skull. When the upper and lower teeth came into contact, the upper jaw moved slightly to the side to allow the teeth to move past one another. In this way, these hadrosaurids were able to chew with a sideways motion, somewhat similar to how cows and horses chew. Muscular cheeks kept food from spilling out of the sides of the mouth.

Brachylophosaurus had very long arms; the reason for this is not known. They were not as long in its relatives *Maiasaura* or *Prosaurolophus*.

CENTROSAURUS
(SEN-troh-SORE-us)

Period:
Late Cretaceous
Order, Suborder, Family:
Ornithischia, Marginocephalia, Ceratopsidae
Location:
North America (Canada)
Length:
17 feet (5 meters)

Centrosaurus, which means "sharp-point reptile," was named by Lawrence Lambe in 1902 from specimens found along the Red Deer River in Alberta. A number of complete skulls and skeletons have since been discovered. An entire *Centrosaurus* herd, ranging in size from juveniles to old adults, was found in a fossil river bed in Dinosaur Provincial Park in southern Alberta. Paleontologists think this herd may have drowned while crossing a flood-swollen river.

Centrosaurus resembled its close relative *Monoclonius. Centrosaurus* had a long, pointed nasal horn; small bumps over its eyes instead of brow horns; and a short, rounded neck frill with moderately large fenestrae (openings). *Monoclonius* and *Centrosaurus* lived at the same time and in the same places. Because they looked alike and because of the poor quality of most *Monoclonius* specimens, *Centrosaurus* and *Monoclonius* have been confused with each other or even considered the same dinosaur. Recent studies have confirmed that they are separate dinosaurs. Part of the proof is the unique paired processes (a hornlike growth) that grew out of the back of the frill of *Centrosaurus.* One pair of processes were long, grooved, banana-shaped tongues of bone that curved forward and down over the fenestrae. A second pair grew backward and curved toward each other.

Other close relatives of *Centrosaurus* included *Styracosaurus, Pachyrhinosaurus, Brachyceratops,* and *Avaceratops.*

CHASMOSAURUS
(KAZ-moh-SORE-us)

Period:
Late Cretaceous
Order, Suborder, Family:
Ornithischia, Marginocephalia, Ceratopsidae
Location:
North America (Canada)
Length:
17 feet (5 meters)

The first *Chasmosaurus* fossil found was part of the neck frill. It was unearthed in 1898 by Lawrence Lambe along the Red Deer River, Alberta. Lambe first thought it belonged to the genus *Monoclonius,* so he named it *Monoclonius belli.* Later, in 1914 after a more complete skull had been found by Charles Sternberg, Lambe realized that his original find was a new ceratopsian and renamed it *Chasmosaurus belli.*

Chasmosaurus had a very long frill with enormous fenestrae (openings) on its surface. The outline of the frill is indented, making it look heart-shaped when seen from above. It is the enormous, or "cavernous," fenestrae for which this dinosaur is named; its name means "chasm reptile."

Skull of Centrosaurus apertus.

Right: *Dromaeosaurs taking advantage of a herd of dead centrosaurs.*

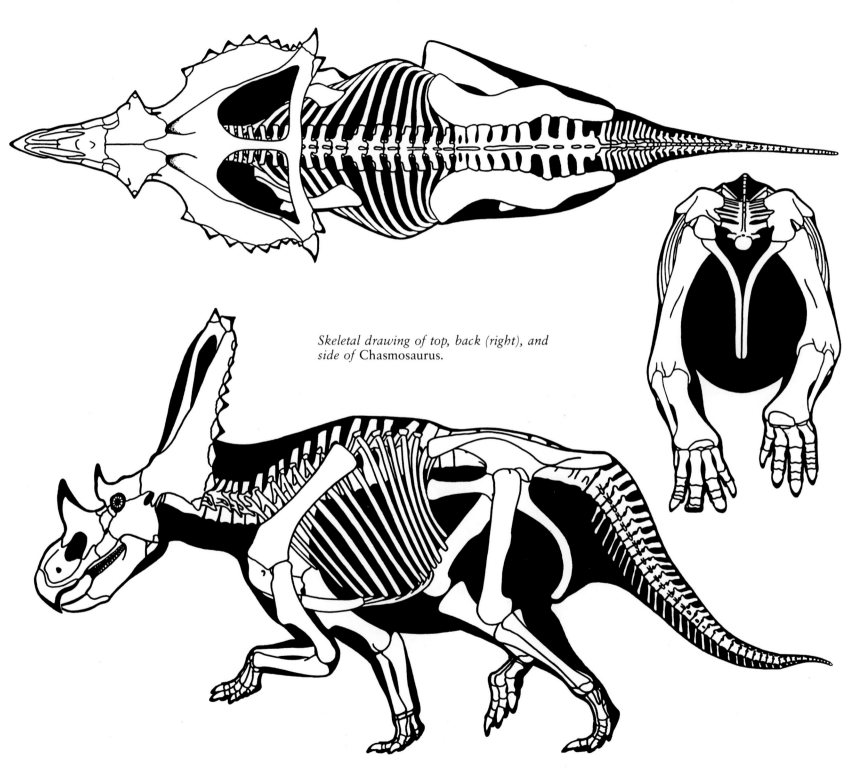

Chasmosaurus had a short nasal horn and brow horns that were different lengths; some species had long brow horns while others had short ones. One speciman collected by Sternberg had impressions of Chasmosaurus skin. These impressions show that the rough skin of Chasmosaurus had large, circular tubercles (or bumps) in regularly spaced rows, with many smaller tubercles between them.

Chasmosaurus was most closely related to Anchiceratops, Arrhinoceratops, Torosaurus, Triceratops, and Pentaceratops. Chasmosaurus was probably the oldest and the smallest of all chasmosaurine ceratopsians.

Skeletal drawing of top, back (right), and side of Chasmosaurus.

Chasmosaurus *skull, as a fossil (top), showing muscles (middle), and as it looked in life (bottom).*

Left: *The scavenger* Dromaeosaurus *finds a carcass of* Chasmosaurus.

163

CONCHORAPTOR
(CONK-oh-RAP-tor)

Period:
Late Cretaceous
Order, Suborder, Family:
Saurischia, Theropoda,
Oviraptoridae
Location:
Asia (Mongolian People's Republic)
Length:
4-6 feet (1-2 meters)

The oviraptorids were peculiar theropods. Smallish, bipedal (they walked on two legs) animals with strong beaks, they may have fed on mollusks by crushing their shells to get the soft meat inside. For many years, only one oviraptorid, *Oviraptor philoceratops*, was known. Paleontologists classified it as an ornithomimid because its skull was toothless. More oviraptorid specimens were discovered in the 1970s. These have been examined and descriptions were published of two new animals: *Oviraptor mongoliensis* and *Conchoraptor gracilis*. The name of the latter species means "slender conch-stealer." Most scientists keep the oviraptorids in their own family, separate from the "ostrich dinosaurs."

Conchoraptor was a smaller animal than its relative *Oviraptor*. The head of *Oviraptor* was decorated with bony crests, but *Conchoraptor* had no decoration. At first, it was thought that *Conchoraptor* was a juvenile *Oviraptor* and that the cranial crest developed at the beginning of sexual maturity. Further study of more skeletons—especially the hands—showed that *Conchoraptor* was a different genus. Its hands seem to be a transitional form, or "missing link," between *Oviraptor* and the oviraptoridlike small theropod *Ingenia*. *Conchoraptor* was found in the Nemegt Formation of Mongolia.

Conchoraptor gracilis

164

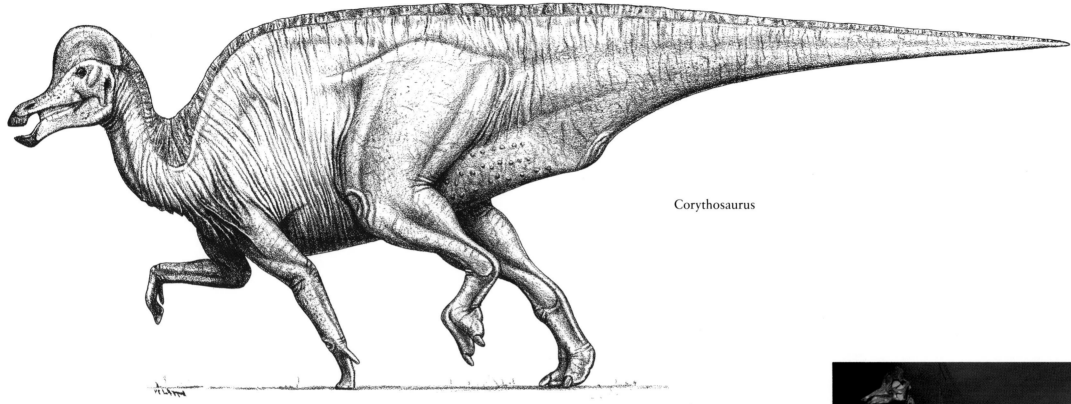

Corythosaurus

CORYTHOSAURUS
(coh-RITH-oh-SORE-us)

Period:
Late Cretaceous
Order, Suborder, Family:
Ornithischia, Ornithopoda,
Hadrosauridae
Location:
North America (Canada, United States)
Length:
33 feet (10 meters)

Corythosaurus, the "corinthian helmet reptile," was one of the most abundant duckbilled dinosaurs from the Late Cretaceous of western North America. Originally found and named by Barnum Brown of the American Museum of Natural History, *Corythosaurus* is also one of the best known of all dinosaurs. Many skeletons of this animal have been found. They ranged from small juveniles to large adults. Some skeletons were fully articulated (attached) with complete skulls, and some skeletons were disarticulated material. Others were partial "mummies" with skin impressions around the body (including impressions of a horny bill), and some specimens still had the small middle ear elements in place. *Corythosaurus* was a remarkable dinosaur.

It had a hollow crest on top of its head above its eyes; this is often considered the most striking aspect of this animal. Its lambeosaurine relatives *Lambeosaurus, Hypacrosaurus,* and *Parasaurolophus* also had crests. The crest, which had different shapes and sizes in males and females and developed only in mature adults, contained the nasal cavity. When *Corythosaurus* breathed, air entered the nostrils. It then went up into the chambers of the crest, into large side pockets, and then to a common chamber in the center of the crest. From there, air traveled down to the back of the throat and into the wind pipe to the lungs.

Returning air took the opposite course. So did sounds that the animal may have made. In fact, it looks like the crest would have made an excellent resonator, like a wind or brass musical instrument. It would have made very low sounds. Scientists think that *Corythosaurus* would have used these low trumpeting notes to make calls to each other or to offspring. But the young, like young alligators today, would have chirped more highly pitched sounds to their parents. Perhaps these calls would have been about food or water, or danger (a tyrannosaur, for instance) in the area.

Corythosaurus skeleton at the Royal Ontario Museum.

165

The duckbilled
dinosaur
Edmontosaurus
wades through a
swamp searching for
food. The duckbilled
dinosaurs had the
most efficient jaws
for chewing plants,
and they became the
most successful
plant-eaters.

167

Daspletosaurus *skeleton at the National Museum in Canada.*

DEINOCHEIRUS
(DINE-oh-KEE-rus)

Period:
Late Cretaceous
Order, Suborder, Family:
Saurischia, Theropoda, Ornithomimidae
Location:
Asia (Mongolian People's Republic)
Length:
Unknown

Deinocheirus ("horrible hand") is a fascinating animal. Its front arms and three-fingered hands are nearly eight feet long. Unfortunately only the shoulder blades, arm bones, hands, and a few pieces of ribs and vertebrae of this animal have been found. These were collected in the Late Cretaceous Nemegt Basin of Mongolia by paleontologists from Poland and Mongolia in 1965. No other fossils have been found.

The size of this specimen is its most amazing feature. The upper arm bone (humerus) is over three feet long. The fingers were not equal in length and each ended in a large claw. The fingers could not move as much as in most other theropods.

Originally *Deinocheirus* was placed in its own family, the Deinocheiridae. But because its arms and hands are similar to the members of Ornithomimidae, *Deinocheirus* is now placed in this family. At least one theropod, *Therezinosaurus,* had even larger hands and claws; its claws were about three times larger than those of *Deinocheirus.*

DASPLETOSAURUS
(das-PLEE-toh-SORE-us)

Period:
Late Cretaceous
Order, Suborder, Family:
Saurischia, Theropoda, Tyrannosauridae
Location:
North America (Canada)
Length:
30 feet (9 meters)

With its massive head and large teeth, there is no question that *Daspletosaurus* was master of its world. It got its name because of its ferociousness; its name means "frightful reptile." It had a huge body balanced upon two powerful back legs. The three-toed taloned feet (much like those of a modern bird) probably held the prey down while it ate. Like all tyrannosaurids, the front limbs were short and had only two fingers each.

Daspletosaurus lived at the same time as *Albertosaurus.* How two large meat-eating dinosaurs could have lived side-by-side is a mystery. Perhaps it was much like the African lion and the cheetah living together in East Africa today. These two cats have different methods of hunting, and they prey on different animals. The lion relies on stealth to get close to its prey (gnu, zebra, etc.), and the slender, fast cheetah runs down its prey. It is possible that *Daspletosaurus,* with its massive head and body, might have stalked the ceratopsians, while the more slender, quick *Albertosaurus* might have run down hadrosaurs. *Daspletosaurus* and ceratopsians are less common than *Albertosaurus* and hadrosaurs in the badlands of Alberta.

A pair of Daspletosaurus.

Right: Daspletosaurus

Denversaurus schlessmani

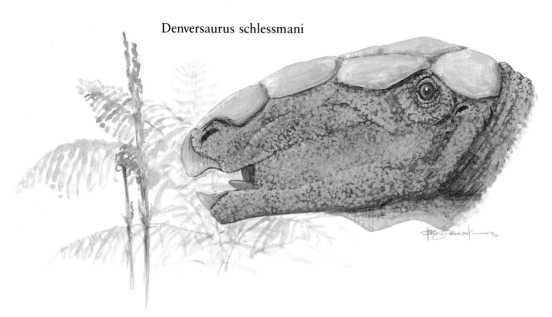

DENVERSAURUS
(DEN-ver-SORE-us)

Period:
Late Cretaceous
Order, Suborder, Family:
Ornithischia, Thyreophora,
Nodosauridae
Location:
North America (United States)
Length:
Unknown

A recently named armored dinosaur, *Denversaurus* is based on a badly crushed skull from South Dakota. No other parts of the skeleton have been found, so it is difficult to estimate how long or heavy the animal was.

Denversaurus, along with *Ankylosaurus,* was found in the lower part of the Hell Creek Formation. *Tyrannosaurus* and *Triceratops* were also found in this formation. But unlike these animals, both ankylosaurs were only in the lower part of the formation. This suggests that some ankylosaurs became extinct long before the end of the Cretaceous. It is not known what

caused their extinction, but it seems to be at the same time a number of other dinosaurs became less abundant.

The skull of *Denversaurus* is very large, and fusion (joining) of the bones may mean it was very old. It is possible that *Denversaurus* is actually an old nodosaurid ankylosaur *Edmontonia.* Few paleontologists believe *Denversaurus* is a valid genus.

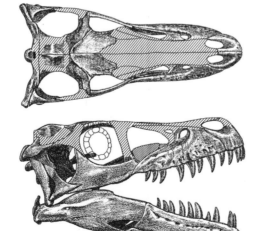

Top and side view of Dromaeosaurus *skull drawing.*

DROMAEOSAURUS
(DROH-may-oh-SORE-us)

Period:
Late Cretaceous
Order, Suborder, Family:
Saurischia, Theropoda, Dromaeosauridae
Location:
North America (Canada, United States)
Length:
6 feet (1.8 meters)

In 1914, Barnum Brown of the American Museum of Natural History collected a nine-inch-long skull and some foot bones from the Judith River Formation in Alberta. It was named *Dromaeosaurus,* which means "running reptile." After that, the genus was often referred to in various publications even though very little was known about it.

In 1969, the skull and foot bones were redescribed. In the process, some important similarities between it and the *Deinonychus* were noticed. Both *Dromaeosaurus* and *Deinonychus* were small theropods with large skulls. Their skulls are similar, and both genera had large sicklelike claws on the second toe of the foot. *Dromaeosaurus* and *Deinonychus* are now placed in the same family, Dromaeosauridae. Other members of this family include *Velociraptor* and *Hulsanpes.*

Not much is known about *Dromaeosaurus* because the only specimen is incomplete. Teeth that may belong to it have been found in several western states and Alberta, but they only tell us that the animal lived in these areas. This was a rare theropod, or at least it was rarely preserved. Scientists are hoping better specimens will be found.

Two small dromaeosaurs attacking a much larger plant-eater.

Dromaeosaurus albertensis

DROMICEIOMIMUS
(droh-MEE-see-oh-MY-mus)

Period:
Late Cretaceous
Order, Suborder, Family:
Saurischia, Theropoda, Ornithomimidae
Location:
North America (Canada)
Length:
12 feet (3.5 meters)

Dromiceiomimus ("emu mimic") has been found both in the Late Cretaceous Horseshoe Canyon and the Judith River Formation of Alberta. It is very similar to *Struthiomimus* and *Ornithomimus,* but had much larger eyes and longer, more slender arms. Also, some of the hip bones were positioned differently.

As in all ornithomimids, the brain of *Dromiceiomimus* was quite large. A large brain does not mean the animal was intelligent. For example, the ostrich and emu also have relatively large brains; they are not very intelligent, but they have very good vision. The enlarged portions of the

brain probably were to coordinate body and limb actions. *Dromiceiomimus* was probably omnivorous; it probably ate fruits, large insects, and small lizards and mammals.

It had birdlike jaws that had no teeth. Another birdlike feature was hollow bones. With its long legs, it ran swiftly.

DRYPTOSAURUS
(DRIP-toh-SORE-us)

Period:
Late Cretaceous
Order, Suborder, Family:
Saurischia, Theropoda, Unknown
Location:
North America (United States)
Length:
18 feet (5.5 meters)

Dryptosaurus is the only carnivorous dinosaur from the East Coast of the United States based on more than a single bone. The partial skeleton was discovered more than a hundred years ago by workers in a

Left: *Male and female* Dryptosaurus. Right: *A fossil claw of* Dryptosaurus.

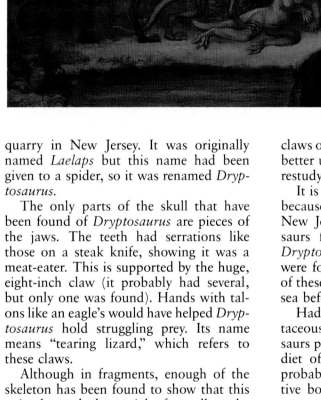

A painting done by Waterhouse Hawkins in 1877 of two dryptosaurs attacking a Hadrosaurus, *with* Mosasaurus *in front.*

quarry in New Jersey. It was originally named *Laelaps* but this name had been given to a spider, so it was renamed *Dryptosaurus.*

The only parts of the skull that have been found of *Dryptosaurus* are pieces of the jaws. The teeth had serrations like those on a steak knife, showing it was a meat-eater. This is supported by the huge, eight-inch claw (it probably had several, but only one was found). Hands with talons like an eagle's would have helped *Dryptosaurus* hold struggling prey. Its name means "tearing lizard," which refers to these claws.

Although in fragments, enough of the skeleton has been found to show that this animal stood about eight feet tall at the hips. The back legs were much longer than the front, so *Dryptosaurus* probably walked on its back legs with its tail acting as a balance.

Dryptosaurus is a puzzle because its relationship to other carnivorous dinosaurs is not known. Although it looked somewhat like a tyrannosaur, it had longer limbs for its size and larger, more curved

claws on its hands. Scientists hope it will be better understood when they have finished restudying the skeleton.

It is not certain what *Dryptosaurus* ate, because the fossil record for dinosaurs in New Jersey is very incomplete. All dinosaurs from New Jersey, including both *Dryptosaurus* and the older *Hadrosaurus,* were found in marine rocks. The remains of these dinosaurs must have drifted out to sea before becoming fossilized.

Hadrosaur bones are in many Late Cretaceous formations in the area, so hadrosaurs probably made up a large part of the diet of *Dryptosaurus.* Ceratopsians were probably not present (none of their distinctive bones have been found), so *Dryptosaurus* did not have to dodge the horns of an angry ceratopsian. Only isolated bone armor plates have been found from nodosaurid ankylosaurs. The body armor of ankylosaurs would have made it difficult for *Dryptosaurus* to kill the animal, but it is possible that *Dryptosaurus* scavenged an already dead body. *Dryptosaurus* may have been like the African lion that feeds on a carcass rather than chasing an antelope.

173

Edmontonia rugosidens

EDMONTONIA
(ed-mon-TONE-ee-uh)

Period:
Late Cretaceous
Order, Suborder, Family:
Ornithischia, Thyreophora,
Nodosauridae
Location:
North America (Canada, United States)
Length:
22 feet (6.6 meters)

Edmontonia would not have made an easy meal for a hungry tyrannosaur. It had a heavily armored body and large, forward-pointing shoulder spines. We know what *Edmontonia* looked like because two specimens were found with their armor and spikes preserved in the position they had in life. The bodies of these specimens may have dried out because of a drought and then been quickly covered by sediment when the rainy season began. Evidence for these changes in the climate is found in the growth rings of fossil wood.

Edmontonia walked on four legs and was a plant-eater. It had a pear-shaped skull (when viewed from the top). The neck and part of the back were protected by large, flat, keeled (ridged) plates. Smaller keeled plates covered the back, hips, and tail. Spines and large spikes along its sides would have made the animal look short and wide when viewed from the front. This made it look more menacing to an enemy.

An *Albertosaurus* was not the only animal it needed to protect itself from. A male *Edmontonia* probably fought with other males for territory and females. The larger males may have used their large shoulder spines for shoving contests. The spines of *Edmontonia* would have been dangerous to rival males or to an *Albertosaurus* or *Daspletosaurus,* if they got too close.

174

Edmontosaurus *skeletal drawing.*

EDMONTOSAURUS
(ed-MON-toh-SORE-us)

Period:
Late Cretaceous
Order, Suborder, Family:
Ornithischia, Ornithopoda,
Hadrosauridae
Location:
North America (Canada, United States)
Length:
42 feet (13 meters)

Edmontosaurus was one of the largest hadrosaurids. This flat-headed duckbilled dinosaur was originally found, described, and named by Lawrence Lambe in 1920. It was one of the last dinosaurs, surviving to the end of the Mesozoic Era along with *Tyrannosaurus* and *Triceratops*.

Like all hadrosaurids, *Edmontosaurus* had a broad snout, long jaws, and large eyes. The snout probably had a horny covering that closed against the horny covering of the lower jaw. This was how the animal bit off leaves and branches from shrubs and low-lying boughs. To chew the food, the animal had many teeth behind its beak that were arranged in a grinding pattern. The teeth, plus the many replacement teeth (there were often a thousand or more in the jaws) formed what is called the dental battery. *Edmontosaurus,* and all other hadrosaurids, were able to move their jaws slightly side-to-side. This made them successful plant-eaters.

The nostrils of *Edmontosaurus* were large and hollow. They may have been covered with loose skin that the animal could have filled with air. When inflated, these bags may have been used to make loud bellowing sounds. Communication was probably important to this animal; it lived in large groups with both adults and offspring. These bags may also have been brightly colored for display to attract a mate or to help other animals from the same species recognize each other.

Edmontosaurus is responsible for the most spectacular of all dinosaur fossils. These are the famous hadrosaur "mummies." These skeletons were found with skin impressions around the head, shoulders, arms, legs, and tail. These impressions show the pattern of tubercles (bumps) that were found on the skin.

Edmontosaurus copei

Workers excavating Edmontosaurus *bones.*

175

The name *Edmontosaurus* means the "reptile from Edmonton," which is the capital of the Province of Alberta, where it was found. It was related to other flat-headed hadrosaurids, including *Shantungosaurus* from the People's Republic of China. It was not as closely related to the solid-crested hadrosaurids, such as *Saurolophus* and *Prosaurolophus,* which lived in the same areas as *Edmontosaurus.* After much study, *Anatosaurus* has been found to be the same animal as *Edmontosaurus,* which was its first and therefore correct name.

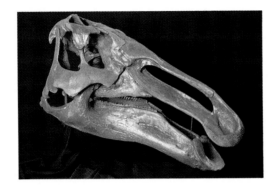

Fossil skull of Edmontosaurus.

A woodland encounter between Daspletosaurus *and* Edmontosaurus *(front).*

ELMISAURUS
(ELM-ee-SORE-us)

Period:
Late Cretaceous
Order, Suborder, Family:
Saurischia, Theropoda, Elmisauridae
Location:
Asia (Mongolian People's Republic),
North America (Canada)
Length:
6–10 feet (1.8–3 meters)

The Joint Polish-Mongolian Paleontological Expeditions of the 1960s produced many new kinds of dinosaurs, many of which were small theropods. Because small dinosaur skeletons were delicate, they were rarely fossilized. One new theropod was named *Elmisaurus.* Its name comes from the Mongolian word *elmyi,* which means beautiful.

In 1981, Halszka Osmólska described the unusual foot bones of *Elmisaurus.* Because these bones were different from other small theropods, she placed it in its own family, the Elmisauridae. This was the only known member of Elmisauridae, but recently the partial skeleton of the small theropod *Chirostenotes pergracilis* from Alberta was described. After the foot bones of *Elmisaurus* and *Chirostenotes* were compared, it was found that *Chirostenotes* was a North American member of

the same family. *Ornithomimus elegans,* also from North America, may be a second species of *Elmisaurus. Elmisaurus* is one of a few Late Cretaceous animals that had both Asian and North American species.

ERLIKOSAURUS
(AIR-lick-oh-SORE-us)

Period:
Late Cretaceous
Order, Suborder, Family:
Saurischia, Segnosauria, Segnosauridae
Location:
Asia (Mongolian People's Republic)
Length:
20 feet (6 meters)

In 1980, Altangerel Perle named *Erlikosaurus andrewsi* after the demon Erlik from Mongolian mythology and paleontologist Roy Chapman Andrews. It was closely related to *Segnosaurus. Erlikosaurus* is the only segnosaurian that was found with a skull, making it a very important segnosaurian. Unfortunately, little of the skeleton was discovered.

The bones of its foot were more slender than those of *Segnosaurus. Erlikosaurus* may have been a smaller, more lightly built animal. The front of the snout was toothless, and the skull bones show that *Erlikosaurus*—and possibly other seg-

Erlikosaurus *skeletal drawing.*

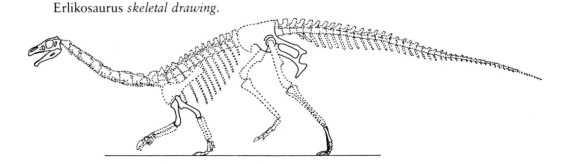

nosaurians—had a horny beak for cropping plants.

The teeth of *Erlikosaurus* show it was a plant-eater. How it used the large, thin, slender claws on its feet is a mystery; perhaps they were useful when the animal waded across rivers.

The segnosaurian *Enigmosaurus mongoliensis* is known only from part of a pelvis; it was found in the same formation as *Erlikosaurus*. Because *Segnosaurus* was closely related to *Erlikosaurus,* scientists think that the pelvis of *Erlikosaurus* was similar to that of *Segnosaurus*. The pelvis of *Enigmosaurus* was very different from the pelvis of *Segnosaurus,* so paleontologist Rinchen Barsbold did not think that it belonged to *Erlikosaurus*. Mongolian dinosaurs are full of surprises, however, and scientists may find that *Erlikosaurus* and *Enigmosaurus* are the same animal.

Erlikosaurus andrewsi

177

Top: Euoplocephalus tutus. Right: Euoplocephalus *skeletal drawing.*

EUOPLOCEPHALUS
(yoo-op-loh-SEF-uh-lus)

Period:
Late Cretaceous
Order, Suborder, Family:
Ornithischia, Thyreophora,
Ankylosauridae
Location:
North America (Canada, United States)
Length:
20 feet (6 meters)

Euoplocephalus lived at the same time and in the same areas as *Edmontonia*. *Euoplocephalus* roamed the forests cropping low plants with its broad beak. It probably ate any type of plant it came across. It used its very small teeth to chew food.

Scientists do not know exactly what *Euoplocephalus* looked like in life because no specimen has been found with the armor preserved in its natural position. We do know that the head and body were well armored; this armor was joined to its head. Even the eyes were protected with bone eyelids. This is how it got its name, which means "well-armored head."

Though scientists do not know the exact arrangement, they do know it did have bands of armor on its back with large spikes protecting its neck and the base of its tail. It probably had smaller spikes all along its back. As in all ankylosaurids, it had a tail club that it used as a weapon.

In a world with dangerous predators, a large, slow-moving animal needed ways to protect itself. All ankylosaurs had body armor. But *Euoplocephalus* may also have had a good sense of smell. The air passage

in the nostrils was looped, so many sensory nerves for smell were probably present. It probably picked up the scent of a predator before it was seen. These looped passages also may have been used to make a bugling noise so *Euoplocephalus* could communicate with other members of its species.

Euoplocephalus was closely related to the other ankylosaurs, including *Talarurus, Saichania,* and *Ankylosaurus.* Some ankylosaurs survived until the very end of the Cretaceous Period.

GALLIMIMUS
(GAL-lee-MIME-us)

Period:
Late Cretaceous
Order, Suborder, Family:
Saurischia, Theropoda, Ornithomimidae
Location:
Asia (Mongolian People's Republic)
Length:
17 feet (5 meters)

Gallimimus ("chicken mimic") was the largest of the ornithomimids (the "ostrich dinosaurs") known. It has been found only in the Late Cretaceous Nemegt Formation of Mongolia. Its form and lifestyle were not very different from its North American relatives *Struthiomimus* and *Ornithomimus.* However, its back limbs were shorter, its toothless skull was much longer, and its hands were smaller when compared to other members of the ornithomimid family. Several juveniles of this species have been found in addition to the giant one.

Gallimimus could not use its hands to grasp, so it may have used them to dig in the ground for food. It is also possible it fed on eggs. It probably ate mostly plants and may have also eaten insects if it could catch them. Like all theropods, it walked on its two back legs (bipedal).

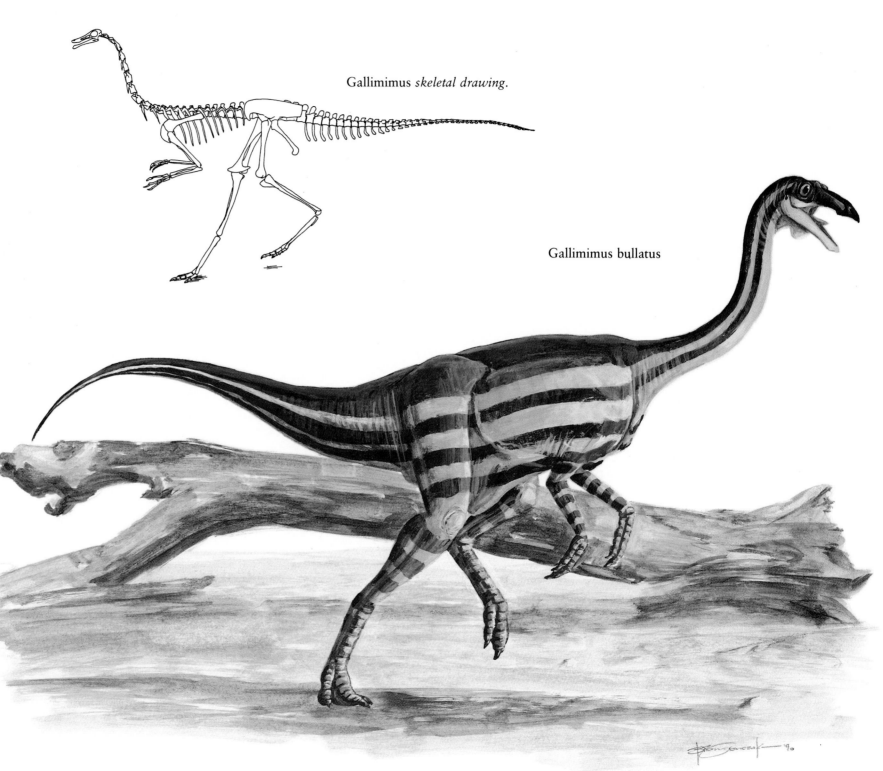

Gallimimus *skeletal drawing.*

Gallimimus bullatus

The duckbilled
dinosaur
Hypacrosaurus *enjoys
some angiosperms
(flowering plants),
which had evolved in
the Early Cretaceous.*

181

GARUDIMIMUS
(gah-ROO-dee-MIME-us)

Period:
Late Cretaceous
Order, Suborder, Family:
Saurischia, Theropoda, Ornithomimidae
Location:
Asia (Mongolian People's Republic)
Length:
12 feet (3.6 meters)

Garudimimus brevipes was one of many dinosaurs found by the Joint Soviet-Mongolian Paleontological Expeditions of the 1970s. It was named for the Garuda bird of Hindu mythology; its name means "short-footed Garuda mimic."

It was a primitive ornithomimid. Although its toothless skull looked like those of the other ornithomimids, it had a short, hornlike crest on top of its muzzle. The pelvis and feet of *Garudimimus* were not as adapted for running as those of its later relatives. Its foot still had a small first toe; this toe was gone in later ornithomimids. *Garudimimus* was placed in its own family, Garudimimidae. But many paleontologists think *Garudimimus* should remain in the family Ornithomimidae.

Despite the differences from its later relatives, it still had many similarities. It was a bipedal (walked on two legs) plant-eater. Its hands were not able to grasp so it may have used them to dig for food.

In 1984, paleontologists described an earlier, even more primitive Mongolian ornithomimid, *Harpymimus okladnikovi*. All other ornithomimids were toothless, but *Harpymimus* had several very small teeth at the front of its snout, which the later ornithomimids did not have. Although they placed the animal in a new family, Harpymimidae, it too probably belongs in the family Ornithomimidae. Because of these two primitive ornithomimids, Mongolia has become an important area for studying the origins of this theropod family.

Drawing of the top of a Garudimimus brevipes *skull.*

Garudimimus brevipes

GOYOCEPHALE
(GOY-oh-cee-FAL-ee)

Period:
Late Cretaceous
Order, Suborder, Family:
Ornithischia, Marginocephalia,
Homalocephalidae
Location:
Asia (Mongolian People's Republic)
Length:
Unknown, but probably no more than
6¹/₂ feet (2 meters)

The flat-headed *Goyocephale* was one of the most unusual pachycephalosaurs. It was found by the Joint Polish-Mongolian Paleontological Expeditions to the Gobi Desert, and was named and described in 1982.

Few pachycephalosaurs are known from more than a skull, but some bones of the skeleton of *Goyocephale* were also found, including the tail and front and back limbs. The skeleton, although poorly preserved, shows that *Goyocephale* was built much like other pachycephalosaurs. The limbs were lightly built, and the backbone was reinforced by ossified (bony) tendons along the spines of the vertebrae (back bones). This strengthened the spinal cord and probably helped reduce stress during head-butting contests. As the name *Goyocephale* ("decorated head") indicates, the skull roof

Goyocephale skeletal drawing.

was rough and pitted. Although flat-headed, *Goyocephale* probably had head-butting contests in which males fought for females and territory during breeding seasons. Also, the prominent, caninelike teeth that were in the front of both the upper and lower jaws probably were a display to scare other animals away. This kind of display was also found in some primitive deer (muntjacs) and the heterodontosaurid dinosaurs.

Goyocephale is one of the few known flat-headed pachycephalosaurs. Its relatives included *Homalocephale* and *Wannanosaurus,* both from the Late Cretaceous of central and eastern Asia.

Goyocephale lattimorei

HADROSAURUS
(HAD-roh-SORE-us)

Period:
Late Cretaceous
Order, Suborder, Family:
Ornithischia, Ornithopoda,
Hadrosauridae
Location:
North America (United States)
Length:
30 feet (9 meters)

Hadrosaurus ("thick reptile") was the first hadrosaur skeleton to be discovered. It was named and described in 1858 by Joseph Leidy, the father of American paleontology. Most of the skeleton was found in marine rocks of Late Cretaceous age in southern New Jersey near Philadelphia. It included many vertebrae, teeth, parts of the front and back limbs, and pelvis.

Hadrosaurus was the first dinosaur to have its skeleton mounted. Mounts of this dinosaur were displayed first at the Academy of Natural Sciences in Philadelphia. It was later displayed at Princeton, the Smithsonian, and at the Field-Columbia Museum in Chicago (now the Field Museum of Natural History).

Leidy was the first scientist to realize that plant-eating dinosaurs such as *Hadrosaurus* and *Iguanodon* did not resemble large, sprawling lizards. Instead they stood upright; Leidy thought they stood like kangaroos.

Hadrosaurus did stand on its back legs. Its front limbs were shorter than its legs. It

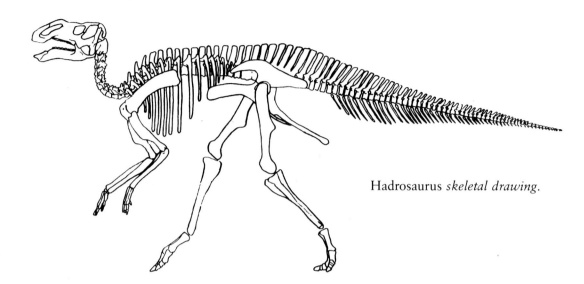

Hadrosaurus *skeletal drawing.*

probably had a horny beak for cropping plants and leaves, and behind its beak it had a complex tooth system for chewing.

For many years, scientists had little idea what *Hadrosaurus* looked like. The skull was not found with the rest of the skeleton. Recent studies have shown that it looked like the hook-nosed hadrosaurids such as *Gryposaurus* and the more poorly known *Kritosaurus*. Both of these animals had a deep, narrow face with a rounded arch above the nostrils (it is not known if *Hadrosaurus* had this arch). This arched snout was probably covered with thick skin and may have been used both as a display and as a fighting structure. If so, it may have been more prominent in males than in females.

These hook-nosed hadrosaurids were close relatives of *Hadrosaurus*. Because they are similar, they have often been confused. *Hadrosaurus* probably lived only in the eastern part of the United States. *Aralosaurus* from the Soviet Union was also a close relative of these hook-nosed duck-billed dinosaurs.

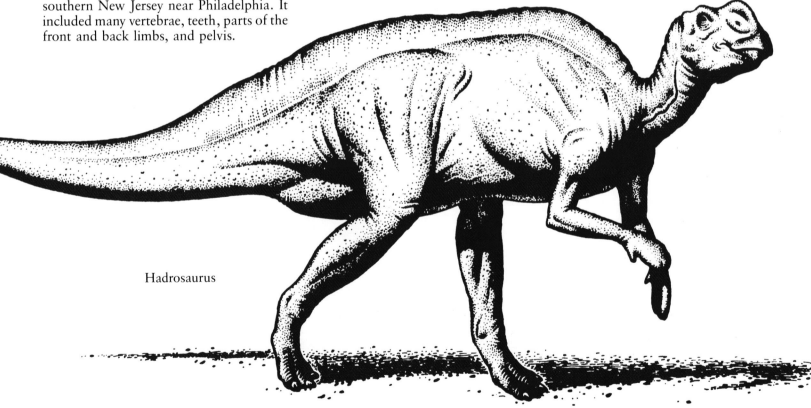

Hadrosaurus

©'85 Walters

HARPYMIMUS
(HAR-pee-MIME-us)

Period:
Late Cretaceous
Order, Suborder, Family:
Saurischia, Theropoda, Ornithomimidae
Location:
Asia (Mongolian People's Republic)
Length:
Estimated 3½ feet (1 meter)

Named after the flying mythical Greek creatures called Harpies that snatched victims with their hands, *Harpymimus* ("snatcher mimic") is the most primitive ornithomimid known. A single skeleton was found in southeastern Mongolia. The bones that were found include all of the neck, back, and pelvic vertebrae and parts of the arm, hand, foot, and lower jaw.

The lower jaw is important because, unlike other members of Ornithomimidae that had no teeth, *Harpymimus* had 10 to 11 very small teeth along each side of the front edge of the beak. The hand of *Harpymimus* is also important. The metacarpal bones of the hand (the long bones that form the palm) were different lengths; this feature is found in most theropods. The metacarpal bones of later Ornithomimids, however, were all the same length. Because of these differences, *Harpymimus* is sometimes put in its own family, Harpymimidae.

Harpymimus represents an advanced "missing-link" between theropods with teeth and grasping hands and the ornithomimids that had no teeth and stiff hands. These later ornithomimids probably used their hands to pull branches within reach of their bills rather than to grasp struggling prey.

Harpymimus okladnikovi

HOMALOCEPHALE
(HOME-ah-loh-SEF-ah-lee)

Period:
Late Cretaceous
Order, Suborder, Family:
Ornithischia, Marginocephalia,
Homalocephalidae
Location:
Asia (Mongolian People's Republic)
Length:
10 feet (3 meters)

As its name ("even head") suggests, *Ho-malocephale* had a flat head unlike most pachycephalosaurs. It is known from limited but very good material. The single skull of *Homalocephale* is missing the front of the snout but is otherwise complete. This skull proves that the animal was a flat, thick-headed reptile. The back of the skull was high and hung slightly over the neck. The sides of the skull were slightly thickened and expanded. The top of the skull, as well as the cheek region and back of the skull, had spikes, bumps, and ridges of bone. The large eye sockets probably mean that *Homalocephale*, like many other pachycephalosaurs, had good vision.

There is other information scientists can find from its skull. There was a large area for the olfactory nerve (the nerve used for smelling). The size of this area suggests that *Homalocephale* had a good sense of smell. This is useful for any animal in the wild; it could have smelled a nearby predator and escaped before the predator saw it.

The teeth of *Homalocephale* show wear; it did a lot of chewing. It probably was a browsing dinosaur, feeding mostly on leaves and probably not eating many fruits.

Perhaps the most important information comes from the skeleton of *Homalocephale*. *Stegoceras* and *Homalocephale* are the only pachycephalosaurs known from both skulls and skeletons. From the skeleton of *Homalocephale*, we know that the thorax, abdomen, and pelvic area were extremely broad, perhaps for a large gut that was needed to digest a diet of plants.

The anatomy of *Homalocephale* provides information about the behavior of this animal. The flat head and rear shelf of the back of the skull may have been for display. They also may have been for head-butting, where males had contests of strength to win females or territory. The spine would have been held horizontally; this would be expected if an animal used its head to butt. Modern big horn sheep use the same behavior when they protect their harem and defend their territory against competitors.

Other flat-headed pachycephalosaurs related to *Homalocephale* included *Wannanosaurus* from the People's Republic of China and *Goyocephale* from Mongolia.

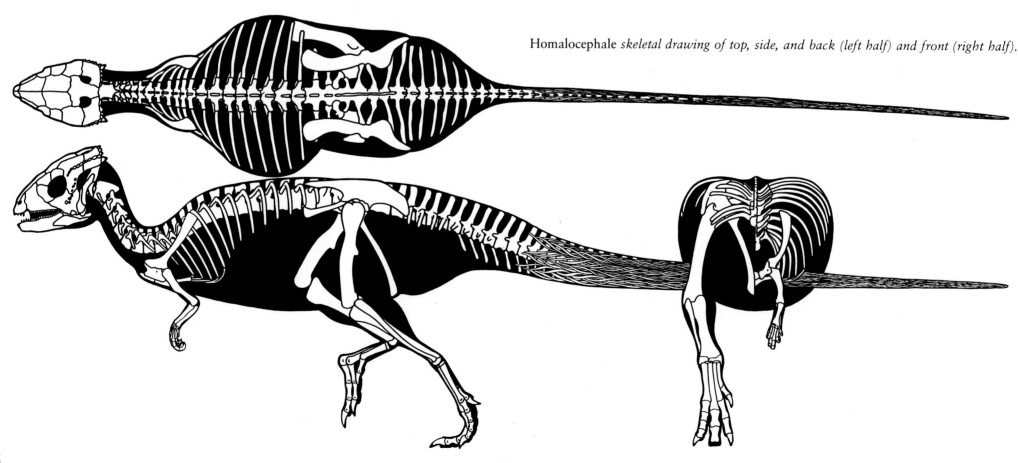

Homalocephale skeletal drawing of top, side, and back (left half) and front (right half).

Homalocephale calathocercos

Hypacrosaurus *muscle drawing*.

HYPACROSAURUS
(hy-PAK-roh-SORE-us)

Period:
Late Cretaceous
Order, Suborder, Family:
Ornithischia, Ornithopoda,
Hadrosauridae
Location:
North America (Canada, United States)
Length:
30 feet (9 meters)

The head of *Hypacrosaurus* looked much like *Corythosaurus*. The snout was somewhat ducklike, although the nostrils were in slightly different places. The crest of *Hypacrosaurus* was shaped like a corinthian helmet, but more pointed at the top. The back of the skull was also similar.

The striking differences between the two were in the skeleton, especially the backbone. *Corythosaurus* had moderate-size spines on its vertebrae (back bones). But *Hypacrosaurus* had very tall spines on its vertebrae. This is how it got its name, which means "high-spined reptile." These tall spines may have allowed for extra back muscles, but they also formed a sail. This sail would have captured the heat of the sun in the morning or released heat to cool the animal off on a hot day. In any case, these long spines would have made the animal look larger.

Like all other lambeosaurines, the crest of *Hypacrosaurus* contained a complex nasal cavity on top of its head. When it breathed, air was drawn in and out of the crest through a series of tubes and chambers that connected the nostrils to the back of the throat. The animal could also make sounds with its crest. Because of the size and shape of the crest, the sounds produced would have been low notes. It probably used these sounds to communicate with other members of its troupe or herd.

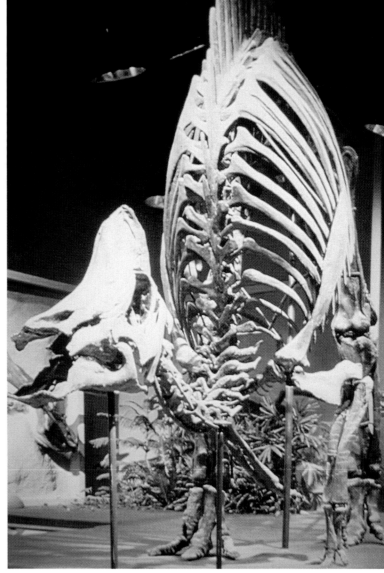

Hypacrosaurus *skeleton on display*.

KRITOSAURUS
(KRIT-oh-SORE-us)

Period:
Late Cretaceous
Order, Suborder, Family:
Ornithischia, Ornithopoda,
Hadrosauridae
Location:
North America (United States)
Length:
30 feet (9 meters)

Kritosaurus was a large, flat-headed duckbilled dinosaur. It had a ridge of bone between the eyes and the snout that gave it a distinguished "Roman nose" appearance. In other ways, *Kritosaurus* was similar to its relative *Hadrosaurus*. One of the largest hadrosaurs, *Kritosaurus* weighed up to three tons and stood around nine feet tall at the hips. The long, heavy tail gave this plant-eater balance when it walked on two legs (bipedal). Its rear feet had three large toes ending with blunt hooves like those of elephants. The front legs were small and seldom used for walking; the animal may have used them in gathering food or in preparing nests.

The skull of *Kritosaurus* was long and slender, with a broad, flat face that looked like the bill of a duck. The ridge of bone in front of the eyes may have increased the nasal cavity to improve its sense of smell, an unusual feature for a reptile.

Kritosaurus had hundreds of tightly packed grinding teeth for crushing the tough plants it ate. To gather food, it probably stood on its tall rear legs and used its heavy tail as the third leg of a tripod. It then could reach high into trees to gather leaves and branches.

Like other duckbills, *Kritosaurus* probably lived in herds and protected the young from giant predators such as *Tyrannosaurus* and *Albertosaurus*. *Kritosaurus* lived throughout western North America from Montana to New Mexico.

LAMBEOSAURUS
(LAM-bee-oh-SORE-us)

Period:
Late Cretaceous
Order, Suborder, Family:
Ornithischia, Ornithopoda,
Hadrosauridae
Location:
North America (Canada, United States, Mexico)
Length:
30 feet (9 meters)

Lambeosaurus lived at the end of the Late Cretaceous. It was a hollow-crested hadrosaurid that lived at the same time and in the same places as *Corythosaurus* and *Parasaurolophus*.

One species of *Lambeosaurus* that was common in Alberta had a crest that looked like a hatchet was embedded in the top of its head. The front part of this crest was stout and pointed forward and up from just above the eyes. The crest was hollow and connected to the nostrils. The nasal cavity went down the back of the throat into the lungs. It is this hollow portion of the crest that could produce low frequency sounds for communication between family members or within large herds. The second part of the crest was farther back on its head and solid. This backward projecting "prong" probably supported a frill of skin that went along the back of the animal to the tail. It seems only males had this prong; only half the skulls found had them.

Another species of *Lambeosaurus* was much rarer. Its crest was very large, flaring forward and upward from the top of the head. The solid prong that extended backward was probably smaller, but it may still have supported a frill of skin down the back of the animal.

The skeleton of *Lambeosaurus* was robust, with long, sturdy front and back legs. The tail was long and was held straight back when the animal walked. Because of the crests, paleontologists once thought *Lambeosaurus* and other hadrosaurids lived in water, using their crests as snorkels or for storing air. They may have gone into the water or enjoyed a swim, but all hadrosaurids lived on land.

The name *Lambeosaurus,* coined in 1923, means "Lambe's reptile" in honor of its discoverer Lawrence Lambe. Lambe described the first specimen of *Lambeosaurus* as *Stephanosaurus* in 1914; at that time he did not think it was a new genus. *Lambeosaurus* was closely related to *Corythosaurus* and *Hypacrosaurus*. Some scientists think that a giant 54-foot duckbill specimen found (fragments only) in Baja California may prove to be a species of *Lambeosaurus*.

A swimming Kritosaurus.

Leptoceratops

LEPTOCERATOPS
(LEP-toh-SAIR-ah-tops)

Period:
Late Cretaceous
Order, Suborder, Family:
Ornithischia, Marginocephalia,
Protoceratopsidae
Location:
North America (Canada, United States)
Length:
8 feet (2.4 meters)

Leptoceratops, the first known protoceratopsid, was found along the Red Deer
River of Alberta, Canada, in 1910. This
partial skull and skeleton was named *Leptoceratops gracilis.* It was the latest protoceratopsid, living through the end of the
Cretaceous Period along with the large ceratopsid dinosaurs *Triceratops* and *Torosaurus.*

Leptoceratops was a lightly built protoceratopsid (its name means "slender-
horned face") with long back limbs and
short front limbs. The feet had tapered
claws. *Leptoceratops* may have run bipedally (on two legs) or stood on its back legs
to feed on tall vegetation. The large skull
of *Leptoceratops* sloped down to a small,
pointed, toothless beak. It did not have nasal or brow horns. The neck frill was only
slightly developed and solid, and it had a
high, raised ridge down its midline.

More partial and complete skeletons
were discovered since the first was found. A
partial skeleton found in the St. Mary
River Formation of Montana in 1916 was
first thought to be a new species of *Leptoceratops;* but it is a new genus, so it was renamed *Montanaceratops cerorhynchus.*
Leptoceratops and *Montanaceratops* are
the only two known North American protoceratopsid dinosaurs.

Maiasaura *with young.*

MAIASAURA
(MY-ah-SORE-ah)

Period:
Late Cretaceous
Order, Suborder, Family:
Ornithischia, Ornithopoda,
Hadrosauridae
Location:
North America (United States)
Length:
30 feet (9 meters)

Since it was named in 1979 by John Horner and Robert Makela, *Maiasaura* has become one of the most famous dinosaurs. It has provided information about how it cared for its young and the early development of dinosaurs.

The name *Maiasaura* means "good mother reptile." This large dinosaur laid her eggs in a mound of dirt in a circular or spiral pattern. Then she covered the mound with vegetation, much like crocodiles do today. The eggs were warmed by the rotting (composting) vegetation. Rather than sitting directly on the nest, mother *Maiasaura* probably sat next to it to keep thieves from stealing the eggs and other maiasaur parents from walking on them. Because females of a herd made nests in the same area, this would have been a danger.

When the eggs hatched, the hatchlings were too immature to leave the nest. Their limbs were not well developed, but there was wear on their teeth. This means the hatchlings stayed in their nests and their parents brought them food. The young *Maiasaura* probably lived in nests until they were a year or two old. They grew from about 16 inches to 58 inches in only a year; this is rapid growth and may mean that they were warm-blooded.

A hatchling *Maiasaura* had a tall, narrow head. As it grew, its head became lower and wider from back to front, with a broad horny beak. Over its eyes was a stout

A Cretaceous inland sea.

Monoclonius

bony crest that probably was used for display and head-butting during breeding season or when defending territory. Because these dinosaurs lived in very large groups, with up to 10,000 animals in a herd, they needed to protect their territory.

All the *Maiasaura* specimens come from the Late Cretaceous Two Medicine Formation of western Montana. *Orodromeus* also lived in this area at the same time, as well as the predators *Albertosaurus* and *Troodon*. *Maiasaura* has not been found in other areas of the west.

We know more about the life of *Maiasaura* than any other dinosaur; we also know a lot about its evolutionary relationships. The closest relative of *Maiasaura* was *Brachylophosaurus* from southern Alberta and Montana. More remotely, these two solid-crested hadrosaurids were related to the more primitive *Hadrosaurus, Aralosaurus,* and *Gryposaurus.*

MONOCLONIUS
(MON-oh-KLONE-ee-us)

Period:
Late Cretaceous
Order, Suborder, Family:
Ornithischia, Marginocephalia, Ceratopsidae
Location:
North America (Canada, United States)
Length:
20 feet (6 meters)

Monoclonius was discovered by Edward Drinker Cope in 1876 along the Missouri River in Montana. The specimen Cope found was very fragmentary and is one of the first ceratopsids found (no one knew what a ceratopsid looked like in 1876 since no skull or complete skeleton had been found). Because the earliest specimens of *Monoclonius* were incomplete, it has often been confused with its close relative *Centrosaurus*. But recent studies have shown they were different dinosaurs.

Charles Sternberg found the first and only complete skull of *Monoclonius* in Alberta in 1937. At least six other species of *Monoclonius* have been named, but they were based on incomplete specimens.

Monoclonius, which means "single horn," was a moderate-size centrosaurine ceratopsid without brow horns but with a well-developed and sometimes curved nasal horn. The neck frill was short and round, with scalloped edges and moderately large fenestrae (openings). The frill was thin along the outer rim and did not have the bony projections that were on the frill of *Centrosaurus*. *Monoclonius* was closely related to *Styracosaurus*, *Brachyceratops*, and *Pachyrhinosaurus*.

Below: Monoclonius *skeletal drawings, front (top left), back (top right), top, and side views.*

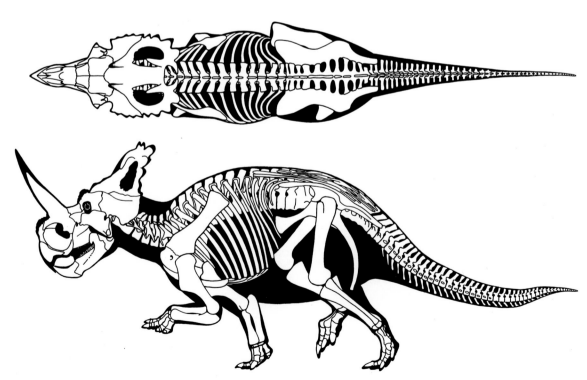

A Cretaceous forest of sequoia trees.

NANOTYRANNUS
(NAN-oh-tie-RAN-us)

Period:
Late Cretaceous
Order, Suborder, Family:
Saurischia, Theropoda, Tyrannosauridae
Location:
North America (United States)
Length:
Estimated 17 feet (5 meters)

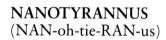

Known from only a single skull and jaw from Montana and three teeth from South Dakota, *Nanotyrannus* was first thought to be an *Albertosaurus*. But it was recently redescribed because it was different in many ways from *Albertosaurus*. One difference was that *Nanotyrannus* had eyes that faced forward. The eyes of *Albertosaurus* were more on the sides of its head, with little overlap of eyesight at the front. *Nanotyrannus* could judge distances, sizes, and angles of attack. It probably roamed around in low plants, waiting in ambush, then leaping on its prey. *Albertosaurus* probably hunted much differently because it could not judge distances.

Nanotyrannus had a curved neck, which gave it more power when it attacked. The back of its skull was expanded for the attachment of muscles from the jaw and neck, which increased the sideways motion of its neck and head. It stood about seven or eight feet tall at the shoulder and probably weighed about one ton.

The teeth of *Nanotyrannus* were not well preserved, but they were serrated blades like most meat-eating dinosaurs. Many parts of the skull of *Nanotyrannus* are puzzling; some of the bones were not fused (joined). This may mean that it was not an adult; some paleontologists think it could have been a juvenile *Tyrannosaurus*. *Tyrannosaurus*, which has been found in the same deposits, also had eyes that faced forward. Also, a number of skulls of *Tarbosaurus*, a close relative of *Tyrannosaurus*, were found in Mongolia. The smallest and probably the youngest looks much like *Nanotyrannus*. Further study may prove that *Nanotyrannus* was a juvenile *Tyrannosaurus*.

Aspideretes, *a soft-shelled turtle, watches as a herd of* Corythosaurus *cool off in the water. A herd of* Chasmosaurus *in the background also enjoy a swim. The carnivore* Troodon, *under a magnolia tree, keeps an eye on the corythosaurs.*

195

Opisthocoelicaudia skarzynskii

OPISTHOCOELICAUDIA
(oh-PIS-thoh-SEE-lee-CAWD-ee-uh)

Period:
Late Cretaceous
Order, Suborder, Family:
Saurischia, Sauropodomorpha,
Titanosauridae
Location:
Asia (Mongolian People's Republic)
Length:
40 feet (12 meters)

Discovered by the Joint Polish-Mongolian Paleontological Expedition in 1965, the sauropod *Opisthocoelicaudia* is known from a skeleton with nearly all the bones of the body except the neck and head. The skeleton was found in the same Late Cretaceous rock layers as the skull of *Nemegtosaurus*. *Euhelopus* may have been a close relative of *Opisthocoelicaudia*, but *Mamenchisaurus* and *Nemegtosaurus* belong in different families.

A member of the family Camarasauridae, *Opisthocoelicaudia* survived its Late Jurassic relatives in North America by 70 million years. It was perhaps 40 to 50 feet long and may have weighed as much as 20 tons.

The name *Opisthocoelicaudia* refers to the unusual trait in the vertebrae (bones of the spine) from the front half of the tail. The side of the vertebra that faced the end of the tail curved deeply inward (it was concave), and the side of the vertebra that faced the front of the animal curved deeply outward (was convex). Its name means "rear cavity tail." This may have allowed the animal to use its tail as a prop, like the third leg of a tripod, when it reached up for higher plants and trees. This would have helped balance the animal and taken some of its weight off its back legs. It also had an extra vertebra in the pelvic area to strengthen the hips, and the hip socket was strong to hold the immense weight of this dinosaur on two

legs. No other sauropod had these features; *Opisthocoelicaudia* may have been a specialized eater.

The hips and tail were also unusual when the animal stood on its four feet (quadrupedal). From the side, its body was almost straight from its neck to the beginning of its tail. Most sauropods had an arched profile. This shape was probably because of the specializations in the tail.

Most of the neck was missing except for several bones. They show that when the animal was moving, *Opisthocoelicaudia* held its neck with the head straight out in front of the body. The neck and skull of *Opisthocoelicaudia* may have been pulled apart by scavengers, which left grooves on the pelvis and on a bone in its leg where their teeth dug into the bone.

ORNITHOMIMUS
(or-NITH-Oh-MIME-us)

Period:
Late Cretaceous
Order, Suborder, Family:
Saurischia, Theropoda, Ornithomimidae
Location:
North America (Canada, United States)
Length:
12 feet (4 meters)

This dinosaur has been found mainly in the Late Cretaceous Judith River and Horseshoe Canyon Formations of Alberta, but less-complete specimens have been found in the western United States as well. *Ornithomimus* ("bird mimic") looks much like a modern flightless bird, such as the

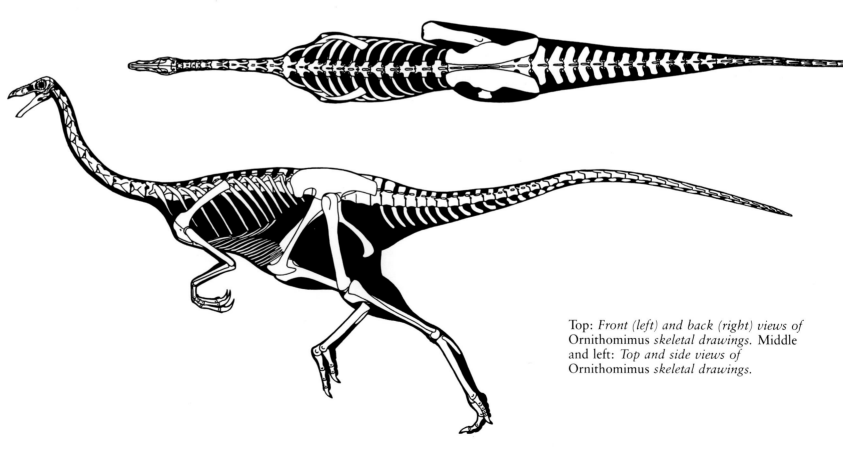

Top: *Front (left) and back (right) views of* Ornithomimus *skeletal drawings.* Middle and left: *Top and side views of* Ornithomimus *skeletal drawings.*

197

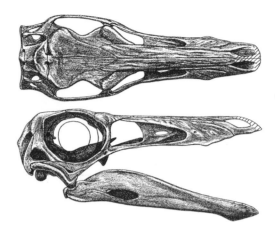

Top and side views of Ornithomimus *skull drawing.*

ostrich. Both have small heads with beaks, long necks, and long back limbs for fast running. But *Ornithomimus* had a long tail and long arms with three-fingered hands that ended in long, slender claws instead of short wings and no tail. The foot of ornithomimids was similar to the foot of some modern flightless birds; they had three toes on long upper foot bones. The ornithomimids may have been able to run up to 30 miles per hour. *Ornithomimus* differs from its close relative *Struthiomimus* because its back and neck were shorter and its limbs were more lightly built.

All ornithomimids had lightly built skulls and no teeth. They may have been omnivorous, eating small vertebrates, insects, and fruits. But some paleontologists think they were only plant-eaters.

Ornithomimus skeleton.

Orodromeus makelai

ORODROMEUS
(OR-oh-DROH-mee-us)

Period:
Late Cretaceous
Order, Suborder, Family:
Ornithischia, Ornithopoda, Hypsilophodontidae
Location:
North America (United States)
Length:
6¹/₂ feet (2 meters)

Orodromeus is a recently discovered dinosaur and one of the most spectacular. *Orodromeus* (the name means "mountain runner") was only about 6¹/₂ feet long as an adult. What makes *Orodromeus* special is that it is known from adult skulls and skeletons, younger animals, juveniles, hatchlings, and even an articulated (the bones are attached) embryo in a whole egg. From all these fossils, we have a rich picture of the life and evolution of *Orodromeus.*

198

The mother *Orodromeus* laid about 12 eggs in a tight spiral, with the first egg in the center of the spiral. These eggs were not large, almost 6 inches high and 2³/₄ inches wide. When the embryos were ready to come out of their eggs, they pecked through the top of the shell and climbed out of the nest. These hatchlings were nearly as fully developed as adults and could leave the nest and feed themselves. Possibly for protection, these hatchlings stayed together after leaving the nest.

Hatchlings had long legs, with short front limbs and large heads. As they grew, their back limbs grew longer in proportion to the rest of their body and their heads got smaller. As an adult, *Orodromeus* was one of the longest-legged hypsilophodontids for its size. It must have been a very fast runner. It had a very long, straight tail, supported by many interwoven bony tendons. The tail balanced the front of the body when it ran.

Orodromeus had simple, primitive teeth, much like the early ornithischian *Lesothosaurus.* From the shape of these teeth, *Orodromeus* probably fed on fleshy fruits and possibly insects, especially when the animal was young.

Orodromeus comes from the Late Cretaceous Two Medicine Formation of western Montana. It was found with the hadrosaur *Maiasaura* and the meat-eating *Albertosaurus* and *Troodon. Orodromeus* may also have lived in southern Alberta. It is closely related to other hypsilophodontids, including *Yandusaurus* from the Late Jurassic of the People's Republic of China, *Zephyrosaurus* from the Early Cretaceous of the United States, and *Hypsilophodon* from the Early Cretaceous of England. *Parksosaurus* and *Thescelosaurus* from the Late Cretaceous of Canada and the United States were two other related hypsilophodontids.

Right: Troodon *chasing an* Orodromeus.

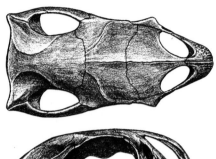

Drawing of top and side view of Oviraptor *skull.*

OVIRAPTOR
(OHV-ih-RAP-tor)

Period:
Late Cretaceous
Order, Suborder, Family:
Saurischia, Theropoda, Caenagnathidae
Location:
Asia (Mongolian People's Republic)
Length:
6 feet (1.8 meters)

The first specimen of *Oviraptor* was discovered by the American Museum of Natural History expedition to Asia in 1923. It was found in the Gobi Desert of Mongolia. This is the same place that *Protoceratops* was found. The specimen was an almost complete skull along with parts of the hands and neck vertebrae (bones in the spine). It was found lying next to a nest of eggs that may have belonged to *Protocera-*

tops. Henry Fairfield Osborn thought the animal may have died while eating the eggs in the nest; perhaps it had been killed by an angry *Protoceratops* parent.

This possible diet of eggs led Osborn to name the genus and species *Oviraptor philoceratops,* which means "egg plunderer, lover of ceratopsians." At first *Oviraptor* was thought to be a member of the Ornithomimidae, but its fingers were not the same length and they ended in strongly curved claws. The ornithomimids had fingers about the same length and almost straight claws.

The skull of *Oviraptor* was short with large eye sockets, a crest above the snout, and a deep lower jaw with a large fenestra (opening) in the middle. Like the ornithomimids, both the upper and lower jaws were beaklike and toothless. The crest was full of sinuses, or cavities, which were filled with air when it was alive. The unusual jaws show that the animal had a specialized diet. Unlike most theropods, except the ornithomimids, *Oviraptor* and other members of the family Caenagnathidae were probably herbivorous (planteaters).

Recently discovered specimens show that aside from the skull, *Oviraptor* was similar to other theropods. An adult was about three feet tall at the shoulder and about six feet long from its nose to the tip of its tail. Its hands were moderately long, and the animal could use them to grasp. The long back legs show it had been a good runner. With no teeth, running may have been its only defense against other theropods.

Since the original specimen was discovered, several other skulls with skeletons have been found. These new specimens show that the size of the crest on each animal was different. The crest ranges from almost none to large. These differences are probably because of the different ages of the animals. This is supported by the fact that the small, nearly crestless forms had

Oviraptor

Pachycephalosaurus grangeri

relatively large eye sockets while the large-crested forms had relatively small eye sockets. In many modern animals the size of the eye socket in proportion to the rest of the head gets smaller as the animal gets older, so the same may have been true for dinosaurs.

Oviraptor was closely related to *Caenagnathus,* from Alberta. Other relatives of *Oviraptor* were *Chirostenotes* and *Elmisaurus.*

PACHYCEPHALOSAURUS
(PACK-ee-cef-AH-loh-SORE-us)

Period:
Late Cretaceous
Order, Suborder, Family:
Ornithischia, Marginocephalia, Pachycephalosauridae
Location:
North America (United States)
Length:
Estimated 15 feet (4.5 meters)

The largest pachycephalosaur was *Pachycephalosaurus.* First found in rocks of Late Cretaceous age in Montana, *Pachycephalosaurus* was named and described by Barnum Brown and Eric Schlaikjer. *Pachycephalosaurus* is known only from a number of large domed skull roofs and a nearly complete skull. As the name *Pachycephalosaurus* ("thick-headed reptile") indicates, the top of the skull was very thick, almost nine inches in some skulls. Unlike other pachycephalosaurs, the snout stuck out, giving it an almost piglike profile. The top of the dome was smooth, much like that of *Prenocephale* and *Stegoceras.*

The back rim of the dome of *Pachycephalosaurus* and the top of the snout were covered with spikes and small horns. The teeth were simple, triangular blades. It ate soft plants.

201

Like its close relatives *Stegoceras, Prenocephale,* and *Stygimoloch, Pachycephalosaurus* probably used its domed head for head-butting contests. The thick skull roof would have protected the small brain from damage. Males protected their territory and females by using this behavior.

PACHYRHINOSAURUS
(PACK-ee-rhine-oh-SORE-us)

Period:
Late Cretaceous
Order, Suborder, Family:
Ornithischia, Marginocephalia, Ceratopsidae
North America (Canada)
Length:
20 feet (6 meters)

Pachyrhinosaurus was probably the most unusual and distinctive ceratopsid. It did not have brow or nasal horns; instead it had a thick, bumpy, spongy pad of bone along the upper surface of its flattened face. This bony pad ran from the front of its nose back to above its eyes. The skull of *Pachyrhinosaurus* was massive; only *Triceratops, Pentaceratops,* and *Torosaurus* had larger skulls. *Pachyrhinosaurus* was the largest centrosaurine ceratopsian.

Charles Sternberg named *Pachyrhinosaurus canadensis* from three partial skulls found in southern Alberta. *Pachyrhinosaurus* means "thick-nose reptile"; the name refers to the bony facial pad, called the boss. Because skulls of *Pachyrhinosaurus* are rare, and because of their odd, gnarled facial boss, some paleontologists thought these specimens were "pathological." That is, they thought the facial pad was formed because a nasal horn broke off and then healed over. So they thought the facial boss was a "scar." Paleontologists recently uncovered a large bone bed with many *Pachyrhinosaurus* specimens in north central Alberta. This proves that the

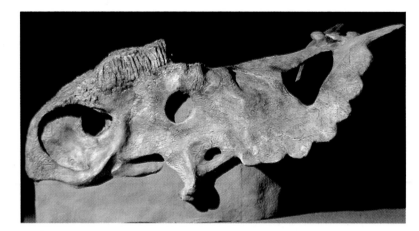

Pachyrhinosaurus canadensis *skull.*

facial pad is a normal feature of *Pachyrhinosaurus* and not a scar.

The rest of the skull of *Pachyrhinosaurus* looked very much like that of other centrosaurine ceratopsians such as *Centrosaurus, Monoclonius,* and *Styracosaurus.* Like them, *Pachyrhinosaurus* had a short frill, a deep face, and a short beak. *Pachyrhinosaurus* was also closely related to *Brachyceratops* and *Avaceratops.*

Pachyrhinosaurus

PANOPLOSAURUS
(pan-OP-loh-SORE-us)

Period:
Late Cretaceous
Order, Suborder, Family:
Ornithischia, Thyreophora,
Nodosauridae
Location:
North America (Canada, United States)
Length:
23 feet (7 meters)

Panoplosaurus is known only from two partial skeletons, one of which preserves some of the armor the way it was in life. This skeleton shows that *Panoplosaurus* was unusual among nodosaurids because it did not have spikes on the sides of its neck.

It is not known how *Panoplosaurus* defended itself from a hungry *Daspletosaurus*. Perhaps the armor covering the rest of its body stopped the hungry predator from trying to attack, or perhaps *Panoplosaurus* used its tail to smack the predator.

Panoplosaurus appears to be closely related to *Edmontonia;* both lived at the same time. Both had large plates on their neck, and smaller keeled (ridged) plates on their body and tail. Their heads were similar and both had large plates fused (joined) to the surface of their skulls. For further protection, both had large oval plates covering their cheeks. Its name means "well-armored reptile." The teeth of *Panoplosaurus* were small for a nodosaurid, and it ate a diet of soft plants.

Panoplosaurus mirus

Parasaurolophus walkeri

PARASAUROLOPHUS
(PAIR-ah-SORE-ol-OH-fus)

Period:
Late Cretaceous
Order, Suborder, Family:
Ornithischia, Ornithopoda,
Hadrosauridae
Location:
North America (Canada, United States)
Length:
33 feet (10 meters)

Parasaurolophus was an interesting-looking dinosaur. While it looked normal from the neck down, it looked almost as if it had a trombone on its head. And in a way, it did.

Parasaurolophus is one of many hadrosaurs from the Late Cretaceous of North America. Its name, which means "like *Saurolophus,*" refers to the resemblance of the crests of these two duckbilled dinosaurs. However, the crest of *Saurolophus* was solid bone and the crest of *Parasaurolophus* was hollow. The hollow space within the crest of *Parasaurolophus* reached the nostrils and looped down to connect to the back of the throat. This crest was the animal's nasal cavity moved on top of its head.

This crest, seen also in other lambeosaurine hadrosaurs, has attracted much attention. At first, paleontologists thought this crest was used underwater, perhaps as a snorkel or a place to store extra air. Other suggestions included extra space to increase the animal's sense of smell or an area used to cool its brain. The function of the crest is now thought to relate to hadrosaur social behavior. Because of their size and shape, crests could have been for display. They may have helped other members of its species identify the animal, and the crest may have shown how old the animal was and its sex.

Also, because the crest was hollow and connected to the lungs, it would have made a resonating chamber. Sounds would have been made by a vocal organ or voice box and "pushed" through the crest, making a deep honking call. In this way, the animal could have communicated. All lambeosaurines would have used their "voices" to announce themselves, to warn their hatchlings, and to challenge other animals that invaded their territory.

PARKSOSAURUS
(PARKS-oh-SORE-us)

Period:
Late Cretaceous
Order, Suborder, Family:
Ornithischia, Ornithopoda,
Hypsilophodontidae
Location:
North America (Canada)
Length:
8 feet (2.5 meters)

Not many fossils of *Parksosaurus* have been found. It is known only from a single skeleton and poorly preserved skull from the southern part of Alberta.

The head of *Parksosaurus* was slightly longer compared to its body size than other hypsilophodontids. The teeth were blunt and peglike, with many rounded ridges. Its teeth were probably used to chew fleshy fruits, thick leaves, and possibly insects if they could be caught.

The body was stocky for a small animal. The limbs were somewhat short and strongly built; it was not a fast runner. Like other hypsilophodontids, the tail had a basket-work of ossified (bony) tendons. Those tendons held the tail out stiffly; the tail acted as a balance for the front half of the body when the animal walked bipedally (on two legs). In this way, the front limbs were free to grasp fruits or move

Right: Parksosaurus warreni

A Cretaceous rocky mountain scene.

branches around and toward its mouth. As with most hypsilophodontids, the hands and feet of *Parksosaurus* were tipped with slightly curved claws.

Charles Sternberg named *Parksosaurus* in honor of W. A. Parks, chief paleontologist of the Royal Ontario Museum early in the 20th century. Relatives of *Parksosaurus* include *Thescelosaurus* and *Orodromeus*, from Canada and the United States.

PENTACERATOPS
(PEN-tah-SAIR-ah-tops)

Period:
Late Cretaceous
Order, Suborder, Family:
Ornithischia, Marginocephalia, Ceratopsidae
Location:
North America (United States)
Length:
Estimated 25 feet (7.5 meters)

Known only from the Late Cretaceous of northwestern New Mexico, *Pentaceratops* had one large horn on its snout, a pair of large horns above its eyes, and a pair of much smaller false horns in the cheek region. Its name means "five-horned face." The horns were actually bone.

Like other large ceratopsians, *Pentaceratops* resembled a rhinoceros in appearance, and probably also in behavior and feeding habits. The skulls found in New Mexico were preserved with the different broadleafed plants the animal ate. These plants resemble figs, willows, magnolias, and other types of hardwood flowering plants. *Pentaceratops* lived in thick forests where these plants grew.

This sturdy herbivore (plant-eater) stood eight feet tall at the shoulder. The

A herd of Pentaceratops.

PINACOSAURUS
(pie-NAK-oh-SORE-us)

Period:
Late Cretaceous
Order, Suborder, Family:
Ornithischia, Thyreophora,
Ankylosauridae
Location:
Asia (People's Republic of China,
Mongolian People's Republic)
Length:
16 feet (4.8 meters)

Pinacosaurus was one of the first armored dinosaurs found in Asia. An expedition from the American Museum of Natural History went to Mongolia to search for traces of early man; instead they found dinosaur eggs and skeletons.

Pinacosaurus must have lived in a fairly dry desert region because almost all of its fossils have been found in sand dune deposits. Scientists do not know what *Pinacosaurus* ate, but it and several other herbivorous (plant-eating) dinosaurs were found in the same deposits, so some food was available. Recently, a group of five juvenile skeletons of *Pinacosaurus* were found huddled together. They probably were caught by a sandstorm and were buried alive.

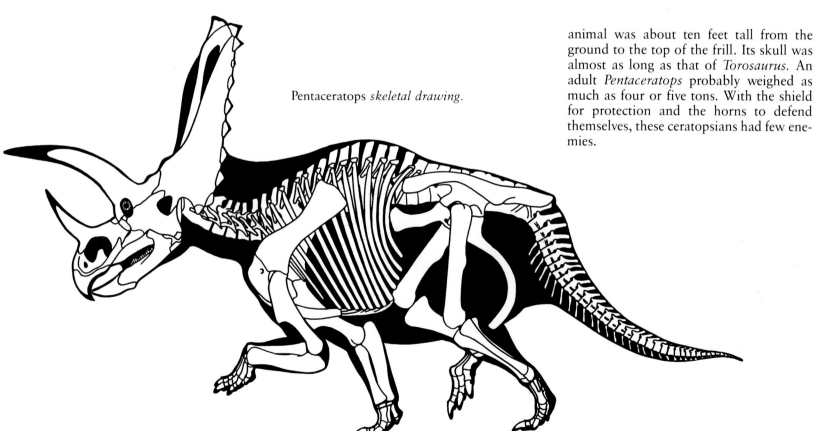

Pentaceratops *skeletal drawing.*

animal was about ten feet tall from the ground to the top of the frill. Its skull was almost as long as that of *Torosaurus*. An adult *Pentaceratops* probably weighed as much as four or five tons. With the shield for protection and the horns to defend themselves, these ceratopsians had few enemies.

Pinacosaurus *skull.*

207

The skull of *Pinacosaurus* is unusual because the entire surface of the skull was not covered with bone plates. Instead, there were few plates and they were small. The plates covered only parts of the skull. But in all other aspects, *Pinacosaurus* looked like most other ankylosaurids. A collar of armor plates covered its neck, plates covered its body and tail, and it had a bone-club on the end of its tail. Except for some unknown large teeth found with *Pinacosaurus*, the only predatory dinosaur was the small sickle-clawed *Velociraptor*. But *Pinacosaurus* had little worry; a blow from its tail club could have killed it.

Syrmosaurus was the name used by Soviet paleontologists to describe *Pinacosaurus*.

Skull of Prenocephale, showing the large dome.

Pinacosaurus *skeletal drawing.*

Pinacosaurus grangeri

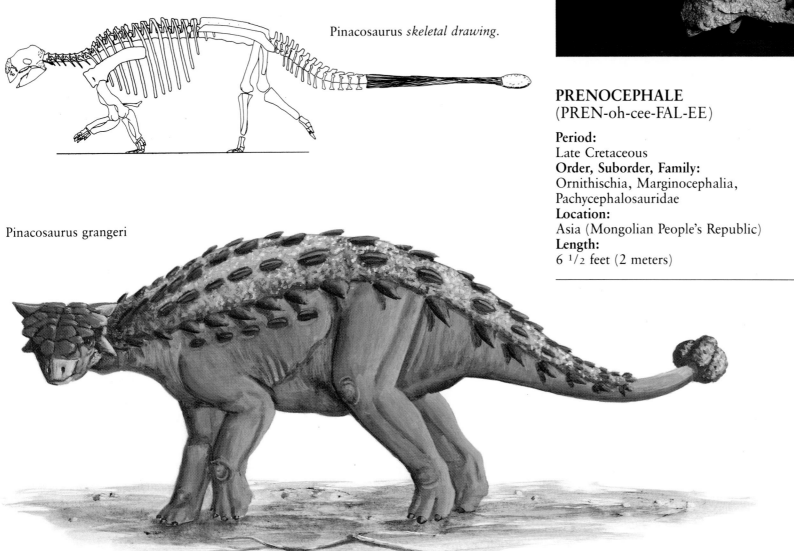

PRENOCEPHALE
(PREN-oh-cee-FAL-EE)

Period:
Late Cretaceous
Order, Suborder, Family:
Ornithischia, Marginocephalia, Pachycephalosauridae
Location:
Asia (Mongolian People's Republic)
Length:
6 ¹/₂ feet (2 meters)

An almost complete skull and most of the skeleton were found for *Prenocephale*. The fossils were well preserved and are some of the finest dinosaur material ever to have been found. It was collected during the Joint Polish-Mongolian Expeditions to the Gobi Desert. The animal was named and described in 1974.

The name *Prenocephale* means "sloping head," which refers to the large domed skull roof. The dome was high and rounded where it covered the braincase (the part of the skull that protects the brain). This dome was so large that it went back to the stout shelf (or frill) at the back of the skull. The animal had many rounded bumps and ridges of bone on the surface of its dome, face, and cheek. The bones of the skull were reinforced and tightly joined.

Prenocephale may have had very good eyesight; its eye sockets were large. Its teeth were simple; it was a herbivore (plant-eater) that probably fed on soft leaves or fruits. It also probably ate insects, if it could catch them.

Like its relatives *Stegoceras* and *Pachycephalosaurus*, *Prenocephale* probably used its dome for head-butting contests. The thick skull roof would have protected the brain from damage during head-on collisions.

Prenocephale prenes

A few ostrich dinosaurs, named Dromiceiomimus, *search for food in a Late Cretaceous forest.*

211

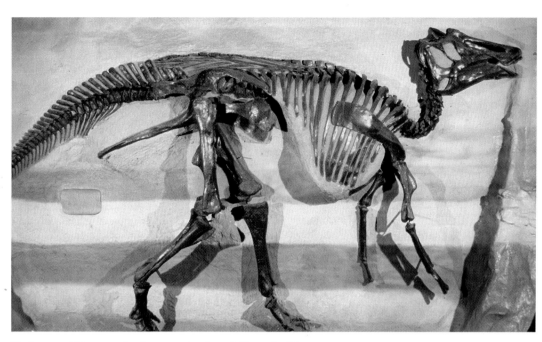

Skeleton of Prosaurolophus *at the Royal Ontario Museum.*

PROSAUROLOPHUS
(PROH-sore-OL-oh-FUS)

Period:
Late Cretaceous
Order, Suborder, Family:
Ornithischia, Ornithopoda,
Hadrosauridae
Location:
North America (Canada, United States)
Length:
30 feet (9 meters)

Prosaurolophus was a common duck-billed dinosaur that lived during the Late Cretaceous in North America. It was discovered, named, and described by Barnum Brown of the American Museum of Natural History in 1916.

Prosaurolophus probably walked and ran on its stout, strong back legs. While resting, it supported itself with its more lightly built front limbs. The animal mostly used its front limbs for grasping and pulling branches, leaves, and fruit. Females may have used their front limbs for building nests.

The head of *Prosaurolophus* was much like other hadrosaurs. It had many teeth, with as many as 50 teeth in each jaw. It also had as many as 250 replacement teeth in each jaw that were below the top teeth. The teeth below would replace the chewing teeth when they were needed.

The snout of *Prosaurolophus* looked much like a duck's. The rim of the beak would have been covered by a stiff bill for cropping foliage and other food. The most unusual part of its skull was the wide, solid bump above its eyes. The bump may have distinguished one animal from another, and males from females.

Prosaurolophus, which means "before *Saurolophus*," was closely related to the longer-crested *Saurolophus*. More distant relatives included *Edmontosaurus* and *Shantungosaurus*.

PROTOCERATOPS
(PROH-toh-SAIR-ah-tops)

Period:
Late Cretaceous
Order, Suborder, Family:
Ornithischia, Marginocephalia,
Protoceratopsidae
Location:
Asia (Mongolian People's Republic)
Length:
6 feet (1.8 meters)

Protoceratops andrewsi was discovered in Mongolia in 1922 by an expedition from the American Museum of Natural History led by Roy Chapman Andrews. Its genus name means "first-horned face," and its species name was in honor of the expedition's leader. *Protoceratops* is one of the most celebrated dinosaurs of the 20th century. Workers also discovered the skeleton of a nimble toothless predator that was later named *Oviraptor philoceratops*, which means "egg-stealer, lover of ceratopsians." In the Gobi Desert were parents, nests, eggs, hatchlings, and egg stealers all in one amazing deposit. This was the first discovery of dinosaur eggs, and the discovery made news everywhere.

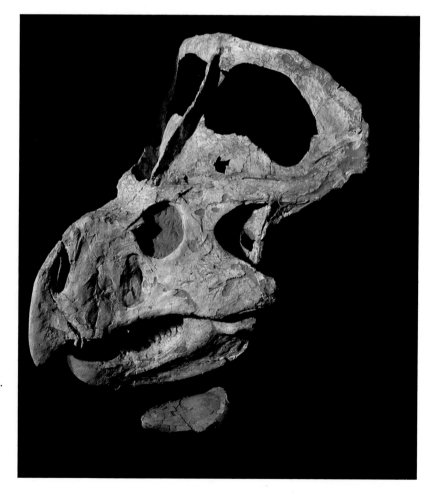

Protoceratops skull.

Left: *Two albertosaurs chasing a* Prosaurolophus *with its young.*

Protoceratops may be the ancestor of all horned dinosaurs. Because of this evolutionary link, and because of all the fossils found, it has been the subject of much study. Like all ceratopsians, *Protoceratops* was from the Late Cretaceous, but it was older than most of its relatives.

Protoceratops was a small, compact dinosaur, only six feet long as an adult and two feet tall at the hips. It weighed less than 400 pounds. Hatchlings were only a foot long, and the eggs were eight inches long and seven inches around. Although small as adults, *Protoceratops* had a sturdy build. The front legs were nearly as long as the back, so it could carry its heavy head and jaws. Its toes had claws that it used to dig in low vegetation for leaves and twigs. Its heavy tail balanced the animal when it walked.

It had a parrotlike beak that was rounded and toothless. The rear of the skull was expanded into great ridges of bone where the jaw muscles attached. The bony frill was small and simple in *Protoceratops* but became large and elaborate in some of its giant relatives. The sides of the frill were open, which lightened the skull without losing strength. The frill extended well past the neck joint. For a small dinosaur, the head and jaws were enormous. Because of this weight, the animal needed to walk on all four limbs so it could support its head when it walked.

Protoceratops had a powerful bite; it cropped low vegetation with its beak. Behind its beak, it had dozens of teeth that chopped the tough leaves and branches into smaller pieces, perhaps in a chewing motion. Food collected in its fleshy cheeks

on the sides of the jaws. Along with low-growing shrubs and trees, *Protoceratops* may also have eaten the newly evolving angiosperms (flowering plants) that appeared in the Late Cretaceous.

Protoceratops did not have horns on its face or a shield like those found on its relative *Triceratops*. *Protoceratops* did have a slight bump on the snout below the eyes. It may have been the beginning of a horn.

Saichania *skeletal drawing.*

The bump was larger on males, which also had larger frills. Males may have used these features to attract females. With the discovery of so many skeletons, scientists concluded that *Protoceratops* lived in herds.

A surprise for paleontologists was the discovery that these dinosaurs lived in the desert. The eggs were laid in shallow holes in the sand. Also, the small pores and the pattern on the shells show that the eggs were adapted for desert conditions. In the 1920s, scientists thought that all dinosaurs lived in swamps and forests.

Relatives of *Protoceratops* included *Montanaceratops* and *Leptoceratops* from North America, and *Bagaceratops* and *Microceratops* from Asia. All are from the Late Cretaceous and are quite similar to their more famous cousin. There may have been land connections between the northern continents in the Late Cretaceous that allowed these small ceratopsians to migrate.

Another group of primitive ceratopsians, the psittacosaurs, also had a beak and

Protoceratops

©'85 Walters

lived earlier than *Protoceratops* and its relatives. *Psittacosaurus* was also found in Mongolia by the Andrews expedition. The psittacosaurs may have been the ancestors of *Protoceratops*.

SAICHANIA
(sigh-CHAIN-ee-uh)

Period:
Late Cretaceous
Order, Suborder, Family:
Ornithischia, Thyreophora,
Ankylosauridae
Location:
Asia (Mongolian People's Republic)
Length:
22 feet (6.6 meters)

Saichania was described from a partial skeleton with the armor preserved the way it was when the animal was alive. The animal died in a sandstorm; it was found squatting on its belly in sandstone. At one time the entire skeleton was present, but erosion destroyed most of the rear of the skeleton. Several other partial skeletons have recently been discovered and these add much to our knowledge of the animal.

The skull of Saichania had odd, domed armored plates fused (joined) to the top. The skull also had large spines on its head that curved slightly down and back. It had two bone collars with keeled (ridged) plates fused to them. Similar keeled plates probably covered the body and tail. The end of the tail had a small club with three plates.

The teeth were small and were suited for a diet of soft plants. Scientists do not know what these plants were, since the sandstone that preserved Saichania was poor at preserving plants. These plants must have been suited to a hot, dry environment. To cope with this harsh environment, Saichania may have moistened the air it breathed with a complex air passage in the skull. If the air was not moistened, then the lungs and other tissue would have lost water; this would have caused the animal's death. Living in such a hot environment would have also required Saichania to get rid of excess body heat. This heat was lost by evaporation of the moisture in its air passage. This is much like a modern dog panting on a hot day.

Saichania chulsanensis

Saltasaurus *skeletal drawing.*

Saltasaurus loricatus

SALTASAURUS
(SALT-ah-SORE-us)

Period:
Late Cretaceous
Order, Suborder, Family:
Saurischia, Sauropodomorpha,
Titanosauridae
Location:
South America (Argentina)
Length:
40 feet (12 meters)

From Salta in Argentina, *Saltasaurus* was described from several incomplete skeletons, none of which were found with a skull. This medium-size sauropod was dwarfed by its giant relative *Antarctosaurus,* also from South America. The armor of *Saltasaurus* consisted of hundreds of small bones about the size of peas, tightly packed in the skin, and a few large oval bony plates. The larger plates were about as broad and thick as a person's palm. This bony protection seems to have covered the back and sides of its body and probably gave it a roughened, bumpy appearance.

Prowling for a meal, a large predator leaping onto the back of a 20-ton sauropod would drive its claws deep into the flesh near the hips. The sudden blow would have harmed most sauropods, bringing them to the ground. But the predator's talons could not break through this sauropod's skin because it was studded with bony plates. An armored sauropod was rare in the world of dinosaurs. Sauropods had lived for more than 70 million years with no defense except their size. *Saltasaurus* was an unusual dinosaur.

Another Late Cretaceous sauropod from South America, *Laplatasaurus,* also had bony plates in its skin. Because these two dinosaurs, both in the family Titanosauridae, had armor, it is possible that other members of the family (*Antarctosaurus,*

Hypselosaurus, and *Titanosaurus* from South America, and *Alamosaurus* from North America) also had bony plates for protection. This trait would distinguish this family from all other sauropod dinosaurs.

Sauropod dinosaurs were not common in most parts of the world by the end of the Cretaceous Period. This may be because they were competing with more-advanced plant-eating dinosaurs and because predatory dinosaurs kept their numbers down. Some predators had become very large (*Tyrannosaurus* weighed up to seven tons) and the size of sauropods was not as much protection as when predators were smaller. The armor on the titanosaurids may be what allowed *Saltasaurus* and other sauropods in this family to survive. *Saltasaurus* and its relatives were successful in South America, and one member of the family established a population in North America. *Alamosaurus* in New Mexico and Utah faced the giant predators *Albertosaurus* and *Tyrannosaurus.*

SAUROLOPHUS
(sore-OL-oh-FUS)

Period:
Late Cretaceous
Order, Suborder, Family:
Ornithischia, Ornithopoda,
Hadrosauridae
Location:
North America (Canada), Asia
(Mongolian People's Republic)
Length:
33-43 feet (10-13 meters)

Saurolophus ("ridged reptile") was a hadrosaurid. It had a large bony spike pointing back over the top of its head between its eyes. The front of this thin crest covered a shallow hole that went down to the nostril area of the snout. This hole may have been covered with a long, fleshy "bag" of skin. The animal inflated the bag to make loud honking sounds. The bag may have also been a colorful display. Both features would have been useful during breeding season. It could call its mate and let another male *Saurolophus* know that it was the dominant male of the herd. The skeleton of *Saurolophus* was much like the

Saurolophus maximus

other hadrosaurids. The back limbs were long and well built, while the front limbs were shorter. The tail was long and held high off the ground and was a balance when *Saurolophus* walked or ran on its back legs.

This Late Cretaceous hadrosaurid has been found in southern Alberta and in Mongolia. There may have been a land connection that allowed this animal to live in central Asia and North America. *Saurolophus* was closely related to *Prosaurolophus* and not as closely to *Edmontosaurus*.

SAURORNITHOIDES
(SORE-orn-ith-OID-eez)

Period:
Late Cretaceous
Order, Suborder, Family:
Saurischia, Theropoda, Troodontidae
Location:
Asia (Mongolian People's Republic)
Length:
6 $^1/_2$ feet (2 meters)

Discovered during an expedition by the American Museum of Natural History, *Saurornithoides* is an example of a birdlike dinosaur. It looked much like a bird. It was found close to where two other birdlike dinosaurs (*Velociraptor* and *Oviraptor*) were also discovered.

This agile 60-pound predator had a long, slender snout and large eyes set in deep sockets. The front limbs of *Saurornithoides* were long for a bipedal (it walked on two legs) predator. On each hand it had three fingers that were covered by sharp claws. The back limbs had feet with four toes each. One toe pointed down, two large toes pointed forward, and the inner toe was held off the ground. This inner toe had a sickle-shaped claw that may have been used as a weapon. Its relative *Deinonychus* also had a sickle-shaped claw on its foot.

The teeth of *Saurornithoides* were different from its closest relatives *Troodon* and *Stenonychosaurus*. Usually the teeth of the animals in the family Troodontidae had large, round roots and serrations (like the edge of a steak knife). The serrations on the teeth of *Saurornithoides* were only on one side and there were no serrations at the tips.

Saurornithoides looked somewhat like a modern flightless bird. Its name means "birdlike reptile." It may have even had a similar lifestyle. It searched for prey, perhaps in twilight (or even at night). *Saurornithoides* may have preferred small mammals, although it probably ate any prey it could catch.

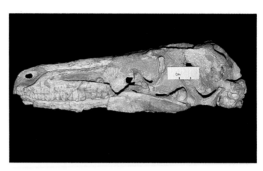

Saurornithoides *skull.*

Saurornithoides mongoliensis

SEGNOSAURUS
(SEG-noh-SORE-us)

Period:
Late Cretaceous
Order, Suborder, Family:
Saurischia, Segnosauria, Segnosauridae
Location:
Asia (Mongolian People's Republic)
Length:
Estimated 20 feet (6 meters)

One of the important finds of the Joint Soviet-Mongolian Paleontological Expeditions of the 1970s was the discovery of a whole new group of dinosaurs, the segnosaurians. *Segnosaurus galbinensis,* or "slow lizard from Galbin" (a region of the Gobi Desert), was first described by Mongolian paleontologist Altangerel Perle in 1979. It was an unusual saurischian that he classified in its own family, the Segnosauridae.

It showed an unusual combination of features of ornithischians, theropods, and prosauropods. Its pelvis looked much like the pelvis of the dromaeosaurids, although it was much larger. *Segnosaurus* had feet with long, slender theropodlike claws and ankles, although it had four toes instead of three on each foot. The teeth, although there were many and they were small, resembled those of some theropods.

The pelvis of *Segnosaurus* was very wide, giving the animal a broad back and a "pot belly." Theropods had pelves (plural of pelvis) that were slender. Its feet were not really theropod feet. Its relative *Erlikosaurus* had a prosauropodlike beak, so *Segnosaurus* probably did, too. After much study, it was found that the teeth of *Segnosaurus* had more in common with prosauropod teeth than with theropod teeth. These and other features suggest that it was more closely related to the sauropods and prosauropods than to the theropods.

Segnosaurus galbinensis

Segnosaurians have been found in several locations in Mongolia and China, and there is a possible *Erlikosaurus* specimen from Alberta. The puzzling dinosaur *Therizinosaurus cheloniformis,* known only from front limbs and hands with claws up to three feet long, was first classified as a turtle, but is probably a huge segnosaurian. Most segnosaurians (*Segnosaurus, Erlikosaurus andrewsi,* and *Enigmosaurus mongoliensis*) came from early to middle Late Cretaceous rocks. *Nanshiungosaurus brevispinus* from China may be younger, and *Therizinosaurus* was even younger.

What the lifestyle of *Segnosaurus* and its relatives was like is not known. The teeth show they were probably plant-eaters. They may have had a large gut for digesting plants. They may have looked like large, wide-bodied prosauropods, and they probably walked on all four legs most of the time. They may have been bearlike or like extinct Ice Age mammals called ground sloths. Segnosaurians were probably not fast runners. If their hands did have claws like *Therizinosaurus,* they would have been used as weapons against predators, including *Alectrosaurus,* which probably hunted *Segnosaurus.*

SHAMOSAURUS
(SHAME-oh-SORE-us)

Period:
Late Cretaceous
Order, Suborder, Family:
Ornithischia, Thyreophora, Ankylosauridae
Location:
Asia (Mongolian People's Republic)
Length:
Estimated 20 feet (6 meters)

Shamosaurus scutatus

Shamosaurus is one of the oldest known ankylosaurs. It lived about the same time as the nodosaur *Sauropelta.*

Little is known of *Shamosaurus* other than two skulls, one of which was found with two armor-plated collars. The skulls were low and broad across the back; they look like triangles when viewed from the top. Armor plates covered the outer surface of the skull, but these were so fused (joined) that no pattern can be seen. Each plate looks like a small bump, making the skull look rough. Large spines were fused to the back of the skull on the sides. Armor was also fused to the outer surface of the lower jaw.

The beak of *Shamosaurus* was narrow. It was probably selective in the parts of plants it ate. The teeth are not well known, but were probably small, leaf-shaped, and made for eating soft plants. It is not known what the rest of the body looked like.

SHANSHANOSAURUS
(SHAN-shan-oh-SORE-us)

Period:
Late Cretaceous
Order, Suborder, Family:
Saurischia, Theropoda, Unknown
Location:
Asia (People's Republic of China)
Length:
6-10 feet (1.8-3 meters)

Shanshanosaurus houyanshanensis

The paleontological expeditions into the Turpan Basin in 1964-1966 turned up several interesting and unusual dinosaurs. In the Subishi Formation, workers discovered the incomplete skeleton of a new, small theropod that was described in 1977 and named *Shanshanosaurus houyanshanensis.* An adult animal, it proved to be so different from other Chinese theropods that a new family, Shanshanosauridae, was created for it.

The foot-long skull of *Shanshanosaurus* had large eye sockets and even larger antorbital fenestrae (openings in front of the eye sockets), which made the skull light. In many ways, its skeleton looks like it may be related to the large theropods such as the tyrannosaurids, but other features suggest that it was related to the dromaeosaurids.

Some scientists have noted that the front teeth of *Shanshanosaurus* look like the teeth of *Aublysodon,* and have suggested it may be related.

Whatever its relationships, *Shanshanosaurus* hunted small animals, such as lizards and mammals. The large eye sockets may mean it was active during twilight, when the light was dim.

The spiny-headed dinosaur Stygimoloch is the latest pachycephalosaur to have been discovered. Its name means "River of Hades devil," and it was found in Montana and Wyoming.

Shantungosaurus giganteus

SHANTUNGOSAURUS
(shan-TUNG-oh-SORE-us)

Period:
Late Cretaceous
Order, Suborder, Family:
Ornithischia, Ornithopoda,
Hadrosauridae
Location:
Asia (People's Republic of China)
Length:
52 feet (16 meters)

Shantungosaurus may have been the largest hadrosaur. It is larger than some of the smaller sauropods. Named and described in 1973, *Shantungosaurus* is known from many disarticulated (not joined) bones from the Shandong Province, People's Republic of China.

Shantungosaurus was a flat-headed hadrosaur, much like its North American relative *Edmontosaurus*. The skull was long, with an extended snout and jaws. The jaws had a lot of room for the many teeth. There were as many as 63 places for teeth in each jaw, and there were six teeth in each place. This was probably the most teeth seen in any dinosaur.

Around the nostrils, there was a large hole where there was probably a fleshy "bag." The animal may have inflated the bag to make sounds or to attract a mate. It may have also used it to defend its territory.

The "reptile from Shandong" had very stout back limb bones, which it needed to support its large size. *Shantungosaurus* probably used both its front and back legs to walk, even when trying to escape from its enemy, *Tarbosaurus*.

SPINOSAURUS
(SPIE-noh-SORE-us)

Period:
Late Cretaceous
Order, Suborder, Family:
Saurischia, Theropoda, Spinosauridae
Location:
Africa (Egypt, Niger)
Length:
40 feet (12 meters)

In 1912, a German paleontological expedition discovered the remains of several new Late Cretaceous dinosaurs in Egypt. *Spinosaurus,* a large theropod, was one of the new dinosaurs. It got its name, which means "spined reptile," because of the tall spines on its vertebrae (bones of the spine). Some spines are over five feet tall. They formed a sail along the animal's back much like those of the Permian mammallike reptile *Dimetrodon.* It is interesting that an unrelated fin-backed dinosaur, the plant-eating ornithopod *Ouranosaurus,* has been found from nearly the same age in nearby North Africa. Two unrelated fin-backed dinosaurs in the same area may mean that the climate influenced the development of fin-backed animals. The fin may have been a thermal regulator, releasing heat on hot days and absorbing heat on colder days. It also may have been used as a display to attract members of its own species and scare other species.

Even though the skeleton is incomplete, *Spinosaurus* shows several other interesting features. It was a long theropod. The teeth are different from other theropod teeth because the serrations (the cutting ridges along the sides) were very small. Even more unusual is that the teeth were shaped like cones rather than blades. These tooth features, along with the shape of the skull bones, show that *Spinosaurus* is similar to *Baryonyx.* They may both belong in the family Spinosauridae. *Spinosaurus* may have eaten fish, but it is difficult to imagine such a large dinosaur catching enough fish to keep it alive. It more likely preyed upon land animals and fish.

The original skeleton of this theropod was destroyed in World War II. Recently, however, a piece of a skull bone belonging to another *Spinosaurus* was found on a shelf in a German museum. Perhaps another expedition to Egypt will uncover more skeletons so that we can learn more about *Spinosaurus.*

STEGOCERAS
(ste-GOSS-er-as)

Period:
Late Cretaceous
Order, Suborder, Family:
Ornithischia, Marginocephalia,
Pachycephalosauridae
Location:
North America (Canada, United States)
Length:
8 feet (2.5 meters)

Stegoceras has been one of the more interesting dinosaurs, partly because of the tangle of names that have been attached to it and also because of explanations that have been attached to its domed skull.

Spinosaurus

This pachycephalosaur was first described in 1902 by Lawrence Lambe. He thought it was a new kind of ceratopsian. However, later material suggested that it was related to the stegosaurs. It was not until 1924 that paleontologists realized it was a pachycephalosaur. Then a nearly complete skull and partial skeleton were described by Charles Gilmore, but he thought it was *Troodon*. Finally it was correctly classified and given the name *Stegoceras* ("horny roof").

Stegoceras was a small pachycephalosaur with a well-developed domed skull roof. It was closely related to the domed pachycephalosaurs, including *Pachycephalosaurus, Prenocephale,* and *Stygimoloch.*

We know much about *Stegoceras* because of a good skeleton (the only other pachycephalosaur preserved with its skeleton is *Homalocephale*) and many partial skulls of young and adult individuals. The dome of *Stegoceras* was flat in young animals but became large and thick in adults. Since there are many *Stegoceras* domes that have become part of the fossil record, we know there are two kinds of domes among adults. The thicker, heavier domes may have been male skulls, while the thinner, lower domes perhaps belonged to females.

Stegoceras may have used its thick dome for head-butting contests. Males would have had these contests to win females or territory. This would also explain why the male skull domes were thicker. There is other evidence that these animals had head-butting contests. The braincase, back of the skull, and backbone all show that forces were sent from the dome through the head, around the braincase, and down the backbone to the limbs. In this way, animals like *Stegoceras* could survive the stress of head-to-head combat, much the same way as goats and sheep of today.

Left: Stegoceras validus

STRUTHIOMIMUS
(STRUTH-ee-oh-MIME-us)

Period:
Late Cretaceous
Order, Suborder, Family:
Saurischia, Theropoda, Ornithomimidae
Location:
North America
Length:
13 feet (4 meters)

Struthiomimus ("ostrich mimic") is the best known of all the ornithomimids. A complete skeleton, which is now displayed at the American Museum of Natural History, was collected from the Judith River Formation of Alberta. Its name points to how similar its skeleton is to the modern *Struthio* (ostrich).

Like other ornithomimids, the skull was small (only ten inches long) and lightly built, and it lacked teeth and had a horny beak. Its eyes were large and it had a slender neck. Just like modern birds, the neck ribs were solidly fused (joined) to the neck vertebrae (bones of the spine). The back was stiff to support the weight of the body, long arms, and neck.

The arms were slender and the hands had three fingers. The inner finger was slightly shorter than the others. The claws at the ends of the fingers were straight and were probably not used to grasp prey. The back limbs and upper foot bones were long, as was the tail. The hands and arms were like those of a modern sloth, which uses its arms to grasp branches of trees. Because of this, some scientists think *Struthiomimus* may have been a herbivore that used its arms to pull branches within reach of its beak. But it may have been omnivorous and eaten plants and whatever small animals it could catch.

Right: *Three* Struthiomimus.

STYRACOSAURUS
(sty-RACK-oh-SORE-us)

Period:
Late Cretaceous
Order, Suborder, Family:
Ornithischia, Marginocephalia, Ceratopsidae
Location:
North America (Canada, United States)
Length:
18 feet (5.5 meters)

Styracosaurus was discovered in 1913 in the Belly River Formation of Alberta by Charles Sternberg. Lawrence Lambe named this animal *Styracosaurus albertensis,* which means "spiked reptile of Alberta," for its unusual neck frill.

Most ceratopsids had small knobs called "epoccipitals" around the edges of their neck frills, giving the frill a scalloped appearance. But *Styracosaurus* had six epoccipitals at the back of its frill that were long, thick, pointed spikes. The two spikes at the back of the frill were the longest. These spikes fan out around the back of the frill and may have made a predator think twice about trying to make a meal of *Styracosaurus.*

The neck frill of *Styracosaurus,* without the spikes, was rounded and short. *Styracosaurus* had small bony bumps over its eyes, rather than long brow horns. It did have a thick, straight, long horn on the top of its nose. Except for the spikes on its frill, *Styracosaurus* looked much like *Centrosaurus* and *Monoclonius.* These three dinosaurs were probably closely related. *Styracosaurus* was also related to *Pachyrhinosaurus, Brachyceratops,* and *Avaceratops.*

Until recently, *Styracosaurus* has been a rare ceratopsian. Paleontologists are now studying a number of *Styracosaurus* skeletons that have been found in Montana. These new skeletons may prove to be a new species.

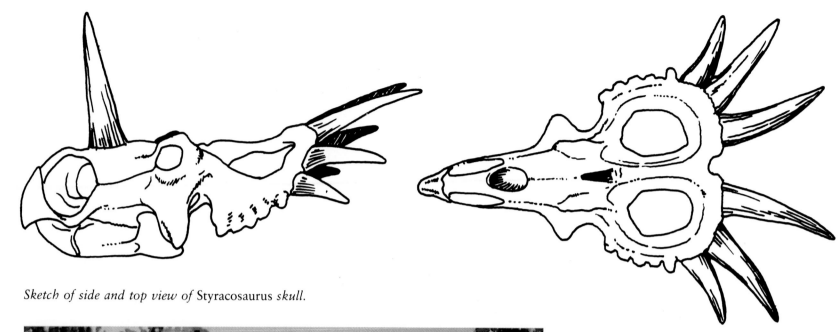

Sketch of side and top view of Styracosaurus *skull.*

Styracosaurus

TALARURUS
(TAL-ah-RUR-us)

Period:
Late Cretaceous
Order, Suborder, Family:
Ornithischia, Thyreophora, Ankylosauridae
Location:
Asia (Mongolian People's Republic)
Length:
23 feet (7 meters)

This is one of the better-known ankylosaurs from Mongolia. Several partial skeletons were excavated by Soviet paleontologists during the 1950s. One of these skeletons is mounted at the Paleontological Institute in Moscow.

Talarurus was a barrel-chested ankylosaur. It had a long, low body; short limbs; and a long tail that ended in a bone club. The skull was triangular, somewhat like the skull of *Shamosaurus.* Bone plates covering the skull were small and different shapes. Its nostrils joined at the front of the snout, making a single large opening.

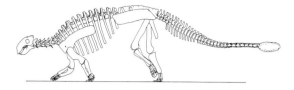

Talarurus skeletal drawing.

The body armor was bands of bumpy plates joined together. The tail club was long and low; the animal could have given a powerful blow to a *Tarbosaurus*. For greater power and strength, tendons were interlaced and attached to the end of the tail. The animal was named after this feature; its name means "basket tail."

TARCHIA
(TAR-kee-uh)

Period:
Late Cretaceous
Order, Suborder, Family:
Ornithischia, Thyreophora, Ankylosauridae
Location:
Asia (Mongolian People's Republic)
Length:
Unknown

This ankylosaur is known from two species. *Tarchia giganteus* is known from a complete skull and a partial skeleton. But,

Tarchia

Talarurus plicatospineus

except for the skull, little of the material has been described. For this reason, neither the length nor weight of the animal is known.

The skull of *Tarchia* was massive, and it had room for a large brain. In fact, its name means "brain" in Mongolian. The skull had large spinelike plates at the top and bottom. Large, knobby plates of armor covered the skull. The beak was broad and rounded. The teeth looked like those of most other ankylosaurs; the animal was a plant-eater. The armor was thin-walled and similar to the armor plates of most ankylosaurs.

Tarchia lived in a dry environment. Other dinosaurs that lived at the same time and in the same place included *Tyrannosaurus*, the ostrich dinosaur *Gallimimus*, and the hadrosaur *Saurolophus*. Scientists do not know what plants *Tarchia* ate because no fossil plants have been found.

229

Thescelosaurus neglectus

THERIZINOSAURUS
(THER-ih-ZIN-oh-SORE-us)

Period:
Late Cretaceous
Order, Suborder, Family:
Saurischia, Segnosauria, Segnosauridae
Location:
Asia (Mongolian People's Republic)
Length:
Unknown

In 1948, several giant claw bones were found by a Soviet-Mongolian scientific team in the Nemegt Basin of the Gobi Desert of Mongolia. Because the shape of the claws is similar to the claws of some turtles and because the claws were found with large, flat bones, workers first thought they belonged to a giant turtle. So the specimen was named *Therizinosaurus cheloniformis* ("turtlelike scythe reptile") by the famous Soviet paleontologist E. A. Maleyev.

Other finds of similar claws, including one with a partial arm, proved that the claws belonged to a dinosaur. The large, flat bones were not part of a turtle, but parts of sauropod ribs. The most interesting feature of these claws is their size. One bony portion of the claw is 28 inches long. In life, the claw would have been covered by hornlike material, making it even longer. It may be from a very large segnosaur.

Unfortunately, the remains of *Therizinosaurus* are too few, are not from parts of the skeleton that give much information (such as the skull or hips), and are in too many pieces to give scientists an understanding of its form and lifestyle. So it is not known what it looked like and what family it belongs to, but many paleontologists place it in Segnosauridae.

Scientists hope to find more fossils that will tell them more about the animal. Another large claw has been found in Niger, Africa, but it is not known if it is related to *Therizinosaurus*.

Thescelosaurus *skeleton.*

THESCELOSAURUS
(THESS-ah-loh-SORE-us)

Period:
Late Cretaceous
Order, Suborder, Family:
Ornithischia, Ornithopoda,
Hypsilophodontidae
Location:
North America (Canada, United States)
Length:
11 feet (3.3 meters)

Thescelosaurus was one of the last hypsilophodontid dinosaurs. It is known from the end of the Late Cretaceous of Montana in the United States, and Alberta and Saskatchewan in Canada. It may have seen what happened to cause the mass extinctions at the end of the Mesozoic.

Meaning "beautiful reptile," *Thescelosaurus* is known from complete skeletons. The front of the jaws lacked teeth. Muscular cheeks along the sides of the face kept food from falling out of the mouth.

This small dinosaur had stocky body and limb proportions. Thescelosaurus must have been a much slower runner than other hypsilophodontids that were about the same size.

TOROSAURUS
(TORE-oh-SORE-us)

Period:
Late Cretaceous
Order, Suborder, Family:
Ornithischia, Marginocephalia,
Ceratopsidae
Location:
North America (Canada, United States)
Length:
25 feet (7.5 meters)

The first two *Torosaurus* specimens were a pair of skulls found in Wyoming in 1891 by John Bell Hatcher. They were described by Othniel Marsh later that same year. These two skulls were named *Torosaurus latus* and *Torosaurus gladius*. Paleon-tologists now believe all *Torosaurus* specimens belong to one species, *Torosaurus latus*.

Its skull had a large flaring neck frill that was over six and a half feet high; it had the largest skull of any known land animal. The size of the skull, along with the two very long and robust brow horns, were the inspiration for the name *Torosaurus*, which means "bull reptile."

Although very large, the neck frill of *Torosaurus* was thin, and the two fenestrae (openings) were large and oval-shaped. Some specimens show extra openings along the sides of the neck frill. *Torosaurus* had a small, drawn out beak that was topped by a short nasal horn. Very little is known about the rest of the skeleton of *Torosaurus*. The few pieces of skeleton that have been found show that it probably looked similar to the other chasmosaurine ceratopsids.

Torosaurus lived during the same time period as its close relative *Triceratops*. But while *Triceratops* is a common dinosaur, *Torosaurus* is rare and may not have existed in such great numbers as *Triceratops*. *Torosaurus* was smaller than *Triceratops*, even though its skull was bigger. *Torosaurus* was also closely related to *Anchiceratops*, *Arrhinoceratops*, *Pentaceratops*, and *Chasmosaurus*.

Torosaurus

TRICERATOPS
(trie-SAIR-ah-TOPS)

Period:
Late Cretaceous
Order, Suborder, Family:
Ornithischia, Marginocephalia,
Ceratopsidae
Location:
North America (Canada, United States)
Length:
30 feet (9 meters)

Triceratops is one of the most spectacular and well known of all dinosaurs. This huge animal, with its long, pointed brow horns and curving neck frill, was one of the last dinosaurs to walk the earth. It lived to the end of the Cretaceous. *Triceratops* was the largest of the ceratopsians.

The first *Triceratops* specimen found was a set of brow horns. Othniel Marsh examined these horns in 1887 and thought they came from an extinct bison. He named the specimen *Bison alticornis;* he did not know that horned dinosaurs existed. Two years later, a nearly complete skull was collected from Wyoming, and Marsh quickly realized his mistake. The new skull was named *Triceratops horridus* in 1889, and the name of the "bison" specimen was changed to *Triceratops alticornis.* Over the next eight years, Marsh added eight more species to the genus.

Triceratops specimens are common and many have been collected. Paleontologist John Bell Hatcher collected more than 30 skulls in one area in Wyoming alone. In fact, so many *Triceratops* specimens have been found that no one knows exactly how many there are. But no complete *Triceratops* skeleton has ever been found.

Although paleontologists have named a large number of species of *Triceratops,* most probably do not exist. Even though all of these "species" differ from one another in little ways, paleontologists now realize that differences should be expected.

Each living animal is not a carbon copy of the other. It is also unlikely that so many species lived together in a small area. All the many named species of *Triceratops* are probably only one or two species.

The body of *Triceratops* was massive with a huge, barrellike ribcage and short tail. Except for its large size, it probably looked like the other large ceratopsids. It was probably not a fast animal. It had heavily built limb bones, and the front limbs were shorter than the back. It probably relied on strength rather than speed for defense.

Although the name *Triceratops* means "three-horned face," not all specimens had three horns. Often the nasal horn was either very short or nearly absent. However, the two brow horns, which grew out of the top of the skull over each eye, were always large and well developed. The brow horns probably had a horny covering. The base of the brow horns in *Triceratops* was hollow; they opened into a large space (called a sinus) above the braincase (the bone that covered the brain). Some modern animals, such as cows, goats, and sheep, also have these sinuses in the tops of their skulls. The sinus acts as a shock absorber for fights; it provides a cushion for the brain.

Some *Triceratops* specimens show healed wounds in their skull or frill, showing that they fought among themselves. They may have fought over females, territory, or leadership. It is also likely that the long, strong horns of *Triceratops* were used as weapons against predators such as *Tyrannosaurus.*

The frill of *Triceratops* was different from all other ceratopsids. It was broad and round, and the bone was thick and had no fenestrae (openings). Traces of blood vessels were present in the frill and skull. These vessels probably supplied the bone and skin with blood. Some paleontologists believe that the broad frill, with its large blood supply, may have helped heat or cool the animal. Blood flowing

Two Triceratops.

close to the surface would give off body heat if the air was cool, or would absorb heat if the air was hot. *Triceratops* could turn its frill toward the sun to warm up, or go to shade to release heat if it was too warm. Modern elephants regulate their body temperature the same way, using their huge ears.

Like the horns, the solid frill may have been used to protect *Triceratops* from predators or from other *Triceratops.* The frill may also have been for bluff; *Triceratops* could put its head down and point its brow horns at another animal, making the frill stand up. This made *Triceratops* appear larger. The frill may also have attracted a mate.

For many years, paleontologists thought that *Triceratops* was most closely related to the centrosaurine (or "short-frilled") ceratopsids, such as *Centrosaurus* and *Styracosaurus.* This was because the frill of *Triceratops* was relatively short; it was much shorter than the frills of the chasmosaurine (or "long-frilled") ceratopsids, such as *Chasmosaurus* and *Torosaurus.* However, all other features of the skull of *Triceratops* are like those of the Chasmo-

saurinae, such as long brow horns, a short nasal horn, and a long snout with a double opening of the nose. *Triceratops* is now considered a chasmosaurine.

Triceratops had a very long and powerful beak. Each jaw had closely packed teeth with a broad grinding surface. With its scissorlike beak and grinding teeth, *Triceratops* was able to bite off and chew even the toughest plants. Because its beak was narrow and pointed, it probably bit off plants with the side of its beak. Muscular cheeks held food in its mouth as it chewed.

Triceratops had a small brain; the ratio of its brain size to its body size is lower than two-legged dinosaurs, such as the duckbills and meat-eaters. Although *Triceratops* probably was not the smartest dinosaur, it was one of the most abundant Late Cretaceous dinosaurs. So, despite its brain size, it was very successful.

The world in which *Triceratops* lived looked quite modern. The landscape had modern-looking trees and shrubs. Animals that lived at the same time as *Triceratops* included *Tyrannosaurus, Thescelosaurus, Torosaurus, Leptoceratops, Ankylosaurus,* and *Ornithomimus.*

Left: *A herd of* Triceratops *in a cypress swamp.*

Troodon formosus

TROODON
(TROH-oh-don)

Period:
Late Cretaceous
Order, Suborder, Family:
Saurischia, Theropoda, Troodontidae
Location:
North America (Canada, United States)
Length:
8 feet (2.4 meters)

Troodon was described in 1856 by Joseph Leidy on the basis of a single small tooth. It was one of the first North American dinosaurs described. However, it was first thought to be the tooth of a lizard. It was not until 1901 that it was known to be a dinosaur tooth.

In the early days of paleontology it was common to name a dinosaur only on the basis of teeth. But often these names were put aside because scientists could not tell what dinosaur the tooth belonged to even with a complete skull with teeth for comparison. Despite this, the name *Troodon* was kept because its tooth was so unusual. But for many years some scientists thought the tooth of *Troodon* was from a pachycephalosaur.

Many scientists believed the original *Troodon* tooth belonged to a theropod. *Troodon* was placed in the family Troodontidae in 1948. Then, in 1983, Jack Horner found the lower jaw of a small theropod with the same type of teeth. This jaw proved that *Troodon* was a theropod. It was also found that all the teeth of *Troodon* were not the same; the shape of the tooth depended on where the tooth was in the jaw. This jaw also showed that the animal called *Stenonychosaurus* was the same as *Troodon*. A close relative of *Troodon* was *Saurornithoides*.

Troodon is now known from several partial skulls and skeletons. These skulls show that it had a large brain for its size, and it probably had the most developed brain of any dinosaur. Its eyes were large, taking up a big part of the skull. Each side of the lower jaw had 35 teeth—more than any other theropod.

Its hands had slender fingers, and the inner finger ended in a large, thin, sharply pointed claw. The foot was similar to the foot of dromaeosaurids, with a large claw on the second toe. The claw was used to slash its prey. However, the claw was higher on the foot and smaller than the claw of a dromaeosaur. The claw on the first finger of the hand of *Troodon* was much larger than the largest claw on its foot. Also, like the dromaeosaurids, the back part of the tail was stiff. The dromaeosaurs may have been the ancestors of the troodontids.

TYLOCEPHALE
(TIE-loh-seh-FAL-ee)

Period:
Late Cretaceous
Order, Suborder, Family:
Ornithischia, Marginocephalia, Pachycephalosauridae
Location:
Asia (Mongolian People's Republic)
Length:
Unknown, but probably no more than 6¹/₂ feet (2 meters)

Tylocephale is one of a group of new dome-headed dinosaurs discovered by the Joint Polish-Mongolian Paleontological Expeditions to the Gobi Desert. Meaning "swollen head," *Tylocephale* was named in 1974 by Teresa Maryanska and Halszka Osmólska on the basis of a skull that was missing much of the snout and the front part of the high dome. It lived during the Late Cretaceous, much like its relatives *Prenocephale* from central Asia, and *Stegoceras, Stygimoloch,* and *Pachycephalosaurus* from North America.

The skull of *Tylocephale* had a high, narrow dome. The bones that formed the dome were tightly joined, making them strong. The back of the dome was flared out into a large, short shelf or frill over the back of the braincase and neck. On this shelf were bony bumps and pits. *Tylocephale* had simple teeth and probably ate leaves and fruit.

The domed skull of *Tylocephale* was not damaged by being hit; it needed this strength during head-butting contests for territory and females.

Tylocephale gilmorei

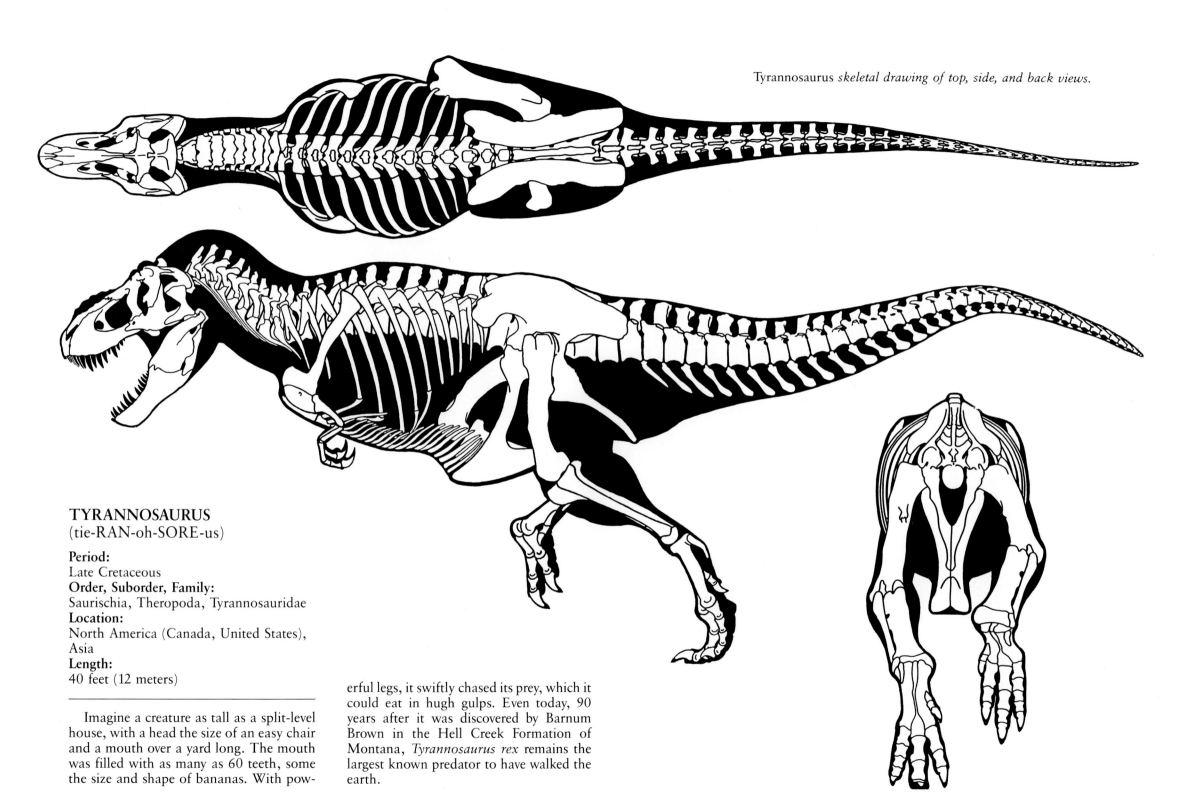

Tyrannosaurus skeletal drawing of top, side, and back views.

TYRANNOSAURUS
(tie-RAN-oh-SORE-us)

Period:
Late Cretaceous
Order, Suborder, Family:
Saurischia, Theropoda, Tyrannosauridae
Location:
North America (Canada, United States),
Asia
Length:
40 feet (12 meters)

Imagine a creature as tall as a split-level house, with a head the size of an easy chair and a mouth over a yard long. The mouth was filled with as many as 60 teeth, some the size and shape of bananas. With powerful legs, it swiftly chased its prey, which it could eat in hugh gulps. Even today, 90 years after it was discovered by Barnum Brown in the Hell Creek Formation of Montana, *Tyrannosaurus rex* remains the largest known predator to have walked the earth.

Left: Tyrannosaurus *attacks an* Edmontosaurus.

237

Probably the most familiar dinosaur, *Tyrannosaurus rex,* the North American species, is known from only seven incomplete skeletons and other assorted remains. *T. rex* has been found in Texas, Wyoming, Colorado, South Dakota, Montana, and Alberta. A few paleontologists think that there may have been two species of *Tyrannosaurus* in North America, but others believe the differences were between males and females. *Tyrannosaurus rex* was about 13 feet tall and over 40 feet long, but a huge upper jawbone at the University of California at Berkeley comes from an animal that may have been 16 feet tall and over 50 feet long, and outweighed even the heaviest modern elephant.

The latest *T. rex* was found in Montana in 1987. It is the most complete specimen found; it has a skull about five feet long and may prove to be nearly 50 feet long when it is finally excavated. It is also the first specimen found with nearly complete forearms. This animal had two-fingered hands, with robust arms. It probably used its front limbs as hooks to hold struggling prey.

Tyrannosaurus was built for hunting. The eyes of most meat-eating dinosaurs were on the sides of their skulls, but those of *T. rex* faced more forward. It may have been able to judge depth and distance. It was not a scavenger, as some paleontologists once thought, but if it found the body of a dead dinosaur, it would not have passed up a free meal. The teeth in the front of its jaws were shaped differently from those in the sides. Different shapes may have had different uses.

Considering its enormous size, the skull of *Tyrannosaurus* was lightly built. It had wide fenestrae (openings) and hollow bones. Some of those bones were not joined tightly, which is one reason *Tyrannosaurus* skulls are often not found whole. Like most theropods, its lower jaw had a hinge that allowed it to open out as well as down, so it could have swallowed large chunks of meat.

Powerful muscles on the thighs and tail made walking and running easy for even the largest theropods. *Tyrannosaurus* could have walked all day at four or five miles an hour in search of food and could have run at a speed of over 30 miles per hour.

A closely related animal, named *Tarbosaurus bataar,* is based on a large partial skull discovered in the Gobi Desert in the late 1940s. Several nearly complete skeletons of this species were excavated. Some of the skeletons were smaller animals and different enough from *Tyrannosaurus* to be considered a new animal, named *Tarbosaurus efremovi.* Some paleontologists believe that *Tarbosaurus* and *Tyrannosaurus* are the same genus, but different species. Recent work has shown that these specimens had probably died before reaching full adult size. So they may be a species of *Tyrannosaurus.* Further studies are being done to find the truth about its relationships.

Tarbosaurus bataar grew to about the same length as *T. rex,* but it was a lighter, more slender animal that lived a few million years earlier. Its eyes did not face forward as much as those of *T. rex.*

Tyrannosaurus *skeleton in foreground.*

VELOCIRAPTOR
(vel-OS-ih-RAP-tore)

Period:
Late Cretaceous
Order, Suborder, Family:
Saurischia, Theropoda, Dromaeosauridae
Location:
Asia (Mongolian People's Republic)
Length:
6 feet (1.8 meters)

The most amazing find in Mongolia may be the discovery of the skeletons of the small theropod *Velociraptor* ("speedy predator") with its right arm clamped firmly in the beak of the small ceratopsian *Protoceratops*. Both skeletons are complete. They are a picture of a Late Cretaceous struggle to the death. Soon after their deaths, they were buried by the drifting sands of a dune. They laid together in this death pose until 1971, when they were unearthed.

In 1923, the first specimen of *Velociraptor* was found by the American Museum of Natural History. Like the famous death-pose specimen, it was found in the Late Cretaceous sandstones of the Djadokhta Formation in the Gobi Desert. And, like the death-pose specimen, it was found lying alongside a skull of *Protoceratops*.

Velociraptor was a small theropod, with a large sickle-shaped claw on the second toe of its foot. It had a low, narrow snout, which is different from other members of its family. The jaws were lined with serrated teeth for tearing flesh. It swallowed its food in gulps instead of chewing, like most theropods. The arms were long and it had strong chest and arm muscles. It looked much like the early bird *Archaeopteryx*, especially its pelvis. Some paleontologists have suggested that *Velociraptor* might have had feathers, but there is no proof for this theory.

Since the death-pose specimen was found with a *Protoceratops*, it probably ate this small ceratopsian, but it may have hunted even larger prey. Its diet also included small animals, such as lizards.

Another dromaeosaurid feature that can be clearly seen in the death-pose specimen are the long pieces of bone along the sides of the bones of the tail to stiffen it. This allowed the tail to act as a balance when the animal walked and ran. The tail, however, was still flexible, especially where it was attached to the hips. The complete "struggle to the death" skeleton has not yet been described, but it will certainly reveal even more new and exciting facts about this fascinating genus.

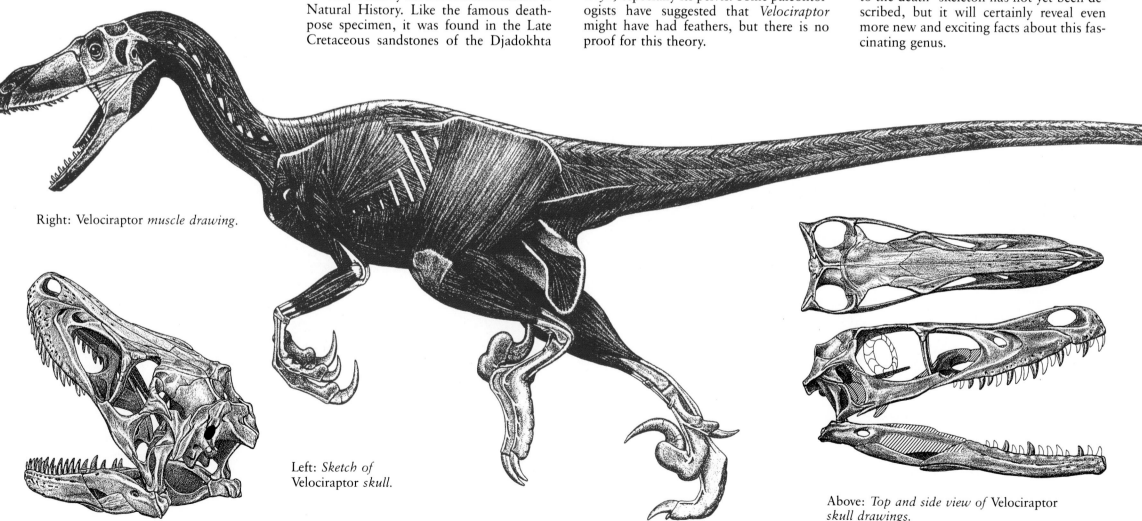

Right: Velociraptor *muscle drawing.*

Left: *Sketch of* Velociraptor *skull.*

Above: *Top and side view of* Velociraptor *skull drawings.*

CHAPTER 8

WHAT CAUSED THE DEATH OF THE DINOSAURS?

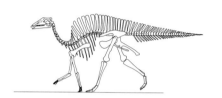

Dinosaurs became extinct at the end of the Cretaceous Period. How and why is a puzzle that paleontologists are trying to solve by studying fossils and rock formations. These fossils and rock formations do not give all the facts, so scientists must take the information and make educated guesses. Sometimes different scientists see the same material but come to different conclusions, so there are many different theories.

Some paleontologists think the extinction was caused by a catastrophe such as a meteorite or comet hitting the earth or a gigantic volcano erupting. Others believe that a more gradual process was responsible. Some theories are that competition between dinosaurs and mammals was the cause, or possibly climate changes. Scientists also disagree about the amount of time it took for the extinction to take place. Some think it happened in several days. Others say it took from hundreds of generations to over half a million years. Any extinction theory must account for the extinctions that occurred in the sea, including some types of clams and coiled mollusks.

The extinction event did not kill all animal and plant life. Many kinds of animals survived, including fishes, frogs, turtles, crocodilians, birds, and mammals. Scientists must take the fossil record and find reasons for all extinctions.

Left: *Two tyrannosaurs watch a comet streak through the sky.*

Far left: Triceratops *lived until the end of the Cretaceous Period*. Left: Triceratops *skeleton.*

The Cretaceous Extinction Event

The extinction event that killed the dinosaurs was worldwide. It affected many plant and animal groups, both on land and in water. Dinosaurs were only a small part—the disappearance of other living things was so great that scientists knew about the extinction 30 years before the first dinosaur was described.

The victims of the Cretaceous extinction included dinosaurs, ammonites (mollusks related to the octopus and the chambered nautilus), pterosaurs, and certain plant groups. But many other animal groups, even some large-bodied reptile groups like champsosaurs, were not affected.

The image of the last majestic dinosaurs passing away and leaving a world of shrew-like mammals and cold-blooded reptiles is false. Instead, many of the major modern land animals were already living in the Cretaceous. Dinosaurs shared their last million years with modern creatures.

Since more than just dinosaurs became extinct, reasons that only explain why dinosaurs died can be ruled out. For in-stance, there is one theory that disease caused the extinction of dinosaurs. But a disease could not have caused the extinction of plants and animals over the whole world.

Fossil Record Information

The relationship between plants and animals that became extinct at the end of the Cretaceous is important to understanding dinosaur extinction. The reasons for extinction in all these different groups are related. Understanding why another group became extinct may give us clues about dinosaur extinction.

Plants and some animals have a better fossil record than dinosaurs. They also give clues about climate that dinosaur fossils do not. Some marine protozoans (single-celled organisms), called foraminifera, have shells that tell the temperature of the water where the animal lived. By studying the chemical make-up of these tiny fossils, the temperatures of prehistoric seas can be found, and changes in the ocean tempera-ture can be shown. Ocean temperature reflects the climate. This can be used to find out what the climate was like before, during, and after dinosaurs became extinct.

But unlike other scientists, paleontologists cannot go into a laboratory and repeat experiments. They can only untangle history by examining fossils. Unfortunately, there is not enough information and it is often incomplete.

Studying the fossil record can be compared to watching a mystery movie. The paleontologist, though, does not have the whole film. The paleontologist has a film with some parts that are almost complete (every other frame) and others where large chunks (whole reels) are missing. The paleontologist must piece these parts together in order to find out how much of the film is missing.

Paleontologists have come up with a measure of how much of the fossil record is present. The term used is "stratigraphic completeness." Scientists must know how complete the record is in order to find out how long the extinction of dinosaurs took. To use the movie example, it's like trying to find how much time has passed since an event (like a murder) occurred. If all of the frames are present, we know the amount of time. If every other frame is present, we can only say that the event happened within the length of the gap.

Scientists have studied the stratigraphic completeness in the rock formations containing the last dinosaur fossils and in the boundary between the Cretaceous and the Tertiary (the period following the Mesozoic Era). In complete rock units, the best we can say is that dinosaur extinction took less than 100,000 years. In rock units where the sections are less complete, the time frame is longer—even as much as a million years.

In marine rocks (rocks formed in seas or oceans) the record is often more complete. It is here that the earliest and some of the strongest evidence for an extraterrestrial

Excavating bones of the Late Cretaceous dinosaur Edmontosaurus.

243

Troodon, *one of the last dinosaurs.*

(something from outside the earth's atmosphere) cause for dinosaur extinction has come. Because the record is more complete in marine rocks, the time units studied are much smaller and more accurate. The stratigraphic completeness in rocks deposited in the San Juan Basin (a rock unit in western North America that includes the final phase of dinosaur history) is 100,000 years. In contrast, marine rocks deposited during this same time in Spain allow an interval as short as 10,000 years to be studied. However, these rocks contain no dinosaur fossils.

A second problem with the fossil record is that sometimes fossils can be collected out of place. Recently scientists reported that some dinosaurs may have survived the end of the Cretaceous and lived into the early Tertiary. Workers collected these specimens in rocks above the Cretaceous-Tertiary boundary, with specimens of early Tertiary mammals.

Many paleontologists feel that these specimens were already fossils in the Early Tertiary. They believe that these fossils eroded out of the rocks, and nature reburied them along with the remains of Tertiary mammals. Scientists call this process "reworking" or secondary deposition. It only looks like these animals lived at the same time, even though they lived millions of years apart. Paleontologists must study every specimen carefully.

Extinction Theories

There are two groups of extinction theories: catastrophic extinction and gradual extinction. Catastrophic extinction would have been caused by a sudden, external event, such as the collision of the earth with an asteroid, or the eruption of a series of gigantic volcanoes. Gradual extinction would have been the result of changes in the earth's land mass and climate shifts. It could also have been because new and better animals won in the struggle for existence.

Until the recent theories about extraterrestrial collisions, some ideas about the disappearance of dinosaurs centered around mammals beating them in the struggle to survive. One theory suggests that mammals killed dinosaurs because they ate dinosaur eggs. Other scientists have suggested that dinosaurs caused their own extinction. According to this theory, too many meat-eating dinosaurs evolved, eating all the plant-eaters, causing all dinosaurs to die. These ideas have the same pitfall described earlier. They explain dinosaur extinction but ignore the extinction of other groups.

Climate Change Theories

Leigh Van Valen and Bob Sloan offered a more complex theory. During the Late Cretaceous, the continents were moving and major new mountain chains began to rise. Many of the shallow Mesozoic seas dried up. Van Valen and Sloan suggest that this caused the world's climate to change. Evidence from fossil plants at their Montana study site suggests that it got about ten centigrade points colder in the Late Cretaceous. A temperature decline that large would affect the earth. It would have become colder in the mountains, and new plants would have replaced the warm-weather plants.

Van Valen and Sloan have argued that dinosaurs were at a disadvantage in the new forests of coniferous trees. So, they left the mountains and moved toward the tropics, to a better climate. This theory suggests that the dinosaurs survived longer in the tropics than in the mountains. Because plants in the tropics survived, something else must have caused dinosaur extinction in these areas.

One suggestion is that placental mammals (mammals that give live birth and have a placenta) became abundant in the mountains, because they no longer competed with dinosaurs. Later, the mammals escaped these regions and went into the tropics, where they drove dinosaurs to extinction. There are problems with this theory. Some studies of foraminifera (the shells of protozoans talked about earlier) show that there was a short-term warming trend in the Late Cretaceous. But they are right about the long-term cooling trend. There is no evidence that dinosaurs lasted longer in one area than another. Although competition between animals may explain the extinction of many living things at the end of the Cretaceous, other groups, especially the foraminifera, seem to have disappeared without competitors.

Another climate change theory is due to recent research. Some living reptiles, turtles and crocodiles, lay eggs. It was recently found that the sex of their offspring is decided by the temperature of the nest. So if the same were true for dinosaurs, cooling temperatures in the Late Cretaceous may have caused all the young to be of the same sex, so the species would not have been able to continue.

Edmontosaurus *skeleton.*

Right: *A duckbilled dinosaur watches a comet.*

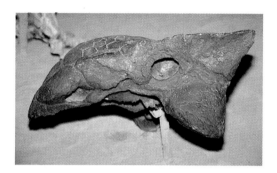

Ankylosaurus *may have been a witness to the extinction event.*

EXTRATERRESTRIAL IMPACT THEORY

One exciting theory is that an extraterrestrial body hit the earth, causing the Late Cretaceous extinctions. Walter and Luis Alvarez and their coworkers found the evidence for this collision during a study of some Cretaceous clay from northern Italy. To their surprise, they found that the clay was rich in the element iridium. Iridium is rare on earth but is more common in extraterrestrial bodies such as meteorites and comets. After further studies, the Alvarezes found the iridium only in a narrow layer. To their amazement, this iridium layer almost exactly matches the Cretaceous-Tertiary boundary. This led them to suggest that a large extraterrestrial body had hit the earth, which caused the extinction of dinosaurs in the Cretaceous.

Since this discovery, scientists have found the "iridium datum plane" (the iridium layer) at the Cretaceous-Tertiary boundary at over 50 sites worldwide. There is other evidence that a large body from outer space hit the earth. For instance, when an asteroid hits the earth, intense heat and pressure develop. The heat and pressure cause changes in the rocks where the comet hit. One of these changes is shock-fractured quartz grains. Bits of quartz (a common mineral in the earth's crust) will break in an unusual way only from intense heat and pressure. The only other place shock-fractured quartz is found is at ground zero of atomic explosions (where a nuclear bomb is exploded). Common elements also act differently when under intense pressure. For example, nitrogen, a usually harmless gas, may have condensed and rained back as nitric acid, a deadly acid rain.

The impact of an asteroid would be a major event in the history of the earth. The iridium layer over the world shows that the comet or meteorite must have been over six miles wide. When it crashed to earth, it would have been traveling 12 miles per second, creating a crater about 100 miles wide.

Because of its speed, the asteroid would have ripped a giant hole in the earth's atmosphere. Parts of the earth's crust would have been blown into the upper atmosphere when the asteroid hit. Later, this would rain down as tiny glass beads, ash, shock-fractured quartz, and parts of the asteroid.

A large amount of dust would have covered the earth. The amount of dust caused by the explosion of Tambora, a volcano in Indonesia, in 1815 caused climate changes worldwide for several years. The dust and debris that would have covered the earth following a meteorite hit of the size suggested by the Alvarezes would have been greater than any volcano.

The dust cloud would have taken weeks or months to settle. First, the temperature on earth would have dropped to below freezing because the dust clouds would have stopped the sun's rays from reaching the earth. This would have harmed the green plants and ocean plankton. Plankton and green plants form the bottom of the world's food chain. They also change carbon dioxide to oxygen.

Late Cretaceous animals might have suffocated because of a lack of oxygen or starved to death. This would have begun with the plant-eaters and carried through to the meat-eaters. After that, the dust cloud would have caused global warming because the heat of the earth would have been trapped. It could not escape through the thick layer of dust in the upper atmosphere.

Since the first Alvarez study, many lines of evidence associated with the iridium layer have all lent support to the contention that an extraterrestrial impact was associated with the end of the Cretaceous. Evidence includes the discovery of an impact structure off the Yucatan peninsula and the discovery of shock-fractured quartz grains. A preponderance of fern spores was also discovered; ferns are usually the first plants to recolonize an area that has been devegetated by a natural disaster.

The dust cloud proposed by the Alvarezes would have killed all plant and animal life—not just dinosaurs. And paleontologists think the extinctions in the marine world lasted thousands of years. This may mean that the marine and land extinctions did not happen at the same time. This has led some scientists to suggest the possibility that many smaller meteors or comets hit the earth over a longer period of time.

Tyrannosaurs attack a herd of Triceratops.

Left: *The comet hits earth, sending debris into the atmosphere.*

CHAPTER 9

NEW DISCOVERIES

Interest in dinosaurs soared to new heights in the 1990s, thanks largely to the blockbuster film *Jurassic Park*. So too did dinosaur discoveries. Since 1990, more than 100 new dinosaur genera have been described and named.

A couple dozen new dinosaurs have been found in western North America. Moreover, paleontologists in South Dakota discovered the most complete *Tyrannosaurus rex* skeleton ever. The story of "Sue" captivated dinosaur buffs around the globe. Dinosaur discoveries in Patagonia included the vertebrae of one of the largest plant-eaters that ever lived, *Argentinosaurus*, which may have been over 100 feet long.

Asia, particularly China and Mongolia, has yielded the largest number of newly discovered dinosaurs. The first feathered dinosaurs, long anticipated because of the close relationship between dinosaurs and birds, finally appeared in the fossil record, at Liaoning, China. The evidence for a dinosaur-bird connection has grown very strong; meat-eating dinosaurs and birds share more than a hundred anatomical features. Although the dinosaur-bird connection was first proposed by paleontologists in the 19th century, the new, computer-oriented methods of classification have finally made this relationship clear.

The remains of Carcharodontosaurus, *an enormous meat-eater, were found in Africa.*

THE STORY OF "SUE"

On a foggy August day in 1990, Susan Hendrickson found a few fossilized dinosaur bones weathering out of a cliff on a ranch near Faith, South Dakota. The ranch belonged to Maurice Williams, who was one-quarter Sioux. Hendrickson's employer, Peter Larson, a founder of the Black Hills Institute of Geological Research at Hill City, South Dakota, was at the time en route to Faith to fix the tires on one of the Institute's vehicles. Hendrickson, driven by a feeling that she would make a great discovery, decided that morning to do some fossil prospecting on the ranch. She could tell at once that the bones visible in the cliff—a few vertebrae and a partial thigh bone—belonged to a large meat-eating dinosaur, almost certainly a *Tyrannosaurus rex*.

By the time she made her way back to camp, Larson had returned. She showed him a few pieces of the find. Larson agreed excitedly

Skeleton of "Sue" on display at the Field Museum of Natural History in Chicago.

The skull of "Sue."

that she had found a *Tyrannosaurus*, and they began making plans to dig the bones out of the ground. They checked to make sure that Williams was indeed the owner of the land where the bones were found, and they obtained his permission to excavate to see how much of the skeleton was there. In a few days, Larson and his crew realized that they were looking at the most complete skeleton of a *Tyrannosaurus*

rex ever discovered. More than 90 percent of the dinosaur's bones were present, including a huge skull nearly five feet long. It was also the largest *Tyrannosaurus rex* ever found, and its bones were especially well preserved.

Larson negotiated with Williams to buy the skeleton for $5,000 and started work. Within 17 days the skeleton was out of the ground, jacketed, and on its way to the Institute's prepa-

ration laboratory. Larson nicknamed the fossil "Sue," after Susan Hendrickson. He had a theory about how one might tell male and female meat-eating dinosaurs apart, and "Sue," he thought, was a large female.

When Williams saw the tremendous publicity the find received, both he and the Sioux tribe began to have second thoughts about the ownership of the bones. The Sioux tribe also

FEATHERED DINOSAURS FROM LIAONING

In 1994, farmers in Liaoning Province in northeastern China began finding exquisitely preserved fossil birds representing a new species, *Confuciusornis*. They were discovered in fine-grained Early Cretaceous sedimentary deposits near the village of Sihetun. Many were so well preserved that even their feathers could be seen. Several kinds of fossil birds were found, but *Confuciousornis* was the most common. Other fossils were also found, including splendid examples of fish and plants. So many fossils were found, and are still being found, that a thriving market has developed in exporting them out of China—a market that the Chinese government considers illegal smuggling.

In 1996, the skeleton of a small dinosaur came to light at Sihetun. Complete practically to the last bone, it belonged to a new kind of theropod about three feet long named *Sinosauropteryx prima*. In size and anatomy, it closely resembled the small European dinosaur *Compsognathus*, but it showed distinct traces of short, brushy structures along the neck, back, and tail. After some arguing back and forth, most scientists now believe that the brushy structures are indeed feathers, somewhat different in structure than those of modern birds. *Sinosauropteryx* is thus the first feathered non-avian dinosaur ever found.

Even as *Sinosauropteryx* was being studied, more feathered dinosaurs turned up in Liaoning: *Protarchaeopteryx*, a larger theropod five feet long, with very birdlike feathers visible along the tail; *Caudipteryx*, a very birdlike theropod about three feet tall, showing good feather impressions along forelimbs and tail; *Sinornithosaurus*, a troodontid-like theropod about the same size as *Sinosauropteryx*, with hairlike feathers; and *Beipiaosaurus*, a theropod more than six feet long, the largest-known theropod with feather impressions (also hairlike). The smallest feathered Liaoning theropod was *Microraptor*, less than 1.5 feet long, classified as a dromaeosaurid. All these feathered dinosaurs had relatively large, powerful hind legs, obviously suited for fast running, and hands with large claws. None had wings.

The discovery of feathered theropods strongly supports the theory that birds are theropod dinosaurs that evolved the ability to fly. But perhaps the most interesting thing about the Liaoning feathered theropods is that they represent several different theropod families. This means that the origin of feathers is not closely linked to the origin of birds, and offers evidence that many different lines of theropod dinosaurs may have had feathers of some sort, not just those most closely related to birds. Depending on how widespread the structures were among theropods, even such giants as *Tyrannosaurus rex* may have had feathers.

Susan Hendrickson discovered the remains of "Sue."

felt that they might be legal owners of the fossil, and they asked the U.S. Government to get involved.

In the ensuing legal struggle, the FBI seized "Sue" from the Institute and locked it away at the South Dakota School of Mines and Technology in Rapid City until the dispute could be resolved. They also seized the Institute's financial and fossil-collecting records—and discovered legal irregularities that eventually placed Larson into a minimum-security federal prison for two years.

Larson never got "Sue" back. The government declared Williams the legal owner and returned the fossil to him. Williams soon contacted Sotheby's in New York City to auction the skeleton. On October 4, 1997, after a huge publicity campaign, "Sue" was sold for a mind-boggling $8.36 million to the Field

Museum of Natural History in Chicago, which received corporate backing from Walt Disney World Resort and McDonald's Corporation.

The Field Museum became responsible for preparing "Sue" for public display. Head fossil preparator Bill Simpson and his team worked the bones out of the matrix, and Phil Fraley designed the mount to hold them. Paleontologist Christopher Brochu was hired to write up "Sue's" scientific description. The skull, crushed and flattened when the dinosaur was buried 67 million years ago, was CT-scanned to reveal its internal structure. Too heavy to mount with the rest of the dinosaur, the skull was replaced on the skeleton by a lightweight cast with the crushing straightened out. On May 17, 2000, "Sue" went on permanent public display in Chicago. The real skull was displayed nearby.

Caudipteryx

Paleontologists discovered dinosaur footprints in Yongjing County in northwest China that dated back to Late Jurassic or Early Cretaceous.

EARLY CRETACEOUS DINOSAURS FROM PATAGONIA

Dinosaurs were first found in South America more than 100 years ago, but only in the past 30 years have enough paleontologists been working there for us to appreciate just how many interesting kinds of South American dinosaurs there were. Paleontologists have discovered South American dinosaurs that date from the middle of the Triassic Period to the end of the Cretaceous Period.

In particular, paleontologists are now putting together a picture of South American dinosaurs from the Early Cretaceous epoch, a stretch of time of which we know little about dinosaurs worldwide. Most of the newly discovered South American Early Cretaceous dinosaurs are various kinds of sauropods, but there are also some new kinds of theropods. Some seem closely related to certain Early Cretaceous dinosaurs from Africa, which is not surprising, because at that time South America and Africa were partly connected. Dinosaurs could have walked from one continent to the other.

Andesaurus was a normal-size sauropod about 50 to 60 feet long. Its gigantic relative *Argentinosaurus* just may be the world's largest known dinosaur. It was about twice the size of *Andesaurus*, with vertebrae about five feet tall. Both it and *Andesaurus*, which were both found in Patagonia, are close relatives of the titanosaurids of Late Cretaceous South America.

Another group of sauropods, called Dicraeosauridae, includes the odd-looking *Amargasaurus*, a tall-spined relative of the African Late Jurassic sauropod *Dicraeosaurus*. These were rather small sauropods (about 40 feet long) related to the giant North American *Apatosaurus* and *Diplodocus*. The vertebral spines of *Amargasaurus* grew especially tall along the back of the neck, where they may have been covered with webs of skin.

Another South American sauropod, *Rayososaurus*, is a close relative of the African *Rebbachisaurus*. Both dinosaurs had tall vertebral spines, but whereas the spines in *Amargasaurus* were paired, single spines were present in the rebbachisaurids. They may have given the animals a tall ridge along the back. The spines of *Rayososaurus* were not quite as tall as those of *Rebbachisaurus*. Both dinosaurs were standard-size sauropods, measuring about 50 to 60 feet long.

A possible relative of the rebbachisaurids is the very strange sauropod *Agustinia*, which had a double row of plates and spines resembling those of *Stegosaurus* along its back. They may have been movable. No dinosaur like *Agustinia* has been found anywhere else in the world.

An Astrodon *battles several* Utahraptors, *who are known for their "killer claws."*

From about the same time and place as the gigantic *Argentinosaurus* comes the correspondingly huge theropod *Giganotosaurus*. Bigger than *Tyrannosaurus*, it is presently the largest known meat-eating dinosaur, as much as 50 feet long. In a lagoonal deposit in Brazil was found the man-size, fish-eating theropod *Irritator*. It was probably related to the much bigger African spinosaur *Suchomimus*.

EARLY CRETACEOUS DINOSAURS FROM NORTH AMERICA

Not much was known about Early Cretaceous dinosaurs of North America until paleontologists discovered new kinds of dinosaurs in Lower Cretaceous rock strata in Utah and Arizona. The North American dinosaurs are more similar to Early Cretaceous dinosaurs of Europe and Asia than they are to those from Africa or South America.

The recent discoveries in Utah and Arizona included two armored dinosaurs: *Gastonia* and *Animantarx*. The first was about 12 to 15 feet long and resembled its close relative, the British dinosaur *Polacanthus*. The second was about half that size and lived several million years later. It was the first dinosaur discovered by tracing the radioactivity of its fossilized bones; they were not visible at the surface where they were buried.

From the same general location where *Gastonia* was found came the scattered bones of the large meat-eater *Utahraptor*. About six feet long and built like a giant *Deinonychus*, *Utahraptor* was armed with "killer claws" more than a foot long on its feet. It may have used them to tear open its prey. Being a dromaeosaurid, it may have

Two Gigantosauruses *corral an* Amargasaurus.

Afrovenator abakensis

been covered with feathers like an ostrich. *Nedcolbertia* was a much smaller meat-eating dinosaur, about six feet long, that lived at the same time as *Utahraptor*.

Sauropods are scarce in the Early Cretaceous of North America, but their partial skeletons are found from time to time. *Cedarosaurus* and the *Sonorasaurus* were smaller relatives, about 50 feet long, of the gigantic Late Jurassic sauropod *Brachiosaurus*. Other Early Cretaceous plant-eating dinosaurs discovered in North America included *Zuniceratops*, the world's earliest known horned dinosaur with well-developed brow horns, and *Eolambia*, an ornithopod dinosaur very close to the ancestry of the later duckbilled dinosaurs.

EARLY CRETACEOUS DINOSAURS FROM AFRICA

Until the 1990s, Africa remained largely unexplored territory for dinosaurs. A few dinosaur-bearing localities were found by German expeditions to Egypt and Tanzania;

French expeditions to Morocco, the Niger Republic, and Madagascar; and South African expeditions within their own country. The 1990s saw the first expeditions organized by American paleontologists to some of the localities previously visited by other countries. American paleontologists returned with more material of previously known dinosaurs and also fossils of dinosaurs not known before. Most of the fossils were from the Early Cretaceous age.

The first *Carcharodontosaurus* remains—teeth—were found by the French in the 19th century, and teeth and jaw fragments continued to turn up in French and German dinosaur digs everywhere across the Sahara Desert during the 20th century. Not until the 1990s did an American expedition, organized by Paul C. Sereno, turn up a good partial skeleton and skull, giving us our first good look at this mysterious giant meat-eater. Closely related to South America's *Giganotosaurus*, *Carcharodontosaurus* was about as large as *Tyrannosaurus* (40 to 45 feet). The American expeditions also found a new, smaller meat-eater about 30 feet long that they called *Afrovenator* and another new

Cryolophosaurus ellioti

meat-eater, *Deltadromeus*, which was similar in size to *Afrovenator* but more slender.

The spectacular Late Cretaceous *Spinosaurus aegyptiacus,* first found by German expeditions to Egypt before World War I, has so far proved elusive; no more *Spinosaurus aegyptiacus* fossils have ever turned up. But a few of its Early Cretaceous relatives, which were smaller (about 35 feet) and evidently had much shorter spines along the back, have been found by French and American expeditions to Morocco. Known from fragmentary fossils are *Sigilmassasaurus, Cristatusaurus,* and *Spinosaurus maroccanus.* Known from a fairly complete skeleton is *Suchomimus.* The spinosaurs are currently being restudied, and *Suchiomimus* may prove to belong to the same species as one of the previously named spinosaurs. A spinosaur hallmark is the elongated, narrow snout with slender teeth, strongly resembling the snouts and teeth of modern fish-eating crocodiles of India. It is the reason we believe spinosaurs were mainly fish-eaters.

New African sauropods found by American expeditions included *Malawisaurus,* a primitive titanosaur from Malawi; *Jobaria,* a large but primitive sauropod similar to *Cetiosaurus* from the Jurassic of Great Britain; and *Nigersaurus,* a peculiar medium-size sauropod perhaps related to the rebbachisaurids. *Nigersaurus* had rows of hundreds of teeth, packed in its jaws like the dental batteries of duckbilled dinosaurs. *Malawisaurus* material had been discovered as early as 1928, but only after better fossils were found in the early 1990s was it possible to identify it as a new kind of dinosaur.

When the French expedition to the Niger Republic in 1972 found the sail-backed ornithopod *Ouranosaurus,* they also found a large, heavily built but otherwise standard iguanodontid in the same general area. This dinosaur was described and named *Lurdusaurus* in 1999.

EARLY JURASSIC ANTARCTIC DINOSAURS

Antarctica was not always covered miles deep with ice. During the Mesozoic, it had a fairly temperate climate in which dinosaurs and other Mesozoic animals and plants thrived. It also served as a land bridge that joined southern Africa, Madagascar, India, and Australia. Unfortunately, today's huge Antarctic ice pack and very cold Antarctica temperatures make it very difficult to collect dinosaur fossils there. But even so, a few scattered dinosaur fossils are now known from Antarctica, one of which, *Cryolophosaurus,* is complete enough to warrant establishing a new species.

Cryolophosaurus was a theropod 26 feet long, described in 1994. It had a unique, flat crest atop its head between the eyes, shaped like two ruffled potato chips stuck together side by side. Quite a bit of the skull was found, so we have a pretty good idea what this dinosaur looked like. Along with it were found the bones of an unnamed prosauropod, perhaps the kind of dinosaur that *Cryolophosaurus* preyed upon. Both dinosaurs lived during the Early Jurassic epoch.

LATE CRETACEOUS DINOSAURS FROM MADAGASCAR

Dinosaurs were first discovered in Madagascar by British and French paleontologists late in the 19th century. The fossils were rather scrappy, but they included Jurassic and Cretaceous sauropod (brachiosaurid and titanosaurid) and theropod bones. In 1926, a fossil tooth from Madagascar was described by the French as belonging to a new species of *Stegosaurus*; the French named the theropod *Majungasaurus.* And in 1979, a thickened skull bone was described as a pachycephalosaur called *Majungatholus.* Every so often a few more scrappy dinosaur bones were found there, but this was essentially where dinosaur paleontology of Madagascar stood as late as the mid-1990s.

In 1996 and following years, American expeditions to Madagascar found fairly plentiful bones of Late Cretaceous dinosaurs, including two kinds of titanosaurids (still undescribed); a large theropod; a new kind of small to medium-size theropod with front teeth that protrude forward almost horizontally; a small, birdlike theropod with a long tail that had large, winglike forelimbs and was probably a good flier; and a "true" bird that was named *Vorona.* The new material settled some doubts about Madagascar dinosaurs. First, the aforementioned stegosaur tooth was found to belong to a peculiar kind of crocodile and was not stegosaurian after all. Then, the so-called pachycephalosaur turned out to be a theropod with a bumpy, thickened skull roof and a short snout. A good skull showed that *Majungatholus* was a close relative of the peculiar South American horned theropod *Carnotaurus*; instead of a pair of horns, it had a single thick knob on top of its head. The earlier name *Majungasaurus* had to be discarded because the material on which it was based was too scrappy to identify; it may or may not be the same dinosaur as *Majungatholus.*

The small theropod with protruding front teeth was named *Masiakasaurus* in early 2001. The available material suggests that it may be related to the small theropod *Noasaurus* from South America, but further work needs to be done before this identification is secure. Some speculate that it was a fish-eater.

The small, birdlike theropod, called *Rahonavis,* is perhaps the most interesting fossil found by those expeditions to Madagascar. Although the describers classified it as a bird about as advanced as the Jurassic bird *Archaeopteryx,* its feet are almost exactly the same as the feet of *Deinonychus* and other dromaeosaurids, right down to the enlarged "killer" claws. The long tail and hips also closely resemble those of dromaeosaurids, but the forelimbs have the long, slender bones of bird wings and little bumps where feathers might have been attached. Thus, *Rahonavis* seems to be a genuine link between small theropod dinosaurs and "true" birds. Only further study, and some more specimens, will resolve the relationship of theropods, birds, and *Rahonavis.*

Archaeopteryx

GLOSSARY

ANGIOSPERMS
Flowering plants that include the familiar hardwood trees, flowers, grasses, and weeds of today. They began as weeds in the Early Cretaceous and are the most successful land plants that ever lived. Their seeds are more complicated than other kinds of plants; they are covered as opposed to the "naked" seeds of conifers.

ANTORBITAL FENESTRA
Means "window in front of the eye." This hole in the skull is in front of the eye. It is one of the features that distinguised an archosaur.

ARCHOSAURS
A group of reptiles that includes dinosaurs, crocodiles, pterosaurs, and thecodonts and their ancestors. Archosaurs had a large opening in front of each eye (antorbital fenestra) and certain other features.

ARTICULATED SKELETON
A skeleton with the bones lying in the position they would have been in life, joined where there would have been joints. The opposite is *disarticulated*, with the bones scattered.

ATMOSPHERE
The air covering the earth.

BEAK
A toothless structure at the front of the mouth of some dinosaurs. It may be sharp (turtlelike), such as in the horned dinosaurs, or blunt (ducklike), such as in the duckbilled dinosaurs, or it may be a variation of either kind. Beaks probably had a horny covering.

BIPED
An animal that stands, walks, or runs on two legs.

BOSS
A blunt raised pad or bump, usually on the head of an animal.

BROWSE
To eat the leaves of shrubs and trees.

CAMBRIAN PERIOD
The oldest period of the Paleozoic, when fossils with hard parts appeared.

CANINE TEETH
The teeth between the front and cheek teeth. They were cone-shaped and pointed, for stabbing prey and slicing flesh.

CARNIVORE
An animal that eats meat.

CENOZOIC ERA
The time of "recent life" or the "Age of Mammals." It was the Era after the Mesozoic, from 65 million years ago to the present.

CHAMPSOSAURS
Crocodilelike reptiles that lived in water during and after the Age of Dinosaurs.

CHEEK TEETH
The teeth behind the front teeth or beak that some plant-eaters, especially duckbills, used for chewing.

CHEVRONS
The small bones below the tail vertebrae of some dinosaurs.

CLADE
A group that includes a common ancestral species and all the species that descended from it, such as archosaurs.

CLASS
A grouping in taxonomy; similar orders are grouped into a class, and similar classes are grouped into a phylum. Dinosaurs, lizards, and turtles form the class Reptilia.

CLASSIFICATION
Putting similar organisms into groupings that show they are related.

COLD-BLOODED
Refers to an animal that gets its body heat from the environment (sun and air), such as modern reptiles. Scientists do not yet know if dinosaurs were warm-blooded or cold-blooded.

CONCRETION
A hard, rounded mass of mineral that forms in sediment, sometimes enclosing a fossil.

CONIFERS
Trees or shrubs that produce naked seed cones, such as firs and pines.

CONTINENTAL DRIFT
The phenomenon by which continents move (or drift), causing land masses and the oceans between them to change and shift.

CONVERGENT EVOLUTION
When two animals or plants have a common feature but did not acquire it through the same ancestral line, such as the wings of birds and bats.

COPROLITES
Fossilized animal dung.

CREST
A hollow or solid structure on the top of the head of the hadrosaurs. It probably was used for ornamentation and display. In the hollow-crested dinosaurs, it may also have been used to produce sound.

CRETACEOUS EXTINCTION EVENT
The event that killed the dinosaurs at the end of the Cretaceous Period. It is not known if the event happened in days or lasted many years.

CRETACEOUS PERIOD
The third and final period of the Mesozoic Era that lasted from 144 million years ago until 65 million years ago. It came after the Triassic and Jurassic Periods. Dinosaurs became extinct at the end of the Cretaceous.

CROP
To pull out the upper and outer parts of a plant for food.

CYCADS
Naked-seed plants that were squat and looked like palm trees.

CYNODONTS
Advanced mammallike reptiles that lived in the Triassic Period.

DENTAL BATTERY
The complicated arrangement of the teeth of duckbilled and horned dinosaurs. The teeth interlocked and overlapped to form an efficient surface for slicing and grinding plants.

DIAPSIDS
Reptiles (including archosaurs, lizards, and snakes) that had two openings behind each eye socket.

DICYNODONTS
Therapsid plant-eaters that lived during the Permian and Triassic Periods. Some had two tusks in their upper jaws.

DISARTICULATED SKELETON
Bones that are separated from the correct position in the skeleton.

DIVERSITY
The variety of types of plants and animals that result from evolutionary changes.

EMBRYO
The early stages of development of a plant or animal, before an egg hatches or an animal gives birth.

EQUATOR
The imaginary circle around the middle of the earth that separates the northern and southern hemispheres. It is the same distance from the equator to the north pole as from the equator to the south pole.

EROSION
The process by which the surface of the land is continuously worn away, exposing underlying rocks and sometimes fossils.

EVOLUTION
A process of changing through generations, usually to better adapt an animal or plant for the environmental conditions it lives in. The process by which diversity is achieved.

EXCAVATE
To dig out and remove, such as a fossil from a rock layer.

EXTRATERRESTRIAL
Describes an object, such as a comet or meteorite, that is not from the earth itself. An extraterrestrial object may hit the earth.

EXTINCTION
Death of a species.

FAMILY
A grouping in taxonomy; similar genera are placed into a family and similar families are placed into an infraorder or family. *Tyrannosaurus* and *Albertosaurus* are placed in the family Tyrannosauridae.

FAUNA
A group of animals that lived (or live) at the same time and in the same place.

FENESTRA
An opening, often in the skull (it is a Latin word that means window). The plural of the word is fenestrae.

FLORA
A group of plants that lived (or live) at the same time and in the same place.

FOOD CHAIN
The order of organisms based on predator and prey relationships. Plankton are the lowest form on the food chain, and they are eaten by small fish, which are eaten by larger fish. *Tyrannosaurus* was the highest form on the food chain in its day.

FORMATION
The name of a unit of rocks or sediment that are of the same age.

FOSSIL
The preserved remains of long dead animals or plants that are made by the process of fossilization. Sometimes it is just the impressions of the remains that are seen.

FOSSIL RECORD
The history of life on earth that is preserved as fossils. It gives us information about the prehistoric world.

FRILL
The bony shelf that covers the back of the neck of ceratopsians.

FUNCTIONAL
Able to perform a normal or specific function. Functional fingers may form a grasping hand.

FUSED
Tightly joined with no joint between, almost as if melted together.

GASTROLITHS
"Stomach stones" that some dinosaurs may have swallowed to help break down tough plants to aid their digestion, similiar to the gizzards of birds.

GENUS
A grouping in taxonomy; similar species are placed into a genus, and similar genera are placed into a family. Some paleontologists believe that the species *Tarbosaurus bataar* belongs in the genus *Tyrannosaurus*, thus *Tyrannosaurus bataar*.

GEOLOGIST
A scientist who studies rocks.

GONDWANALAND
The southern land mass that was made up of South America, Africa, India, Antarctica, and Australia. It broke apart during the Mesozoic Era.

HABITAT
The area that an animal lives in. The habitat is characterized by temperature, climate, plants, and anything else that affects the animal.

HATCHLING
A newly hatched animal.

HEMISPHERE
Half of the world, divided at the equator. There is the northern hemisphere and the southern hemisphere.

HERBIVORE
An animal that eats plants.

ICHTHYOSAUR
Marine reptile that looked like a dolphin. It lived during the Mesozoic Era, but was not related to dinosaurs.

ILIUM
One of the bones of the pelvis that is attached to the backbone.

INFRAORDER
A subdivision of taxonomy; similar families are placed into an infraorder, and similar infraorders are placed into a suborder or order. The families Tyrannosauridae and Allosauridae form the infraorder Carnosauria.

IRIDIUM
A rare element that is found in the earth's core or in extraterrestrial objects.

IRIDIUM LAYER
A thin layer of iridium found at the boundary between rocks of the Cretaceous and Tertiary Periods. It may be linked to the Cretaceous Extinction Event.

ISCHIUM
One of the bones of the pelvis that points down and back from the hip socket.

JURASSIC PERIOD
The second of the three periods of the Mesozoic Era that lasted from 213 million years ago until 144 million years ago. It came after the Triassic Period and before the Cretaceous Period. Dinosaurs became the dominant land creatures during this period.

KEELED
Ridged

KINGDOM
The highest grouping of taxonomy. Many phyla are included in the kingdom Animalia and many others in the kingdom Plantae.

LAURASIA
The northern land mass that was made up of North America, Europe, and Asia. It was separated from Gondwanaland by the Tethys Sea. It began to break up during the Mesozoic Era but new connections were formed between Alaska and Asia.

MAMMALS
Warm-blooded animals that are covered by hair and feed their young by producing milk, including humans.

MARINE
Relating to the sea. For example, a marine reptile lived in the sea.

MARSUPIAL MAMMALS
Mammals that lack a placenta, and so keep babies in the womb for only a short time. Marsupials may, like possums and kangaroos, carry their babies in a pouch after birth.

MESOZOIC ERA
The time of "middle life" or the "Age of Reptiles." It was divided into three periods, the Triassic, Jurassic, and Cretaceous, and was the time when dinosaurs rose to dominance. The Era lasted from 248 million years ago to 65 million years ago.

METACARPAL BONES
The long bones of the hand that form the palm.

METATARSAL BONES
The long bones of the foot.

MOSASAURS
Large reptiles that were predators and lived in water. They appeared in the Cretaceous Period, but they became extinct at the end of that period. They were lizards that were not related to dinosaurs. Mosasaurs were mostly large, with long heads, sharp teeth in sockets, and long jaws with joints.

OMNIVORE
An animal that eats both plants and animals.

OORT CLOUD
A swarm of comets located just outside the solar system. If the Death Star (this star is only a theory) disturbs the cloud, the cloud may send comets that hit the earth. The theory is that this happens every 26 million years.

OPPOSABLE FINGER
A finger that can be placed against another finger, to form a grasping hand. Human hands have opposable thumbs.

ORDER
A grouping of taxonomy; similar suborders are placed into an order, and similar orders are placed into a class. The suborders Theropoda and Sauropodomorpha belong in the order Saurischia.

ORGANISM
A living thing. An organism can be a plant or animal, and can be complex, such as a human or dinosaur, or simple, such as a microscopic one-celled protozoan.

ORNITHISCHIA
One of two major groups of dinosaurs, the "bird-hipped" dinosaurs. All dinosaurs in this group were plant-eaters.

PALATE
The bony arch that forms the roof of the mouth.

PALEONTOLOGY
The study of fossils. A paleontologist is a scientist who studies fossils.

PALEOZOIC ERA
The time of "ancient life" or the "Age of Fishes and Invertebrates." It was divided into six periods, the Cambrian, Ordovician, Silurian, Devonian, Carboniferous, and Permian. This Era came before the Mesozoic Era and lasted from 600 million years ago to 248 million years ago.

PANGAEA
The single land mass during the Permian Period. It began to divide into Gondwanaland and Laurasia in the Triassic Period.

PELVIS
The hip area of a skeleton. The pelvis is made up of the ilium, the ischium, and the pubis.

PERMIAN PERIOD
The last period of the Paleozoic Era. It came right before the Mesozoic Era and saw the rise of mammallike reptiles and the first archosaurs. Many animal groups became extinct at the end of the Permian.

PHYLUM
A grouping of taxonomy; similar classes are placed into a phylum and similar phyla are placed into a kingdom. The phylum Chordata includes all animals with backbones.

PHYTOSAURS
Crocodilelike archosaurs of the Triassic Period.

PLACENTAL MAMMALS
Mammals that have a special membrane, the placenta, that surrounds the developing baby in the womb. The placenta provides nourishment and stores wastes. Like marsupials, placentals give birth to live young and feed them milk.

PLANKTON
Single-celled plants and animals that live in water and are the first step in the food chain. Phytoplankton (plant plankton) produce great quantities of oxygen.

PLESIOSAURS
Marine reptiles that swam by using their paddlelike forelimbs. They lived during the Mesozoic Era, but they were not related to dinosaurs.

PREDATOR
An animal that kills other animals for food.

PREDENTARY BONE
A bone at the tip of the lower jaw in ornithischian dinosaurs. It may have formed the lower beak but never had teeth.

PREY
The animal that is killed by a predator.

PRIMITIVE
The earliest and usually least advanced forms that lack special features. The earliest dinosaurs, *Staurikosaurus* and *Herrerasaurus,* were the most primitive.

PROCESS
A bony projection.

PROTEROSUCHIANS
The earliest archosaurs. They were large, four-legged meat-eaters that lived during the Permian Period.

PROTOZOAN
A single-celled microscopic animal.

PTEROSAURS
Flying reptiles of the Mesozoic. They were archosaurs and cousins of dinosaurs.

PUBIS
A bone of the pelvis that points down and forward in saurischian dinosaurs but is backward and parallel to the ischium in ornithischian dinosaurs.

QUADRUPED
An animal that stands, walks, or runs on all four legs.

RED BEDS
A type of soil in which the iron in the soil is oxidized (rusted) because of the climate. Red beds are indeed red. Many Triassic fossil beds are red beds.

REPTILES
Cold-blooded animals with scales that lay eggs on land. Living reptiles are turtles, snakes, crocodiles, and lizards. Dinosaurs were reptiles but were more advanced than any living reptiles and may have been warm-blooded.

REWORKED
Describes fossils that have eroded and then been reburied in another time period. It then appears as if the fossilized animal had lived in the later time period. Also called *secondary deposition.*

RHYNCHOSAURS
Late Triassic plant-eating archosaurs that had an upper jaw that ended in a downcurved beak.

ROSTRAL BONE
A bone found at the tip of the upper jaw only in ceratopsian dinosaurs.

SACRUM
The part of the backbone that attaches to the pelvis.

SAURISCHIA
One of two major groups of dinosaurs, the "lizard-hipped" dinosaurs. This group includes the carnivorous theropods, the plant-eating sauropodomorphs, and the strange segnosaurians.

SEDIMENTARY ROCK
Rock that was formed by layers of sediment, such as mud, clay, sand, and lime, that hardened to rock. Bones may be preserved in these types of rocks.

SERRATED
Having sharp notches along the edges, like a steak knife. The teeth of the meat-eating dinosaurs were serrated.

SCUTES
Bony or horny plates that are produced in the skin.

SHOCK-FRACTURED QUARTZ
Quartz is a common element on earth. It breaks in an unusual way when subjected to extreme heat and pressure, such as an atomic bomb blast or an asteroid hitting earth.

SKELETON
The bones of the body that support the soft tissues. Usually only the skeleton is fossilized.

SPECIES
The lowest grouping in taxonomy; similar species are placed into a genus. Species are the kinds of plants and animals. *Tyrannosaurus rex* is a kind of dinosaur.

STRATIGRAPHIC COMPLETENESS
How much of the geologic record (record found in rocks) is present for a specific amount of time.

SUBORDER
A subdivision of taxonomy; similar infraorders are placed into a suborder, and similar suborders are placed into an order. The Ornithopoda are a suborder of the order Ornithischia.

SYNAPSIDS
Mammallike reptiles that include the ancestors of mammals. Pelycosaurus of the Permian Period and therapsids of the Triassic Period were the main groups of synapsids.

TAXONOMY
The study of the classification of living things.

TERRESTRIAL
Relating to land. An animal that lives on land is said to be terrestrial.

TERTIARY PERIOD
The period following the Mesozoic Era, when mammals became the dominant land animals. It lasted from 65 million years ago to two million years ago.

TETHYS SEA
The shallow sea that separated Gondwanaland and Laurasia during the Mesozoic Era.

THECODONTS
"Socket-toothed" reptiles that were probably the ancestors of dinosaurs, crocodiles, and pterosaurs, all of which made up the infraclass Archosauria.

THERAPSIDS
The synapsid reptiles that had a semi-erect or fully erect stance. They were the dominant land animals in the Late Permian Period and Early Triassic Period.

THEROPOD
Bipedal meat-eating saurischian dinosaurs.

TRACKWAY
Fossilized footprints.

TRIDACTYL
An animal that walks (or walked) on three toes.

TUBERCLES
Bumps and nodules, found on fossilized skin impressions.

TRIASSIC PERIOD
The first period of the Mesozoic Era, coming before the Jurassic and Cretaceous Periods. Dinosaurs first appeared late in the Triassic Period, which lasted from 248 million years ago to 213 million years ago.

VERTEBRA
A spool-shaped bone, many of which joined together to form the spine, or backbone. The plural of vertebra is vertebrae.

VERTEBRATE
An animal with a backbone, such as fish, humans, and dinosaurs.

VERTISOLS
A type of soil that is produced by a wet season followed by a dry season. This soil is found in Triassic formations.

WARM-BLOODED
Refers to an animal that generates its body heat internally and so does not depend directly on the sun for heat. Birds and mammals are warm-blooded.

INDEX